MARY'S BREAD BASKET
AND SOUP KETTLE

MARY'S BREAD BASKET AND SOUP KETTLE

by Mary Gubser

drawings by Pat Biggs

QUILL
NEW YORK

Gubser, Mary.
  Mary's bread basket and soup kettle.

  Reprint. Originally published: New York
Morrow, 1975, © 1974.
  Includes index.
  1. Bread. 2. Soups. I. Title.
TX769.G78 1985   641.8'15   85-6281
ISBN 0-688-05886-8 (pbk.)

Printed in the United States of America

5 6 7 8 9 10

To my husband, Gene
For his patience, understanding,
and willingness to taste anything

FOREWORD

Immediately after World War II there was a baker's strike in our city. We had three vigorous young sons and action was necessary. I opened a cook book and made my first loaf of bread. I learned what home makers have known for centuries — that kneading a beautifully made resilient dough, watching the rising process, smelling the delicious aroma as the bread bakes, and, finally pulling out a golden-brown loaf is one of the most satisfying experiences in caring for a household.

Bread is older than written history. Its tantalizing fragrance has floated through many civilizations. Wars have been and are waged over rich grain lands. Breads became a part of religions through mystical shapes. Greek bread baked in a ring means a continuity of life, a braided Jewish Challah symbolizes a ladder to heaven. Breaking of bread is an expression of Christ's body in a Christian Communion. Bread is still used as an eating implement in many countries. Strict laws have governed bakers from ancient times to the present era.

The rediscovery of home breadmaking in the past ten years is one of the delightful results to come out of our complex world. If you wish to get back to the "basics" of creating a food with your own hands, there is no better way than to bake bread and make a big pot of soup. Although bread and soup making still take a little time and patience, a great deal has been done to improve methods over the past fifty years. Now that American industry has provided us with excellent home freezers, one or two days a month devoted to baking and soup making will give much pleasure to family and friends.

Teaching classes in bread and soup has shown me the kind of recipes people are looking for with a clearer understanding of their problems. In presenting this book it is my desire to give you a better perspective of all phases of breadmaking, with recipes easy to follow and ingredients available in most sections of our country. Further, my purpose is to show how delightful, exciting and fulfilling the art of bread and soup making can be.

ACKNOWLEDGMENTS

Without the help of family and friends, the culmination of my efforts to produce a cookbook would not have been possible. My deepest thanks to my three sons, Nick, Peter, and Mike and superb daughters-in-law, Margaret and Annie for years of steady inspiration. I can never repay my niece, Pat Biggs, for all the time and thought she has given to make this a unique and artistic book. My sister, Kathryn Loring, was especially helpful at the beginning of my project. To my inimitable mother-in-law, Elsie, my deep appreciation for she has been pushing me several years to write a cookbook.

I wish to particularly recognize and thank friends who have been of inestimable assistance.

Linda Harbert and Ethel Kulhanek for their laborious work of correcting my manuscript.

To Nancy Feldman, Fran Ringold, Ruth McAfee, and Sue Schempf, my cooking companion, for their excellent practical assistance and encouragement.

My international friends who have helped give my cuisine a distinctive "spice" — Ethel George of London, Denise Minard of Paris, Maria Stini in Greece, Svante Haglund in Sweden, and Helen Yeni-Komshian in Beirut.

All of my friends who have shared ideas and recipes throughout the years.

To my husband's office staff for their constant delight over my culinary efforts and assistance in the mechanical task of preparing my manuscript for the printer.

And last, to my students, who were the final motivation and exciting stimulus for the creation of my book.

TABLE OF CONTENTS

MARY'S BREAD BASKET
AND SOUP KETTLE

THE STORY OF BREAD

Sixty to eighty thousand years ago man first crunched on wild seed that pleased him. Forty thousand years later, after the last ice age, primitive man could no longer solely depend on animals for food as they were fast disappearing. He began to supplement his diet with roots, nuts, tubers, vegetables, and seeds. Then he found that he need not move from place to place hunting food. By staying in one spot longer, he could harvest the wild grasses and ultimately in a crude manner plant the seeds and cultivate more grain. Over 10,000 years ago nomadic agriculture was born. Next man began to find that he could grind those seeds and produce a kind of meal. Some intelligent cave woman finally mixed a little water with the meal, slapped it on a hot rock and had unleavened bread. Unfermented cakes and biscuits have been found in the remains of the ancient Swiss Lake Dwellings, one of the oldest sites for such artifacts. These discoveries show definite evidence of milling and baking.

It was in the Fertile Crescent that breadmaking first became an art. This area encompassed the Tigris-Euphrates valley to the Persian Gulf and around to Egypt. Wild grasses called einkorn and emmer, the ancestors of wheat, grew in this region. These wild plants still can be found today as far north as Iran. Bread of this primitive man was unleavened — flat, hard sheets made by mixing pulverized grains with water and spread on hot stones. All indications show that the Egyptians were the first to have leavened bread. There is no record of how fermentation began but there are many pictographs in the ancient tombs showing grinding and sifting flour, mixing and baking loaves. Their administrative system was based on wheat and bread. As a result, Egyptian bakers rose to the status of priests. Although their breads were not the highly aerated loaves that we know, great ingenuity was shown in the use of honey, spices, herbs, and nuts for making a large variety of exotic shapes. There is also evidence the Egyptian baker saved a part of each day's dough for use later — a method similar to saving a starter for our sourdough breads. Laborers working on the Pyramids were paid in beer and bread. The famous Book Of The Dead gives elaborate instructions concerning the protection of bread.

In the era of history belonging to the Greeks that followed, improvement was made in ovens. The Greeks developed a thin bread rolled like a parchment. Little advancement was made, however, until the Romans conquered Macedonia in 168 B. C. Greek bakers were then brought to Rome. The Romans made great strides in improving the milling, grinding, and sieving. However, leavened bread was eaten by only the upper ten percent of the population. Roman soldiers were not allowed to have raised bread as it was thought unhealthy. As with the Egyptians, Greeks, and others through the centuries, fine white flour was used only for the aristocracy. Heavy, coarser breads were given to the slaves and lower classes.

Up to the time of Emperor Trajan, most bread was baked in homes or small community ovens. During his reign, public bakeries became widespread and the first school for bakers was established. From the ruins of Pompeii, we know that much of the Roman bread was round and rather flat. It was more like our bread because of the finer grinding, but still was a heavy loaf that could sink immediately in water. For several centuries, there was a custom for a baker to make a personal mark on his breads. The Romans made bread into a political element; they ruled, conquered, and lost through wheat and bread.

Bread and wheat moved across Europe in two different directions, ultimately coming to Britain well in advance of the first Roman legions. With the fall of the Roman Empire, agriculture came to a stand still.

By the late middle ages an agricultural revolution had taken place with development of an improved plow, making possible cultivation of greater quantities of grain. Trade guilds were established and one of the strongest was the Baker's Guild. The Worshipful Company of Bakers, established in London during the year 1155 is still in existence. From the time of Egypt to the present day, laws have been enacted by each country governing the weights and grades of breads to protect the populace but also in defense of the baker. During this period the milling process began to undergo a rapid change. From mortars, pestles and querns the advance was to power by water and wind or by man and animal.

Columbus took a "starter" with him on his cruise to the New World. A few years later wheat was introduced into both Americas. Jesuit priests carried wheat into Arizona and California. Our western Indians still eat an unleavened bread taught them by these wandering men of the cloth. But more exciting was the opening of the new country and the important role that wheat and bread played.

Wheat had been grown in the coastal areas during colonial days but with little success. Men began moving west and found perfect farmland for grain growing. Most settlers became farmers and by 1860 the vast majority of the occupied territories was farm land. Between 1860 and 1870 our population increased from 31 million to over 50 million. At this point the greatest progress was in the improvement of farm machinery by such men as McCormick and Deere. With this came a rapid development and change in milling. The slow stone grinding could not keep pace with the population growth of either the United States or Europe.

Fast roller milling was first developed in Hungary and soon came to the United States. With automatic milling, the flour industry was able to supply a rapidly growing country. For by 1880 the population had increased sixty percent over 1860. Because of the perishable nature of

2

bread, large bakeries were established over the States rather than localized in a few communities. At present fifty million loaves of bread are baked each day in our country. To supply the enormous quantities needed, it was a natural sequence for breadmaking to pass out of the home and into bakeries.

Bread is the history of civilization. Slowly grains led man from savagery and barbarism to advancement in social culture. Primitive men became nomadic farmers and began to group together to form a tribe. From tribal life, small communities were created, then towns and cities, and finally nations and empires. Bread was man's first manufactured food. Baking, the world's oldest food industry, is still the largest food processing business in the United States. There is no cuisine that is loved so universally. "Breaking bread" together has symbolized friendship for centuries. It is the "staff of life".

THE SAGA OF SOUP

The simplicity of French peasant living has produced some of our most exciting and nourishing food. One of the best is soup. There is little record of soup making until Medieval days. Frequently meat would be stewed and since there were no eating implements, a peasant broke off huge chunks of bread to dip into the juices. This was called a "sop". By the 12th century broth was discovered and called "soupe". During the 13th century, monks turned soup making into an art along with their excellent breads and wines. La Soupe became the name of the evening meal in rural France for hundreds of years.

As has happened many times in history, the aristocracy was a bit slow but they finally became aware of what could be done with soups. French kings especially loved soups, consuming as many as four different kinds at one meal. By the time Louis XIV arrived, soups had to take a new turn. Louis mistrusted everyone including his cooks, so he had a taster. To become a taster was an honor but the taster wishing to be protected also had a taster. By the time the food finally reached poor Louis, it was either lukewarm or cold. Louis demanded that cold soups be served and thus initiated development of such lovely ideas as M. Diat's Vichyssoise.

The French Revolution scarcely interrupted haute cuisine but it did change life for the royal cooks. In 1765 there was one cafe in Paris owned by a M. Boulanger who served only soups. He posted the word "restaurant" in front of his establishment and the idea stuck although it actually meant restorative. Since the royal chefs had lost their employers as well as their jobs, they began to open "restaurants" and by 1794 Paris had five hundred cafes. During the latter part of the 18th century, the English aristocracy accepted soups, serving them regularly as a separate and elegant course.

Soup was a mainstay of American settlers. The iron soup kettle could simmer and bubble all day leaving time for the frontier woman to do her interminable chores. Besides soup was an economical dish as every bit of left over meat, vegetables, noodles, and rice could be thrown into the pot.

Soups can be made to fulfill any desired purpose in planning a meal or party — a main course, an appetizer, a first course, served as a beverage, and even a dessert. A fragrant soup can be a lovely introduction to dinner creating a leisurely and elegant atmosphere. For the younger generation who desire easy, informal entertaining, nothing is better than a large pot of soup-stew and hot home made bread. Soup is universally enjoyed whether it is a small demi-tasse of bouillon or a hearty bowl of black bean with sausage.

Following will be a description of Basic Stocks — beef, chicken, and fish. Prepare these stocks on days that you are baking bread and freeze in small quantities for future use. Stock will stay fresh three to four days in the refrigerator. If it is to be frozen after this period, it should be reboiled, placed in plastic containers, labeled and frozen. This provides a fine base for many soups. If you are pressed for time, there are excellent canned bouillons and consommes as well as concentrated cubes. With pungent herbs, spices, vegetables, fruits, and good wines, you are ready for soup making. Bread baking in the oven and soup simmering on top of the stove gives a warm glow of real satisfaction and accomplishment.

BEEF STOCK

4½ pounds beef bones, including
   marrow bones
2 pounds beef stewing meat
5 quarts water
2 cups water for deglazing
1 cup celery and leaves, coarsely
   chopped
2 carrots, sliced

2 medium onions, peeled and
   chopped
1 clove garlic
4 sprigs parsley
1 bay leaf
8 black peppercorns
1 teaspoon thyme

Place the soup bones and stewing meat in a roaster. Bake in a preheated 400° oven about 40 minutes or until brown. Remove bones and meat to a large soup kettle and add 5 quarts of water. Discard fat from the roaster and add the 2 cups of water. Boil and stir until all the scrapings are loose from the pan. Transfer liquid and scrapings to the soup kettle. Bring slowly to a boil uncovered and skim. Add remaining ingredients. Allow to boil and skim again. Lower heat to simmer, cover the kettle and let soup bubble lightly 5 hours without stirring.

Place a wet cheesecloth in a colander over a large bowl. Ladle out as much stock as possible without disturbing contents of the kettle and strain through the cheesecloth. This top broth may be placed in a separate container and used for clear soups. Strain the remaining stock. Allow stock to cool and skim off the fat. If the flavor is weak, boil down rapidly to concentrate. Salt may be added now to taste or later when using for specific recipes. The stock is ready for immediate use or freezing.

CHICKEN STOCK

*6 pound chicken, cut in pieces or
chicken backs, necks, wings,
and giblets*

6 black peppercorns
4 quarts water, approximately
2 onions, quartered
2 celery stalks with leaves, chopped
2 leeks, cleaned and sliced (optional)
2 cloves garlic, peeled

2 carrots, sliced
1 bay leaf
3 sprigs parsley
½ teaspoon thyme
½ teaspoon savory

Place chicken in a large soup kettle with the peppercorns and water
to cover. Bring slowly to a boil. Reduce heat and simmer uncovered
1 hour, skimming frequently. Prepare vegetables, herbs, and seasonings.
Add to the soup pot and bring back to a simmer. Cover and continue to
cook 2 hours. Remove from heat and skim as much fat as possible.
Strain broth through a fine sieve or several thicknesses of wet cheese
cloth in a colander placed over a bowl. Cool and skim off fat again.
If the flavor is weak, boil down to concentrate. The broth is ready for
immediate use, refrigeration or freezing.

SUGGESTIONS

Save bones and scraps of leftover chicken and skin. Freeze in
plastic bags. When about 6 pounds has accumulated, prepare stock as
above, adding 1 can of rich, condensed chicken broth to give more
flavor.

FISH STOCK

*2 pounds of lean, bony fish, fish
heads, bones or trimmings*
2 quarts of water, approximately
1 cup dry white wine
1 carrot, sliced
1 onion, sliced

2 sprigs fresh parsley
½ bay leaf
½ teaspoon thyme
1 teaspoon lemon juice
6 peppercorns

Place all ingredients in a soup kettle with sufficient water to cover.
Bring to a boil and skim. Lower heat to simmer and cook uncovered
30 minutes. Strain the stock through several thicknesses of wet cheese
cloth in a colander over a large bowl. Fish stock will keep in a refrigerator about 3 days or freeze broth in small quantities. Label each container
with name and amount.

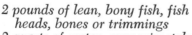

THE ART OF BREADMAKING

Explanation of the ingredients used in breadmaking, techniques to apply, an explanation of terms, difficulties to expect and other information are on the following pages. All are short and informative. As you proceed to delve into the art of breadmaking and encounter the inevitable problems, turn back to these pages and find the help you need.

BASIC INGREDIENTS FOR EXCELLENT BREADS

Yeast. Working with yeast is an exciting experience simply because it is alive! For a beginner: sprinkle a cake or package of yeast in ¼ cup of warm water, add a teaspoon of sugar and stir with a fork until it is dissolved. Watch it begin to work. Soon the yeast comes alive, bubbles and doubles in size with an aroma that is earthy and fragrant. Now you can see that it is a living organism, dependent upon warmth and food. As yeast grows in dough, carbon dioxide is formed, expanding the elastic cell structure in the glutenous part of the flour and causing bread to rise.

Yeast may be purchased in two forms; compressed or cake yeast, and dry yeast sealed in a packet. Either is excellent. The cake yeast is more perishable and will keep well sealed two weeks in the refrigerator. A date is on each package stating when it was made: for example — 0314, the 3 being the month and 14 the day. When fresh, cake yeast should crumble easily. If not, throw it away. Dry yeast is far more available and will keep for weeks outside the refrigerator and indefinitely inside if well covered. A date is stamped on each packet of dry yeast stating how long it will last.

The warmth of water to dissolve yeast is a problem for many cooks. Cake yeast likes lukewarm water — 80 to 90°. Dry yeast prefers warmer water — 110°. As a beginner use a candy thermometer. Touch the water with a finger each time until you get the "feel" of the correct warmth. If you have no thermometer, allow water to run over your hand until there is a slightly biting warmth. Always sprinkle yeast over the water, *stirring with a fork* until it is dissolved. Try the experiment suggested at the beginning of this section. If the yeast mixture does not bubble, the water is too hot, too cold, or the yeast is old. If so, throw it away and try again.

Flour.   This basic ingredient of bread contains a protein substance called gluten. When gluten is wet an elastic framework is formed. Remember when as a youngster you made paste out of flour and water? It is this sticky construction that enables dough to hold the leavening gas or bubbles produced by yeast fermentation. The amount and strength of gluten varies with flours. The same brand of flour will have different absorption powers. As a result, *an exact amount of flour can never be given in a recipe.* Temperature and humidity will have a direct effect on the amounts used, since flour absorbs water from the atmosphere. In high altitudes and on the desert, flour will dry out. A sunny day versus a rainy day makes a difference. It will be great fun and a test of your skill to know how a dough should feel when the mixture is correct. Do not be concerned about the variables in flours. As your kneading proficiency develops, you will become aware that dough has enough flour when it becomes smooth, elastic, and the stickiness almost disappears.

There are two basic white flours — soft and hard wheat. Unbleached hard wheat all-purpose flour makes the best bread because of its high protein content. The higher the protein content, the stronger the gluten. Unbleached flour is found mainly at health food stores, and specialty shops. Now that the demand is stronger, super markets are beginning to stock unbleached and stone ground flours. The regular all-purpose flour obtainable in all grocery stores is a combination of hard and soft wheats and produces very good breads. *The recipes in this book are adaptable to any all-purpose flour.*

Never sift flour unless specified. Sifting aerates the flour unnecessarily for breadmaking. Whole wheat and rye flours are never sifted simply because it is not necessary. Be careful when measuring not to pack the flour. Dip a measuring cup into the flour container and scrape off the excess with a knife. I love storing my flours on a kitchen cabinet in large colorful glass jars with wide tops for easy availability. Wherever flour is stored, be certain that it is dry and has a secure lid. Flour that is not to be used soon should be placed in a freezer or refrigerator. A more complete explanation of flours is given under Wheats and Flours.

Liquids. A number of liquids may be used, each producing a different texture and flavor.

Water generates an earthy flavor with a crisper crust. Because it creates a sturdy texture, this kind of bread holds together well for sandwiches.

Potato water and potatoes makes a coarser bread with a distinctive, tasty flavor. The dough has more moisture and thus becomes a higher, larger loaf. Instant potatoes may be used in place of regular potatoes quite successfully. Follow the directions on a package of instant potatoes but use only hot water for mixing. To make potato water: add 3 teaspoons of instant potatoes to ½ cup hot water.

Milk produces a more nutritious bread that is creamier in texture. Sweet milk, buttermilk, canned, and powdered skim milk all may be used. Unpasteurized milk must be scalded and cooled. Pasteurized milk need only be heated to lukewarm. Powdered skim milk is particularly popular with dieters and health food devotees besides being most convenient.

Various liquids such as fruit and vegetable juices are used in breads for enticing flavors.

Fats lubricate the glutenous framework of dough so that it can expand more easily. They also produce flavor and tenderness. Butter and margarine are used predominately in this book, mainly for flavor. Vegetable shortening, lard, and oil will create a fine texture, but lack the lushness of butter. For those on a cholesterol free diet, use an oil such as a safflower.

Suggestion: When preparing to bake, melt sufficient butter or margarine in a small saucepan for the selected recipe plus enough more to grease bowls and baking pans.

Sugar activates yeast quickly. It adds flavor and a golden crust. A variety of sugars such as white, brown, raw, honey, and syrups are used in breadmaking and may be interchanged in recipes. Dough which contains a large amount of sugar must be baked in a moderate oven or the bread will brown too fast. When large quantities of eggs and fats are used, the activity of yeast is retarded and a longer rising period is required.

Salt partially coordinates the flavor of bread although it is not so important that it cannot be eliminated. Fermentation is slightly controlled by salt. For those on a salt free diet, do not hesitate to cut or eliminate salt content. Salt substitutes are unsatisfactory. The flavor of good bread reduces the need for salt. Never use more salt than specified or growth of yeast may be harmed.

Eggs create a delicate structure, flaky crust, and good flavor. When a large number of eggs is used, the dough is easily handled, slower rising, and will have a drier texture. You may substitute one whole egg for every two egg yolks, or use two yolks for one egg. Do not forget that egg whites freeze and refrigerate well about two weeks.

TECHNIQUES OF BREADMAKING

PREPARATION
MIXING
KNEADING
RISING
SHAPING

BAKING
FREEZING AND STORAGE
HIGH ALTITUDE BAKING
PROBLEMS THAT MAY ARISE

PREPARATION

Select a recipe and read it completely. Get everything ready — ingredients, bowls, measuring and mixing spoons, cups, rubber spatula, pastry brush, and pans. *Reread your recipe.* Through careful planning and organization at the beginning, the whole process will ultimately become easier. With experience you can be more casual. It is preferable to make a whole recipe. Small recipes double easily. As long as you are devoting a day to breadmaking, make two or three recipes and start a pot of soup. Don't forget that bread is always a most welcome gift.

MIXING

There are several methods of bread mixing; batter, plain dough, sponge, overnight, and a combination of new procedures.

Batter or casserole bread is literally what it says, a mixture too soft to be kneaded. It rises quickly and takes the shape of the pan or bowl in which it bakes.

Plain or conventional dough combines all ingredients, is kneaded thoroughly, and allowed to rise as the recipe specifies.

Sponge method is a longer way in which yeast, liquid, sugar, and a portion of the flour are combined and allowed to double. The remaining ingredients are added, a thorough kneading applied, and the dough allowed to double again.

Overnight sponge is similar to the above, except that the first mixture is allowed to set overnight before the final ingredients are combined.

New methods are as follows:

1. Coolrise combines all the ingredients, the dough is kneaded, formed, and placed in the refrigerator from 2 to 8 hours before baking.

2. Can-Do-Quick is an idea developed by the Betty Crocker Kitchens in which only buttermilk is used as a liquid. All ingredients are combined with a light kneading and immediately formed into a loaf for one rising.

3. Rapidmix is the most popular of the newer methods. The process combines a portion of the dry ingredients including dry yeast, beaten thoroughly in an electric mixer with lukewarm liquids, then kneaded and allowed to rise as in the conventional way. Any of my recipes may be adapted to the Rapidmix method.

Conventional and Sponge systems will be used predominantly in this cookbook. Through these, you gain the real sense of breadmaking and the pleasure of working with yeast.

After everything is assembled, you are ready for mixing. Some recipes will combine the liquids and add them to the flour, while others will do just the reverse. After the first two or three cups of flour are beaten into the liquid, add only *one* cup at a time until the dough is of the right consistency. Following this technique of mixing, lessens the chance of adding too much flour. When the dough begins to pull away from the bowl, stop the addition of flour and place mixture on a lightly floured surface for kneading. *The exact amount of flour* can never be given due to variables in weather and flours. Too much flour makes a heavy dough. After kneading begins, add as little flour as possible. When mixing liquids into the flour, always start with a minimum amount of flour, then proceed as directed. Adding the correct amount of flour is one of the challenges of breadmaking.

KNEADING

Now comes the time when you can get your hands into the dough and push, pull, pat, slam, and spank to your heart's content. The first three secrets of excellent bread are *KNEAD, KNEAD, and KNEAD*. If there is no kneading surface built into your kitchen, purchase a marble slab (18x22"), or a good bread board. To hold either kind steady, a wet tea cloth may be placed underneath or small round sponge discs can be applied. A heavy pastry cloth works quite well but has more of a tendency to slip than the board or marble.

The technique of kneading is as follows: place the dough on a

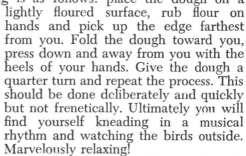

lightly floured surface, rub flour on hands and pick up the edge farthest from you. Fold the dough toward you, press down and away from you with the heels of your hands. Give the dough a quarter turn and repeat the process. This should be done deliberately and quickly but not frenetically. Ultimately you will find yourself kneading in a musical rhythm and watching the birds outside. Marvelously relaxing!

If possible, purchase a dough scraper (refer to suggested utensils). It is especially useful when beginning to knead and the dough is sticky. Pick up the dough with the scraper and knead with one hand until the dough becomes smoother, then proceed to finish the process with both hands. A dough scraper is invaluable for cleaning bread boards and kitchen cabinets.

If the dough is quite sticky, sprinkle more flour on your board and hands. With some dough, buttered hands solve the problem of stickiness. Do not expect to completely eliminate a moist feeling.

If the dough becomes dry and floury, then too much flour has been added. There is more danger of under kneading than over kneading, so work away. It is hard to ruin your dough. You can slam it on the counter, throw it on the floor or at one of the kids and that dough will still be alive and happy. Knead until the dough is smooth, satiny, and bouncy with tiny bubbles or blisters underneath the skin. With a forefinger, punch the dough, if it pops right back, then you have kneaded enough. The average amount of time for kneading will be about 10 minutes. Larger recipes require 15 minutes. Perhaps you may tire; cover the dough and rest a few minutes. You could knead for an hour or longer, and the dough will still be happy.

If you are lucky enough to have a mixer with a dough hook, combine ingredients as described under *MIXING*. Never dump everything in at once as this is too hard on the motor. Allow the mixer to knead 5 minutes at the number one position after the correct amount of flour has been added. Finish kneading by hand 3 to 5 minutes.

Why is kneading so important? Yeast forms gas bubbles which must be distributed evenly in the glutenous structure of the flour. By thoroughly kneading, the ingredients are well blended in the elastic framework of dough. Kneading is one of the charming delights of breadmaking. To all my female readers — your arms will become stronger, the bust firmer, and many problems solved. Men are excellent breadmakers for with their strength, they can make a beautifully textured bread.

RISING

Heavy crockery bowls are the best for proofing dough (refer to Glossary). They are quite inexpensive and can be purchased at most hardware and feed stores. *Rinse the bowl with hot water, dry thoroughly and brush with melted butter or margarine.*

After kneading, form the dough into a ball, drop into the greased bowl turning once to coat the top. Cover loosely with plastic wrap (do not seal) and a clean kitchen towel, preferably the terry cloth type. Be careful not to cover tightly as yeast needs air as well as warmth. The purpose of covering is to avoid forming a crust on the dough and to create a warm, cozy atmosphere. Place the bowl in a draft-free, warm spot. This can be on the back of the stove (never on a burner or pilot light), in an unlighted oven, or a cozy utility room. Modern kitchens are usually free of draft but each will have a comfortable, warm corner.

To understand the rising process: 1 cake or package of yeast will raise 8 cups of flour. For faster action, 1 cake to each 4 cups of flour is generally used. If you wish to give your bread an even faster push, add ¼ teaspoon of ginger to the liquid dissolving the yeast. When the dough has doubled in bulk, press a finger into the dough and pull it away quickly. If a deep indentation remains, the dough is ready for molding. If the depression springs back, cover and continue to let it rise.

If a second rising is specified, punch your fist down into the dough, knead lightly in the bowl, cover as before and allow to double. A second rising requires a shorter time than the first. Even though a recipe does not call for a second rising, but you are busy and cannot finish the bread, a second or third rising will never hurt. Do not allow the dough to over rise and fall back into itself. The bread will then be sour and heavy.

SHAPING

Turn the dough out on a lightly floured board and knead one or two minutes. Cover with a towel or plastic wrap and allow to rest 10 minutes. The dough will become more relaxed and easier to handle. Here are three of the most effective ways to mold a loaf of bread.

1. Cut the dough with a dough scraper into specified number of portions. With a rolling pin, roll one piece into a rectangle. Rolling helps eliminate bubbles. Press out any bubbles on the edges with your hands. Beginning with the narrow side, roll up like a jelly roll, seal the ends and seam by pinching the dough together. Be careful not to break the dough. Place seam side down into a greased loaf pan.

2. Roll into a rectangle as in the first method. Fold ⅓ of the narrow end to the middle and fold the other third on top so that they overlap. Seal the side and ends; place seam side down in a greased pan. Pat into a smooth shape.

3. A simple but effective method is patting and shaping the dough with your hands into a loaf. Do not be afraid of the dough; make it do what you want. If it does not mold as you wish, cover and allow to rest another 5 to 10 minutes. Other methods of shaping will be described with recipes.

BAKING

Standard loaf or bread pans are 9x5x3″ and 8½x4½x2½″. Other sizes available are 7½x3½x2¼″ and an individual size, 4½x2½x2½″. Any utensil used for baking should be brushed with melted butter, margarine or shortening. Never use oil as it absorbs into the dough and causes bread to stick to the pan.

Check the accuracy of your oven with a thermometer. In most communities, the utility companies will calibrate ovens free of charge. *Preheat oven during the last rising for at least 20 to 30 minutes.* The dough should rise to the top of pans or just curved over the tops. Bread is ready to bake when a light press of a finger leaves a small depression. Place bread on the center shelf or next to the lowest. Be sure the pans are spaced so that heat can circulate. Bread rises rapidly during the first fifteen minutes of baking, a fine skin is formed and the bread is "set". The oven may be opened after this period.

Metal baking pans are preferred. If glass loaf pans are used, lower the temperature of the oven 25°. If the bread becomes too brown, place a sheet of foil or heavy brown paper over the top during the last 15 minutes. Usually the specified cooking time will be adequate. If in doubt that the bread is done, thump with a knuckle or finger tips on top or side of bread. If there is a hollow sound rather like thumping a watermelon, and the bread has pulled slightly away from the pan, it is done. Another check is to turn loaf out of pan and if lightly browned on sides and bottom, it should be finished. If still in doubt, pop the bread back in the oven for another five minutes.

Turn loaves out on wire racks to cool — the bread should fall right out of the pan. If a soft crust is desired, brush with melted butter. It is better to allow bread to cool before cutting. However, if you cannot keep the family away, lay the bread on its side and cut with a good bread knife warmed in hot water and dried.

FREEZING AND STORAGE

The majority of breads freeze beautifully and if well wrapped will keep six months to a year. Allow bread to cool thoroughly. Wrap in foil, place in a plastic sack and label. When ready to use, remove the plastic sack and pop into a preheated 375° oven 35 to 45 minutes. If allowed to thaw first, then heat in the oven 25 minutes if you wish to serve the bread hot.

Uncooked dough may be formed into loaves after one rising, placed in a flat pan, and wrapped airtight with foil or plastic wrap. Store in the freezer. These loaves will keep about 2 weeks. Remove bread from freezer, place in a loaf pan and allow to stand at room temperature covered with a towel about 6 hours, or until doubled in bulk.

Another method is to place frozen loaves in the refrigerator overnight, remove next morning, and allow to double in bulk at room temperature. Rolls: the dough may be allowed to double, then formed, placed on a flat surface, wrapped airtight, and stored in the freezer for a two week period. Two or three hours before baking, remove from freezer, place on a greased baking sheet, and allow to double in size. Cook as directed.

Freezing uncooked dough is a fairly successful method for short periods of time. I have found that baking first, and then freezing is better. When storing bread for daily use, place in a plastic bag and keep in a well ventilated breadbox or drawer. Bread may be stored in the refrigerator but this does consume a large amount of space.

HIGH ALTITUDE BAKING

The higher you live, the faster the dough rises. Less yeast is necessary than at sea level or the bread will rise too fast. If a recipe calls for 3 cakes of yeast, use only 2. The timing element of fermentation will then become more equalized. First risings at 5000 feet will take about 65 minutes. The same bread at 7500 feet will double in 45 minutes. At 10,000 feet 40 minutes is usually ample time. Second bowl risings are always faster anywhere.

PROBLEMS THAT MAY ARISE

1. Porous Bread is caused from over rising or cooking at a temperature too low. Thorough kneading will also help eliminate this difficulty. When shaping loaves, press or roll out as many bubbles as possible.

2. Failure of bread to rise may be caused by old yeast or by dissolving yeast in water too hot which kills the action. It is better to have water too cool — use a thermometer.

3. Streaked Bread may be caused by under kneading and not kneading evenly. Too much flour will produce a heavy bread. I cannot emphasize enough the importance of adding flour in small portions, mixing thoroughly, and careful kneading.

4. Uneven Baking will be from using old, dark pans or too much dough in a pan. Crowding an oven shelf, allowing no air space, and temperatures too high can also contribute to this problem.

5. Rising Pointers: *be patient with the dough* — leave it alone to have a full rising. Set a timer and do other chores. Under rising makes a crumbly bread with a strong sour smell.

6. Temperature. Each kitchen is different as to amount of humidity and warmth. Do not forget that a rainy day makes a difference in the amount of flour required and in the rising time. Learn to do the finger test (page 12) and this will give you a better idea of your own environment.

7. Shaping. In most of my recipes a resting period is suggested before forming the dough into loaves. This gives the dough a chance to relax, which makes easier manipulation. A rest period is especially important in forming rolls and braided breads.

8. Crusts. Do not expect to produce a crust that compares with fine bakeries. They are equiped with specially built ovens sometimes lined with tile or brick and with piped in steam. However, methods will be described showing how to produce a lovely, crusty bread that you will be proud of. No commercial bakery can produce the luscious home made texture that you can. If a crust is quite dark and blisters, it is usually from under rising.

9. Interruptions. Dough can be made to adjust to your time schedule if emergencies arise. If interrupted when kneading, cover the dough with a towel and leave it 15 to 20 minutes. If you have to feed the baby, punch the dough down and allow it to rise again. If loaves over rise in the pans, take them out, knead lightly, allow to rest 5 minutes and reshape. Bread dough can take a lot of punishment, so relax and enjoy your adventure.

SUGGESTED UTENSILS FOR BREAD AND SOUPS

Breadboard, marble slab or pastry cloth
Measuring cups for dry ingredients
Measuring cups for liquids with lip for pouring
Standard measuring spoons
Large bowls, preferably crockery
Small bowl for dissolving yeast
Sauce pans for heating liquids and melting butter
Wooden spoon
Rubber spatula
Dough scraper
Kitchen scissors
Ruler
Variety of bread or loaf pans, baking sheets, cake pans, soufflé bowls,
    casseroles, charlotte mold, and muffin tins
Wire Racks
Rolling pin
Electric mixer, egg beater and/or whisk
Soft pastry brush, 1" wide
Feather brushes
Spatula
Plastic wrap and bags
Foil
Tape for labeling
Kitchen towels, preferably terry cloth
Two-quart crocks with lids for sourdough starters
Cheesecloth
Doughnut and biscuit cutters
Sharp knives
Razor blade
Straight-edge knife for leveling flour
Candy thermometer
Fancy pans such as Kugelhoff, Savarin, Bundt, Brioche tins, Popover
Soup pot
Skimmer
Ladle
Kitchen scales
Sharp grater for citrus fruit
Electric blender
Coffee cans of various sizes
Ring molds

DOUGH SCRAPERS

KUGELHOFF

SOUFFLE BOWLS

BUNDT PANS

CHARLOTTE MOLDS

BRIOCHE TINS

MUFFIN TINS

SAVARIN

TUBE PAN

BASIC
WHITE BREADS
WITH VARIATIONS

SOUPS:

> *Minted Green Pea*
> *Chicken Broth with Mushrooms*
> *Cream of Zucchini*
> *Gazpacho or "Soup Salad"*

BASIC WHITE BREAD I

My first recipe is especially adaptable for a beginning baker. The ingredients are simple and the dough easy to manipulate. Treat your family to the joy of a wonderful aroma, and eating hot bread right out of the oven! *Read the chapter on Techniques before your first endeavor.*

2 packages dry compressed yeast
2½ cups warm water
2 teaspoons salt
2 tablespoons sugar
¾ cup dry skim milk

3 tablespoons melted butter or margarine
6 to 6½ cups white flour
Melted butter or margarine

Sprinkle yeast over the warm water in a large mixing bowl. Stir with a fork until dissolved. Blend in the salt, sugar, dry milk, and butter. Beat in 3 cups of flour with a rubber spatula until mixture is smooth. Gradually add enough flour to make a soft, workable dough that pulls away from sides of the bowl. Turn dough out on a lightly floured board and knead until smooth and satiny, about 10 minutes. If you tire, cover the dough with a towel and rest a few minutes. Sprinkle more flour on your board and hands when necessary but do not allow dough to become dry. Place dough in a warm, greased bowl, turning to coat the top. Cover loosely with plastic wrap and towel. Set aside to double in bulk, about 1 hour.

Punch down the dough, knead lightly in the bowl, recover, and allow to double again, about 45 minutes. Turn out on a floured surface and knead 2 or 3 minutes. Cover with a towel or plastic wrap and let rest 10 to 15 minutes. Divide into 3 portions. Mold in loaves and place in greased 8½x4½x2½" loaf pans. Cover with a towel and let rise to tops of pans, about 1 hour. Bake in a preheated 375° oven 30 minutes. Remove from pans and cool on wire racks. Brush tops of bread with melted butter while loaves are hot, if desired.

DIRECTIONS FOR VARIOUS SIZES OF LOAVES—BASIC BREAD I

9x5x3" loaf
Produces 2 loaves
Pan rising time: 45 minutes to 1 hour
Baking time at 375° is 35 to 40 minutes.

4x7½x2" loaf
Produces 4 loaves
Pan rising time: 1 hour
Baking time at 375° is 25 minutes.

6x3x2″ loaf

Produces 8 loaves
Pan rising time: 1 hour
Baking time at 375° is 25 minutes.

2½x4x2″ loaf

Produces 16 loaves
Pan rising time: 45 minutes to 1 hour
Baking time at 375° is 20 minutes.

NOTE:

Refer to GLOSSARY on pages 277-279 for words or phrases you do not understand. If the glossary does not give an explanation, check your local dictionary.

BASIC WHITE BREAD II

A larger recipe than Basic Bread I with a sturdy texture that makes it exceptionally great for a large family. If left alone for a day, the bread is excellent for sandwiches.

3 packages dry or compressed yeast
4 cups warm water
3 tablespoons sugar
1 tablespoon salt

⅓ cup melted butter or
margarine
11 to 12 cups white flour

Combine yeast and water in a large mixing bowl (refer to Ingredients, page 7). Stir with a fork until dissolved. Blend in the sugar, salt, and butter. Beat in 4 cups of flour with a rubber spatula until the batter is smooth. Gradually add sufficient flour to make a soft, workable dough that pulls away from sides of the bowl. Turn dough out on a lightly floured board and knead 15 minutes, or until smooth and elastic. Add more flour in small portions if necessary to cut stickiness, but do not allow dough to become dry. Rest, if you tire kneading. When using a heavy mixer with a dough hook, follow directions as described. Knead at the Number 1 position for 8 minutes and finish by hand 4 or 5 minutes. Place the dough in a large, warm, greased bowl, turning to coat the top. Cover loosely with plastic wrap and a towel. Allow to double in bulk, approximately 1 hour.

Punch down the dough, turn out on a floured board and knead 3 to 5 minutes. Place dough back in the bowl, recover and allow to double a second time, about 45 minutes.

Turn dough out on a floured surface and knead lightly. Cover and let rest 10 minutes. Shape in 4 loaves and place in greased loaf pans (8½x4½x2½″) Cover with a towel and let rise to tops of pans, about 45 minutes. Bake in a preheated 400° oven 35 minutes. Remove from oven and turn out on wire racks to cool. Brush tops of loaves while hot with melted butter if a softer crust is desired.

OPTION

4 cups of warm milk, or half milk and half water may be substituted for the warm water. Milk will give a slightly softer texture; it is equally delicious and will add enrichment. Follow directions as described.

FREEZER WHITE BREAD

Freezing uncooked dough is a simple and successful process. Uncooked dough must be wrapped thoroughly and will keep no more than four weeks in the freezer.

Directions are as·follows: when you have finished kneading either the Basic White Bread I or II, cover dough with a towel and allow to rest 20 minutes. Divide dough into 3 or 4 portions. Form each piece in a smooth ball. Place on greased baking sheets. Cover with plastic wrap and freeze until firm. Remove and wrap the frozen loaves in foil and place in plastic bags. Label date of freezing and kind of bread. When ready to use, remove a loaf from the freezer. Remove from wrapping and place on an ungreased pan. Cover with a towel and let stand at room temperature until thawed, about 4 hours. You may then mold into a loaf and place in a greased bread pan or leave it in the round shape and place in a greased cake tin. Cover and let rise until doubled in bulk, about 1½ hours. Brush loaf with melted butter or margarine. Bake in a preheated 350° oven 35 to 40 minutes. Cool on wire racks or serve piping hot.

Any plain, simple dough may be frozen by following the above directions. Do not attempt to freeze uncooked doughs heavy with sugar, butter, and eggs.

BUTTERMILK BREAD

This recipe produces the kind of luscious, firm texture that epitomizes a home made bread — one of my favorites.

2 packages dry or compressed yeast	4 tablespoons sugar
½ cup warm water	2 teaspoons salt
2 cups buttermilk	¼ teaspoon baking soda
½ cup melted butter or margarine	8 to 9 cups flour

Sprinkle yeast over the warm water in a small bowl; stir with a fork until dissolved. Set aside. Heat buttermilk in a small saucepan to lukewarm. Curdling of milk will not hurt. Transfer milk to a large mixing bowl. Blend in the butter and yeast mixture. In a separate bowl, combine sugar, salt, soda, and 2 cups of flour. Add to the milk mixture and beat thoroughly with a rubber spatula. Gradually stir in enough more flour to make a soft, workable dough that pulls away from sides of the bowl (refer to Techniques, page 11). Turn out on a lightly floured surface. Knead about 10 minutes or until smooth and satiny. Place dough in a warm, greased bowl, turning to coat the top. Cover loosely with plastic wrap and towel. Allow to double in a draft free spot about 1 hour. Punch down, knead lightly in the bowl, recover, and allow a second rising, approximately 45 minutes. Turn out on a floured board and knead 1 minute. Cover with a towel and let rest 10 minutes. Divide dough in 3 portions. Shape in loaves and place in greased 8½x4½x2½" loaf pans. Cover with a towel and let rise until nicely curved over tops of the pans, about 40 minutes. Bake in a preheated 350° oven 35 to 40 minutes. Remove from pans to wire racks. Brush with melted butter if desired.

WHITE BREAD WITH EGGS

Beautiful brown loaves with just a faint aroma of honey and a golden crust that melts in your mouth!

2 packages dry or compressed yeast	2 cups warm milk or water
½ cup warm water	1½ teaspoons salt
1 tablespoon sugar	¼ cup honey
2 eggs, lightly beaten	8 to 9 cups flour
½ cup melted butter or margarine	Melted butter or margarine

The Sponge: Combine in a large mixing bowl, the yeast, ½ cup of warm water, and sugar. Stir with a fork until dissolved. Cover with a towel and set aside for 20 minutes.

When the sponge is bubbling nicely, add eggs, butter, milk or water, salt, and honey, stirring until smooth. Beat in 2 cups of flour. Gradually add enough more flour to make a soft, workable dough that leaves sides of the bowl. Turn out on a lightly floured surface and knead until smooth and resilient, about 10 minutes. Add only enough more flour to make a smooth dough.

Round dough into a ball and place in a warm, greased bowl, turning to coat the top. Cover loosely with plastic wrap and towel (refer to Techniques, page 12). Set in a draft free spot until double in bulk, about 1 hour. Knead lightly in the bowl, recover and allow to double again, approximately 45 minutes. On a lightly floured board, knead 2 or 3 minutes, cover and let rest 10 minutes. Cut in 3 portions, shape in loaves and place in greased pans 8½x4½x2½″. Cover and let rise to tops of pans, 45 minutes to an hour. Bake in preheated 375° oven 35 minutes. Remove and turn out on wire racks to cool. Brush with melted butter while hot, if desired.

OVERNIGHT WHITE BREAD

A delicately textured bread that can be started before retiring and finished by noon the next day.

1 package dry or compressed yeast	¼ cup melted butter
¼ cup lukewarm water	2 tablespoons sugar
1 cup warm milk	1½ teaspoons salt
1 cup warm water	6 to 7 cups flour

The Sponge: (Refer to Techniques, page 10). Sprinkle yeast over the ¼ cup of warm water, stirring with a fork until dissolved. Set aside. In a large mixing bowl, combine warm milk and water, melted butter, sugar, salt, and yeast mixture. Beat in 3 cups of flour, mixing thoroughly until smooth. Cover carefully with plastic wrap and towel. Place bowl in a warm, draft free spot to rise overnight.

Next morning, at your leisure, stir the sponge down and add enough remaining flour to make a firm dough. Turn out on a lightly floured board. Knead until smooth and elastic, about 10 minutes. Form into a ball, place in a warm greased bowl, turning to coat the top. Cover loosely with plastic wrap and a towel. Allow to rise until *tripled* in bulk, about 2 hours.

Remove dough to a lightly floured surface, knead lightly, cover and allow to rest 10 minutes. Shape in 2 loaves and place in greased pans

(8½x4½x2½"). Cover with a towel and let rise in a draft free spot until doubled in bulk, about 1 hour. Bake in a preheated 350° oven 50 to 60 minutes. Remove from pans and turn out on wire racks to cool. Brush with melted butter while hot, if desired.

SESAME POTATO BRAIDS

A lovely dough to manipulate into golden braids or a cottage loaf and sprinkled lavishly with healthful sesame seeds.

1 cup lukewarm mashed potatoes	2 teaspoons salt
2 packages dry or compressed yeast	¼ cup dry skim milk
½ cup warm water	5½ cups flour, approximately
1 cup warm potato water	1 egg white beaten with 1
½ cup melted butter or margarine	tablespoon water
3 tablespoons sugar	Untoasted sesame seed

Prepare 1 cup mashed potatoes with either regular or instant potatoes. If using instant, combine 1¼ cups boiling water with 1 cup instant potatoes. Beat until smooth. Measure out 1 cup of potatoes and use the remainder to make the potato water. Set mashed potatoes aside to cool.

Combine yeast and ½ cup warm water in a large mixing bowl, stirring with a fork until dissolved. Add the potato water, butter, sugar, salt, dry milk, and potatoes. Blend until mixture is smooth. Add 2 cups of flour and beat thoroughly. Gradually add sufficient flour until dough pulls away from the bowl. Turn out on a lightly floured board and knead until smooth and satiny, about 10 minutes. Place in a warm, greased, bowl, turning to coat the top. Allow to double in bulk, about 1 hour. Punch the dough down, cover and let rest 10 minutes.

Divide dough in half and cover one portion. Cut the other piece in 3 equal portions. Roll into 14" smooth ropes. Braid, starting from the center and working out toward each end. Place on a greased baking sheet and tuck ends under. Divide remaining dough in 3 pieces and roll in 12" ropes. Braid and place in a greased 9x5x3" loaf pan. Cover and allow to double, about 45 minutes. Brush loaves with egg glaze and sprinkle liberally with sesame seed. Bake in a preheated 400° oven 10 minutes. Lower heat to 350° and bake 30 to 35 minutes. Cool on wire racks.

VARIATIONS

Cottage Loaf: Divide dough in half. Set one portion aside and cover with a towel. Cut 1/3 off the other piece of dough. Place the larger portion in a greased 1 quart souffle bowl. Pat dough to cover the bottom. With your hands, make an indentation in the center. Round the smaller portion into a ball and set in center of the prepared dough. Cover and let rise until doubled, about 45 minutes. Repeat with remaining dough. Brush with egg glaze, sprinkle with sesame seed and bake as directed.

Caraway Bread: When mixing ingredients together, add 1 tablespoon of caraway seeds. Proceed as directed.

CASEROLE BREAD

A quick, versatile batter bread with an unusually good flavor adaptable to variations. (Refer to Techniques, page 10).

2 packages dry or compressed yeast
2 cups warm milk
¼ cup sugar
1 teaspoon salt

¼ cup melted butter or
*   margarine*
1 egg, beaten
4½ to 5 cups flour

Sprinkle yeast over the warm milk in a large mixing bowl, stirring with a fork until dissolved. Add sugar, salt, melted butter, and egg, mixing until well blended. Gradually begin adding the flour, beating until the mixture becomes a smooth batter. This may be done with a wooden spoon, rubber spatula (especially good for scraping the sides) or an electric mixer. Cover the bowl with a towel. Place in a warm, protected spot to double, about 45 minutes.

Stir down and pour into a thoroughly greased 2½ quart souffle bowl or casserole. Cover with a towel and allow to rise ½ inch from top of bowl, about 25 minutes. Do not let rise above the rim, or batter will spill over in the oven. Bake in a preheated 350° oven 1 hour. If bread becomes too brown, place a sheet of foil over top the last 10 minutes. Turn bread out and cool on wire rack. This bread may be baked in 2 greased loaf pans (8½x4½x2½") 40 minutes.

VARIATIONS

Raisin-Batter Bread: At end of the first rising, beat in 1 cup of scalded and dried raisins or currants. Proceed as directed.

Cheese Batter Bread: At end of the first rising, add 2 cups of grated cheddar cheese and proceed as directed,

HERB FILLED BREAD

A delicious and tantalizing aroma will float through your house when this bread is baking—marvelous for a buffet dinner. Makes one large loaf.

2 tablespoons butter
1½ cups finely chopped parsley
1 cup finely chopped green onions
1 garlic clove, minced
½ teaspoon salt
Freshly ground black pepper

2 dashes of Cayenne
1 egg, lightly beaten
½ Basic White Bread I or II
   or Buttermilk Bread
Melted butter

Melt butter in a small skillet. Sauté parsley, onions, and garlic over moderate heat. Stir until wilted, reducing mixture to half the original volume, but do not allow to brown. Season with salt, a few grindings of black pepper and Cayenne. Set aside to cool.

At end of the second rising of either Basic White Breads I or II or the Buttermilk bread, cut off suggested amount of dough. On a lightly floured board, roll dough in a rectangle, 9x14″. Brush lightly with part of the beaten egg to ½″ of edges. Mix remaining egg into the cooled vegetable mixture. With a rubber spatula, spread herb mixture over the dough, leaving ½″ free edge. Roll tightly jelly roll style starting from the narrow end. Pinch edge and sides to seal. Place rolled dough in a greased 9x5x3″ loaf pan, seam side down to avoid leakage. Pierce loaf with a toothpick about 6 times. Brush top with melted butter, cover with a towel, and allow to rise in a warm, draft free place until slightly curved over top of pan, about 45 minutes. Bake in a preheated 400° oven 50 minutes. Remove loaf from pan and cool on a wire rack. This bread freezes well so several loaves can be made ahead for a party.

MIKE'S PEANUT BUTTER SWIRL

This idea originated with my youngest son — so here is a tribute to children of all ages who are lovers of peanut butter and grape jelly!

¾ cup peanut butter, crunchy or plain	⅓ recipe of Buttermilk or Basic White Dough II or
½ cup grape jelly or jam	½ recipe Basic White I

At end of the last rising before baking, roll selected dough into an oblong 9x14". Combine the peanut butter and jelly, stirring until well blended. With a rubber spatula, spread peanut butter mixture over the dough to ½" of edges. Roll tightly from narrow end, jelly roll fashion. Seal the side and ends by pinching thoroughly. Place seam side down in a greased loaf pan, 9x5x3". Pierce loaf 6 times with a toothpick almost to the bottom. This helps hold the swirls together. Cover with a towel and let rise to top of pan, about 45 minutes. Bake in a preheated 350° oven 45 minutes. Turn out on a wire rack to cool. If you have to cut the loaf while hot, do so carefully with a warmed knife, and the bread turned on its side. If the children will allow it to cool, the bread will be much easier to handle. Try it toasted for breakfast!

VARIATION

Combine ¾ cup peanut butter with ½ cup honey or light molasses. Proceed as directed.

BUBBLE LOAVES

Here are two loaves of bread that are great fun to make and amusing to eat. Just pull off a bubble and pop it in your mouth. Both loaves are especially adaptable to Basic White, Buttermilk or White Bread with Eggs.

POPPY SEED BUBBLE LOAF

⅓ cup poppy seeds	Melted butter or margarine

At the end of the second rising of any above suggested breads, pinch or cut off small portions of dough about 1" in diameter. Round quickly into balls. Dip the *top* of each ball in melted butter and then in poppy seeds. Place buttered side up in a greased pan — either a loaf or tube pan. Pile balls on top of each other until the pan is ½ to ¾ full. Cover with a towel and place in a warm spot to rise 30 minutes. Bake in a preheated 375° oven 40 minutes for smaller pans and 50 minutes for a large loaf. Turn out on wire racks to cool.

CINNAMON BUBBLE LOAF

⅓ cup Cinnamon-Sugar mixture, page 131   Melted butter or margarine

Follow directions given for the Poppy Seed Loaf. If desired, you may sprinkle ½ cup raisins among the balls of dough. Baked in a 10" angel food cake pan, makes this a most attractive loaf for a brunch.

RAISIN-CINNAMON BREAD

Any of the white breads may be used for this recipe. Suggestions: ⅓ of Basic White II, Potato, Egg Bread, Buttermilk or ½ of Overnight and Basic White I.

1 cup raisins or currants	*½ cup chopped nuts, optional*
½ cup sugar	*Melted butter or margarine*
1 tablespoon cinnamon	*Confectioner's Icing*

Place raisins or currants in a sieve and run hot water over them; shake off excess water and pat dry on paper towels. At end of the last rising, before forming into loaves of any suggested bread, cut off desired amount of dough and place on a lightly floured board. Put the raisins or currants on top of the dough. Begin kneading carefully until well distributed. Cover and allow to rest 5 minutes. Roll into an oblong 8x12". Brush with butter or margarine to within ½" of edges. Mix sugar and cinnamon together. Sprinkle over the dough. Add nuts at this time if desired. (Option: instead of kneading raisins into the dough, they may be sprinkled over the sugar mixture.) Roll tightly from narrow end, jelly roll fashion. Pinch the ends and side to seal thoroughly. Place seam side down in a greased pan, 9x5x3". Pierce the loaf in 6 places with a toothpick to release air. Cover with a towel, place in a draft free spot, and let rise to top of pan, about 45 minutes. Bake in a preheated 350° oven 35 to 40 minutes. Cool on a wire rack. The loaf may be dribbled with Confectioner's Icing, page 268.

MINTED GREEN PEA SOUP

A refreshing, light green soup that is lovely served in glass bowls or cups. Serves six.

3 cups chicken stock
1 garlic clove, peeled
1 small onion stuck with 1 clove
1 large sprig of fresh mint or
   1 teaspoon dried mint

1 package frozen green peas
   (10 ounce box)
1 cup heavy cream

In a large saucepan, combine the chicken stock, garlic, onion, mint, and peas. Bring quickly to a boil and cook partially covered, about 10 minutes or until peas are tender. Remove onion and clove. Whirl the soup through a blender and transfer to a clean saucepan. Return to moderate heat and slowly pour in the cream, stirring constantly. Serve hot immediately. For a summer soup, chill thoroughly. Serve in cold soup bowls with a bit of chopped fresh mint sprinkled on top.

CHICKEN BROTH WITH MUSHROOMS

A most gratifying soup that can utilize left overs. Chicken bouillon cubes, canned, or home made broth may be used.

½ cup finely chopped celery
2 tablespoons butter or margarine
½ cup sliced mushrooms
6 cups chicken broth
1 cup cooked rice

Salt
Freshly ground black pepper
Lemon juice
Minced parsley or watercress

In a small saucepan, saute' celery in butter or margarine until almost tender. Add mushrooms and cook five more minutes, stirring constantly.

Bring chicken broth to a boil in a large container. Add the celery-mushroom mixture and cooked rice to the broth. Bring soup to a boil, adjust for salt and pepper. Add drops of lemon juice to bring out the full flavor of combined ingredients. On each serving, sprinkle a portion of minced parsley or watercress. Serves 8.

CREAM OF ZUCCHINI SOUP

One of my most popular recipes — a refreshing, lovely green soup that freezes and doubles beautifully.

1½ pounds zucchini, washed and sliced
¾ cup water
¾ teaspoon salt
¾ teaspoon sugar
½ teaspoon basil
2 tablespoons finely chopped onion
3 tablespoons butter or margarine

3 tablespoons flour
½ teaspoon salt
Freshly ground black
  pepper
2 cups warm milk
Finely chopped parsley

Combine zucchini, water, the ¾ teaspoon salt, sugar, and basil in a saucepan. Bring to a boil; cover and simmer until tender, about 15 minutes. Purée the zucchini and liquid in a mixer or blender. Set aside.

In a large saucepan, sauté onion in butter or margarine until tender, but do not allow to brown. With a small whisk, blend in flour, ½ teaspoon salt, and several grindings of black pepper. Add milk and puréed zucchini, stirring with a wooden spoon until smooth. Taste and correct seasoning. Stir until mixture thickens and comes to a boil. For presentation, sprinkle a little freshly chopped parsley on each serving. Serves 8 to 10.

GAZPACHO OR "SOUP-SALAD"

For a summer patio party, try serving this soup from a huge brandy snifter. Guests will love the beautiful color and fresh taste. Recipe doubles and triples easily.

3 hard boiled eggs, separated
2 tablespoons oil
2 cloves garlic, crushed
2 teaspoons Worcestershire
1 teaspoon dry mustard
2 or 3 dashes of Tabasco
Salt to taste
Freshly ground black pepper
Juice of 1 lemon or 2 limes
1 quart tomato juice

1 small finely minced cucumber
1 medium size mild onion, chopped
* very fine*
*   •   •   •*
1 sweet green pepper, finely
* chopped*
Thin slices of lemon
Ice cubes
Hot croutons

Work egg yolks and oil with a fork into a smooth paste in a wooden salad bowl. Add the crushed garlic, Worcestershire, dry mustard, Tabasco, salt, black pepper, and lemon juice. Slowly stir in the tomato juice, blending well. Add the finely cut cucumber and onion. Place in a crock or jar, cover and allow to chill at least 3 hours, preferably overnight.

PRESENTATION

Cut egg whites into thin strips. Place on bottom of chilled soup bowls with the chopped green pepper and thinly sliced lemon. Ladle soup into bowls. Add an ice cube to each serving and sprinkle with piping hot croutons. Serves 8 to 10.

WHOLE WHEAT AND OATMEAL BREADS

SOUPS:

Beef Wine Stew with Wild Rice

Hearty Split Pea

Old Fashioned Potato and Onion

Navy Bean

Mid-Eastern Lentil Soup with Spinach

BASIC WHOLE WHEAT BREAD

An excellent bread for beginners in the use of whole wheat flour. It is a simply made recipe producing loaves with an earthy aroma and flavor.

2 packages dry or compressed
   yeast
2 cups lukewarm water
2 teaspoons salt
3 tablespoons sugar
3 cups unbleached white flour

½ cup hot water
⅓ cup butter or margarine
⅓ cup brown sugar,
   molasses or honey
4 to 5 cups stone ground
   whole wheat flour

The Sponge: Sprinkle yeast over the warm water in a large mixing bowl. Stir with a fork until dissolved. Add the salt, 3 tablespoons of sugar, and white flour. Beat well with a rubber spatula until smooth. Cover with towel and set in a warm spot until light and bubbly, about 1 hour.

Meanwhile, combine hot water, butter, brown sugar, molasses or honey; stir and cool to lukewarm. When the sponge is bubbly, add the sugar mixture and enough whole wheat flour to make a soft, workable dough. Turn out on a lightly floured board and knead until smooth and bouncy, about 10 minutes. If dough is sticky, add small amounts of white flour while kneading (refer to Techniques, page 11). Place dough in a warm, greased bowl, turning to coat the top. Cover loosely with plastic wrap and a towel. Set in a warm spot about 1 hour or until double in bulk. Turn dough out on a board and knead lightly. Cover with a towel and allow to rest 10 minutes. Divide in 2 portions and shape into loaves. Place in greased loaf pans 8½x4½x2½″. Cover and let curve slightly over tops of pans, about 30 minutes. Bake in a preheated 350° oven 45 minutes. Turn out on racks to cool. Brush with melted butter if a soft crust is desired.

ONE HUNDRED PERCENT WHOLE WHEAT BREAD

A firm entirely whole wheat bread. Using a stone ground flour will enhance the nutritive value plus creating a delightfully nutty flavor.

3 packages of dry or compressed
   yeast
1 cup warm water
½ cup butter or margarine
1 tablespoon salt
1 cup boiling water

1 cup honey or light molasses
1 cup dry skim milk
2 cups water
10 to 11 cups stone ground
   whole wheat flour

The Sponge: (Refer to Techniques, page 10.) Sprinkle yeast over the cup of warm water, stirring with a fork until dissolved. Set aside. In a large mixing bowl, combine butter or margarine, salt, ½ cup of the honey or molasses, and boiling water. Blend thoroughly. Add the dry milk and 2 cups of water. Stir in the yeast mixture. Measure in 4 cups of flour, beating until smooth with a rubber spatula or an electric mixer. Cover with a towel, set in a warm place until light and doubled in bulk, about 30 minutes.

When the sponge has doubled, blend in the remaining honey or molasses and sufficient flour to make a *soft dough*. Be careful to add no more flour than necessary, for with whole wheat the dough can soon become stiff and unworkable. Turn out on a lightly floured surface. Knead 10 to 15 minutes or until smooth and elastic. Brush hands and board with flour when needed. Place dough in a large, warm, greased bowl, turning to coat the top. Cover loosely with plastic wrap and a towel. Allow to double in bulk, about 1½ hours. Grease 3 large loaf pans (9x5x3") or 4 smaller ones (8½x4½x2½"). Punch down the dough, shape in desired number of loaves, and place in prepared pans. Cover and allow to curve over tops of pans, about 1 hour. Bake in a preheated 350° oven 45 minutes for small loaves and 55 for larger ones. Cool on wire racks. Brush with melted butter, if desired.

RAISIN ORANGE LOAF

Whole wheat has an affinity for the flavor of orange and white raisins. Try this toasted with the Orange Crunchy Butter on page 267.

> ½ cup white raisins, scalded
>   and dried
> ½ cup chopped candied orange peel

> ½ One Hundred Percent Whole
>   Wheat Dough
> Confectioner's Icing (optional)

At end of the second rising, divide the One Hundred Percent Whole Wheat dough in half. Knead the raisins and orange peel into the dough until the fruit is well distributed. Cover and let rest 10 minutes. Shape in 2 loaves and place in greased loaf pans, 8½x4½x2½". Cover with a towel and allow to double, about 1 hour. Bake in a preheated 350° oven 40 to 45 minutes. Turn out on racks to cool. If desired, these loaves may be frosted with Confectioner's Icing, page 268 using orange juice as the mixing liquid.

CRACKED WHEAT BREAD

A healthful, crunchy loaf with a marvelous crust; one of my husband's favorites. Great to keep in the freezer when unexpected guests arrive.

1½ cups cracked wheat	¼ cup melted butter or margarine
2 cups boiling water	2 teaspoons salt
2 packages of dry or compressed yeast	½ cup brown sugar or molasses
½ cup warm water	2 cups whole wheat flour
1 cup warm milk	4 to 5 cups unbleached white flour

Combine cracked wheat and boiling water in a large mixing bowl; stir and cool to lukewarm. Sprinkle yeast over the warm water, stirring with a fork until dissolved. To the cooled cracked wheat mixture, add the warm milk, butter, salt, brown sugar or molasses, and yeast mixture. Stir with a rubber spatula until well mixed. Add the whole wheat flour and beat until smooth. Stir in enough white flour to make a soft dough. Turn out on a lightly floured surface and knead 10 minutes. This dough can be sticky; if necessary add a bit more white flour while kneading. Place in a warm, greased bowl turning to coat the top (refer to Techniques, page 12). Cover loosely with plastic wrap and a towel. Set in a draft free spot and allow to double, about 1½ hours. Turn out on a board and cut in 3 portions. Cover with a towel and let rest 10 minutes. Mold into loaves and place in greased pans, 8½x4½x2½". Allow to double in bulk, about 30 minutes. Bake in a preheated 350° oven 1 hour. Turn out on racks to cool. Brush with melted butter while loaves are hot, if desired.

WHEAT GERM – WHOLE WHEAT BREAD

The addition of wheat germ in this recipe gives a toasty flavor. Unusually good for family loaves, for if allowed to cool, the bread will make excellent sandwiches and toast.

¾ cup hot milk	3 cups stone ground whole wheat flour
½ cup wheat germ	3 to 4 cups unbleached white flour
2 packages dry or compressed yeast	Melted butter or margarine
1¾ cup warm water	
½ cup melted butter or margarine	
1½ teaspoons salt	
½ cup honey, molasses or brown sugar (packed)	

Combine hot milk and wheat germ in a small mixing bowl. Set aside until lukewarm. In a large mixing bowl, combine yeast and warm water, stirring with a fork until dissolved. Blend in the butter, salt, and choice of sugar. Add the wheat germ mixture. Beat in the whole wheat flour until batter is smooth. Gradually add sufficient white flour to make a soft, workable dough. Turn out on a lightly floured board and knead until smooth and elastic, about 10 minutes. Place in a warm, greased bowl turning to coat the top. Cover loosely with plastic wrap and a towel. Set aside in a protected spot to double in bulk, about 1½ hours. Punch the dough down, turn out on a lightly floured surface (use white flour), cover, and let rest 10 minutes. Shape in 3 loaves and place in greased 8½x4½x2½" pans (refer to Techniques, page 14). Cover and let rise to tops of pans, about 1 hour. Bake in a preheated 400° oven 10 minutes. Reduce heat to 350° and bake 30 minutes. Remove from pans. Brush with melted butter, if desired, and cool on wire racks.

SESAME WHOLE WHEAT BREAD

Sesame seeds, shredded wheat, and whole wheat combines this bread into a triple, rich flavor. A favorite of my students and one of the best toasting breads.

2 cups boiling water	*⅓ cup brown sugar*
2 shredded wheat biscuits	*2 teaspoons salt*
1 package of dry or compressed yeast	*½ cup toasted sesame seeds**
¼ cup warm water	*2 cups whole wheat flour*
¼ cup melted butter or margarine	*2 to 3 cups white flour*

Pour boiling water over the shredded wheat biscuits in a large mixing bowl. Cool to lukewarm. Sprinkle yeast over the warm water, stirring with a fork until dissolved. Add melted butter, brown sugar, salt, sesame seeds, and whole wheat flour to the cooled shredded wheat mixture. Beat well with a rubber spatula or an electric mixer. Stir in the yeast mixture and enough white flour to make a soft dough. Turn out on a lightly floured board. Knead until smooth and elastic, about 10 minutes (refer to Techniques, page 12). Place dough in a warm, greased bowl turning to coat the top. Cover loosely with plastic wrap and a towel. Allow to rise until doubled, about 1½ hours. Punch the dough down, cover and let rest 10 minutes. Shape in 2 loaves. Place in greased pans (8½x4½x2½"), cover with a towel and let rise to tops of pans, about 30 minutes. Bake in a preheated 375° oven 35 to 40 minutes. Turn loaves out on a rack to cool. Brush with melted butter if desired.

*TOASTED SESAME SEEDS

Spread seeds in a shallow pan. Toast in a preheated 300° oven 20 to 30 minutes, stirring occasionally. Do not allow to burn!

WHOLE WHEAT EGG BREAD

A light whole wheat bread that is easy to handle, makes a crisp toast, and usable in several variations.

2 cups hot water
½ cup honey or brown sugar
⅓ cup butter or margarine
2 packages dry or compressed yeast
½ cup warm water
2 eggs, lightly beaten

1 teaspoon salt
½ cup wheat germ
3 cups stone ground whole
   wheat flour
4 to 5 cups unbleached
   white flour

Combine the hot water, honey or brown sugar, and butter in a large mixing bowl. Cool to lukewarm. Sprinkle yeast over the ½ cup warm water, stirring with a fork until dissolved. Add yeast mixture, eggs, salt, wheat germ, and whole wheat flour to the cooled ingredients. Beat with a rubber spatula until smooth. Gradually stir in enough white flour to make a soft dough that pulls away from sides of the bowl. Knead on a lightly floured surface until smooth and elastic, about 10 minutes. Place in a warm, greased bowl turning to coat the top. Cover loosely with plastic wrap and a towel. Allow to double in a warm, protected spot about 1½ hours. Punch the dough down in the bowl, knead lightly; cover, and allow to rise again until doubled, about 30 minutes.

Turn dough out on a floured surface and knead one minute. Cover with a towel and allow to rest 10 minutes. Shape in 3 loaves (refer to Techniques, page 13) and place in greased loaf pans, 8½x4½x2½". Cover with a towel and let rise to tops of pans, about 30 minutes. Bake in a preheated 350° oven 35 to 40 minutes. Cool on wire racks.

WHOLE WHEAT CINNAMON-RAISIN SWIRL

½ of Whole Wheat Egg Dough
Melted butter or margarine
½ cup sugar
1 tablespoon cinnamon

½ cup white or dark raisins
   rinsed in hot water and dried
Confectioner's Icing (optional)

At end of the second rising, roll the whole wheat dough into an oblong, 9x14". Brush with melted butter to within ½" of edges. Combine sugar and cinnamon. Sprinkle over the rectangle of dough. Scatter raisins on top of sugar mixture. Roll tightly jelly roll fashion from the short side. Pinch the side and ends to seal. Place loaf seam side down in a greased

9x5x3" loaf pan. Pierce with a toothpick six times almost to the bottom of loaf to release air. Cover with a towel and allow to double, 30 to 45 minutes. Bake in a preheated 350° oven 35 to 40 minutes or until golden brown. Cool on a wire rack. When cooled, the loaf may be iced with Confectioner's Icing, page 268.

WHOLE WHEAT BUBBLE LOAF

Follow the directions for Cinnamon Bubble Loaf on page 29, using all the Whole Wheat Egg dough to fill a greased angel food cake pan or ½ the recipe for a single loaf pan (9x5x3"). Scatter white raisins among the bubbles.

WHOLE WHEAT-WHITE SWIRL

A charming swirl that is easy to make and a delight for your guests in both eye appeal and flavor, plus being adaptable in several forms.

2 packages dry or compressed yeast
¼ cup warm water
3 cups warm milk
⅓ cup sugar
⅓ cup melted butter or margarine

2½ teaspoons salt
5 to 6 cups white flour
5 tablespoons molasses
2½ cups whole wheat flour, approximately

Sprinkle yeast over the warm water; stir with a fork until dissolved and set aside. In a large mixing bowl, combine the milk, sugar, butter, and salt. Stir until well blended. Add the yeast mixture and 3 cups of white flour. Beat until smooth with a whisk or an electric mixer. You will have about 4 and ¾ cups of batter.

Divide batter in half. To one portion, gradually stir in sufficient white flour to make a soft, workable dough. Turn out on a floured surface and knead until smooth and satiny, about 8 minutes. Round in a ball, place in a warm, greased bowl, turning to coat the top. Cover loosely with plastic wrap and towel. To the remaining batter, add the molasses and enough whole wheat flour to make a workable dough. Turn out on a lightly floured surface and knead until smooth and satiny, about 8 minutes. Place in a warm, greased bowl and cover as directed with the white dough. Set both bowls aside in a protected area to double in bulk, about 1½ hours.

Punch the dough down, turn out on a lightly floured board, knead lightly, and let rest 10 to 15 minutes. Divide each dough in half. Roll out half the white and the dark in rectangles, 9x14″. Place the whole wheat on top of the white. Roll tightly from the narrow end. Pinch side and ends. Place in a greased 9x5x3″ loaf pan. Repeat with remaining dough. (Optional: 2 portions may be kneaded together lightly instead of rolled, making a different type of swirl.) Cover and let rise until just curved over tops of pans, about 45 minutes. Bake in a preheated 375° oven 40 to 45 minutes. Cool on wire racks.

MINIATURE LOAVES

Roll half the white and dark in rectangles, 8x17″. Place the whole wheat on top of the white. With a dough scraper divide the rectangle down the center lengthwise. Cut each side in 4 portions. Roll each portion in a tiny loaf; pinch side and ends. Place in greased loaf pans, 4½x2½x1½″. Place pans on a baking sheet for easy handling. Cover and let rise to tops of pans, about 40 minutes. Bake in a preheated 375° oven 25 minutes. Cool on wire racks. These loaves may be stored in the refrigerator for 1 day, then sliced and toasted to use with hors d'oeuvres or soups.

OATMEAL RAISIN BREAD

A dark bread with a rich texture and flavor — great for a Sunday morning breakfast.

3 cups oatmeal	1 cup lukewarm water
2 teaspoons salt	½ cup molasses
⅓ cup butter or margarine	1 cup bran buds
1½ cups raisins	2 cups whole wheat flour
3 cups boiling water	4½ to 5½ cups white flour
2 packages dry or compressed yeast	Melted butter or margarine

In a large mixing bowl, combine oatmeal, salt, margarine or butter, and raisins with the boiling water. Stir until well mixed and cool to luke-warm. Sprinkle yeast over the warm water, stirring with a fork until dissolved (refer to Ingredients, page 7). Add yeast mixture, molasses, bran buds, and whole wheat flour to the cooled oatmeal mixture. Beat vigorously with a rubber spatula until smooth. Gradually add enough white flour to make a soft dough. Turn out on a lightly floured surface and knead 5 minutes, using only enough more flour to avoid stickiness.

Place dough in a warm, greased bowl, turning to coat the top. Cover loosely with plastic wrap and a towel. Place in a warm spot to double in bulk, about 1½ hours. Punch down, knead lightly, and mold in 3 loaves. Place in well greased pans, 8½x4½x2½". Cover and let rise until just curved over tops of pans, about 45 minutes. Bake in a preheated 350° oven 40 minutes. Cool on wire racks. Brush with melted butter while hot.

OPTION

For a change, bake this bread in a greased 2 quart souffle bowl and 2 small one quart bowls. Cook larger loaf 45 minutes and smaller ones 40.

OVERNIGHT OATMEAL BREAD

One of the most popular breads with all my classes, as it is combined in the evening, baked the next morning, and produces two flavorful loaves. The finished bread is similar to a sourdough.

2 cups boiling water
1 cup oatmeal
6 tablespoons butter or margarine
1 package dry or compressed yeast

½ cup warm water
½ cup sugar
1 teaspoon salt
4 to 5 cups flour

In a large mixing bowl, combine the boiling water, oatmeal, and butter; stir and let stand until cool. Sprinkle yeast over the warm water, stirring with a fork until dissolved. Add the sugar, salt, and yeast mixture to the cooled oatmeal mixture. Blend well. Beat in 2 cups of flour until batter is smooth. Gradually add enough remaining flour to make a soft dough. Turn out on a floured board and knead about 5 minutes, using ½ cup more flour if necessary. The dough will be sticky; do not attempt to eliminate all the stickiness as it should be a soft dough. Place in a warm, greased bowl turning to coat the top. Cover loosely with plastic wrap and a towel. Set in a protected spot overnight.

The next morning, knead down and divide in 2 portions. Pat and shape in 2 well greased loaf pans, 8½x4½x2½". Cover and let rise to tops of pans, about 1½ hours. Bake in a preheated 450° oven 10 minutes. Lower heat to 350° and continue to bake 35 minutes. Remove from pans and cool on wire racks.

BEEF STEW WITH WILD RICE

A different kind of soup-stew that is superb in flavor. Excellent used for a bread and soup party. Serves 10.

⅓ cup oil
4 pounds cubed stewing beef
2 large onions, sliced
3 cloves garlic, minced
½ teaspoon thyme
½ teaspoon oregano

¼ cup chopped-parsley
1½ cups dry red wine
Water to cover
2 cups fresh or 1 box frozen
　peas (10 oz. size)
4 large tomatoes, peeled and
　cut in eighths
10 to 12 small peeled onions

6 medium carrots, scraped and
　sliced
1 pound fresh mushrooms, sliced
1 cup dry red wine
Grindings of black pepper
Salt
¾ cup wild rice, thoroughly
　washed

Heat oil in a skillet and sauté cubed meat until well browned. Transfer meat to a soup kettle. Add onion and garlic to skillet; cook and stir until tender and golden in color. Remove to soup pot. Add a little red wine to the skillet and boil rapidly stirring until scrapings are free. Pour into soup. Season with the thyme, oregano, and parsley. Measure in 1½ cups wine and enough water just to cover ingredients. Bring to a simmer, cover, and cook about 1½ hours or until meat is very tender.

Add fresh peas (frozen peas should be added with wild rice at end of recipe), tomatoes, onions, carrots, mushrooms, and 1 cup red wine. Add a few grindings of black pepper and adjust salt to your taste. Stir the stew, bring to a boil and cook 15 minutes uncovered. Add the wild rice and frozen peas if used. Cover, bring back to a simmer, and cook until done, about 45 minutes to 1 hour.

HEARTY SPLIT PEA SOUP

With a good sturdy whole wheat bread, a bowl of split pea soup, a glass of wine, logs burning in the fireplace, you can have a lovely winter's evening.

1 pound split peas (2 cups)
Ham bone with meat, turkey carcass,
*   or ham hock*
3 quarts of water

• • •

1 medium onion stuck with 2 cloves
1 clove of garlic, minced
1 cup celery with leaves, chopped

2 leeks, cleaned and sliced
½ cup carrots, chopped
½ teaspoon thyme or
*   marjoram*
1 bay leaf
Dash of Cayenne
Salt to taste
Grindings of black pepper

Combine the split peas, ham bone or turkey carcass, and 3 quarts of water in a large soup pot. For those on a cholesterol free diet, the turkey is excellent. Bring to a boil, skim, and lower heat. Simmer uncovered 1 hour, stirring occasionally.

Add onion, garlic, celery, leeks, carrots, thyme or marjoram, bay leaf, and Cayenne. Cover and simmer 2 hours. Remove bones, strip off meat, and cut in small pieces. Purée soup in a blender. Transfer soup back to a clean soup pot, add pieces of meat, and reheat. Taste for seasoning. Add salt if necessary and a few grindings of pepper. This recipe doubles easily and freezes well. Serves 12.

VARIATIONS

For a piquant flavor, add ½ teaspoon ginger — different and delicious. To make a full meal soup, slice a cooked Polish sausage and add to the soup. For devotees of beer — add 1 can of beer (12 oz.) or malt liquor and 1 can of beef broth. Simmer until soup stops foaming, about 10 minutes.

OLD FASHIONED POTATO AND ONION SOUP

When the children have the sniffles, your husband is grumpy, and you feel certain you are coming down with a miserable cold, make this old favorite and everyone will feel better.

4 cups diced peeled potatoes
4 cups chopped onions
Water to cover
6 tablespoons butter or margarine

6 tablespoons flour
4 cups hot milk
Salt to taste
Grindings of black pepper

Combine potatoes and onions in a large saucepan. Cover with water and bring to a boil. Allow to cook rapidly uncovered until vegetables are tender. Mash half the onions and potatoes through a sieve — or all if your family prefers a smooth soup. Add remaining water in the pot and set mixture aside.

In a 4 quart saucepan, melt the butter. With a whisk, stir in the flour cooking until smooth and bubbly. Add hot milk all at once, beating vigorously to keep it smooth. Change to a wooden spoon and stir well until thick. Add potato-onion mixture, salt and pepper to taste. If everyone is hungry enough, add sliced frankfurters and with good hot bread, the whole family will feel better!

NAVY BEAN SOUP

1 pound navy beans (2 cups)
Meaty ham bone or ham hock
Boiling water
   • • •
1 cup onion chopped
½ cup carrots, chopped
½ cup celery, diced
1 clove garlic, minced

1 or 2 leeks, cleaned and sliced
  (white part only)
2 tablespoons oil
1 bay leaf
Grindings of black pepper
Salt to taste

Wash and pick over beans, place in saucepan, and cover with water to soak overnight. The next morning, drain and place beans in a large soup pot. Add the ham bone and boiling water to cover. Bring to a boil, lower heat and simmer covered 1 hour.

While the beans are bubbling, sauté onion, carrots, celery, garlic, and leeks in the oil until tender, stirring occasionally to avoid burning. Add vegetable mixture to the soup with bay leaf and pepper. Simmer one hour. Remove ham bone, strip meat, and dice in small pieces. Return meat to the soup pot and taste for seasoning. The amount of salt needed depends on the ham used. Simmer another 30 minutes. Remove the bay leaf. Mash part of the soup ingredients with a fork or purée in a blender. Return to the soup kettle and bring back to a boil. Serves 10.

VARIATION

If one-half the soup is left, add 2 cups of canned tomatoes. Refreshing and good for a second day revival!

MID-EASTERN LENTIL SOUP WITH SPINACH

An exciting, nourishing soup that is good either hot or cold. When in season, fresh swiss chard is unusually tasteful in place of the spinach. Serves 6 to 8.

1½ cups lentils	1½ teaspoons salt
2 quarts water	2 pounds fresh spinach or
½ cup olive oil	1 box frozen spinach (10 oz.)
¾ cup chopped onions	¾ cup lemon juice
2 stalks celery, chopped	Grindings of black pepper
5 garlic cloves, minced	Yogurt (optional)
3 tablespoons dried mint	

Wash and pick over lentils. Place in a soup pot. Cover with water and bring to a boil. Reduce to simmer, cover, and cook until done, approximately 1 hour. Meanwhile, sauté onions, celery, and garlic in oil until tender, about 10 minutes. When lentils are soft, add the onion mixture, salt to taste, and dried mint. Simmer 30 minutes. Add chopped spinach, lemon juice, and grindings of black pepper. Again bring to a simmer and cook until spinach is done. This soup is quite good cold. Try a dollop of yogurt on each serving.

SOURDOUGH STARTERS AND BREADS

SOUPS:

Oklahoma Bouillabaisse

Spanish Bean Soup

Oyster Stew

Brunswick Stew

Shrimp and Crab Gumbo

SOURDOUGH BREADS

Since World War II the popularity of Sourdough Breads has spread rapidly from San Francisco to New York City. All shapes and sizes of loaves may be purchased in airports, supermarkets, specialty shops, fish markets, and even some department stores.

So many erroneous stories have been written about handling sourdough starters and breads, that it is time these floating myths be cleared.

One does not have to buy a starter nor borrow one. Excellent starters can be made right in your own kitchen. All are easy to do and great fun to watch, because you are actually creating something — living yeast.

The quality of texture produced through sourdough seems to give a third dimension to breads. Once you have a clear understanding of what a starter is and how to produce it, I am certain you will be as enthusiastic with this form of breadmaking as I. San Francisco type of sourdough is only one of many varieties to be made.

The history of sourdough goes back to the beginning of leavened bread, for undoubtedly this was the way it all started. Alaskan miners have romanticized sourdoughs and created a tradition of friendship in Alaska by sharing their starters, but they were not the first to use such a method. However, these intrepid men did find other uses for their starters, such as drinking the liquid alcohol that forms on top. Certainly that would keep a person warm in such a frigid atmosphere. One can get tipsy just smelling!

Your great-great grandmother crossing the prairies carried her sourdough with her as one of her most precious possessions. She made many quick breads, but when there was time, she was able to produce loaves of bread with her starter. Chuckwagons supplying food for hard working cowboys always had a small wooden cask of sourdough starter. If the weather became too cold, the cook slept with his cask. Many immigrants to the United States carefully carried a crock of dough across the sea. Don't forget there was no commercial yeast available until the 20th century.

There has been much written maintaining that it is impossible to create bread such as is found in San Francisco. Do not let this deter you. Certainly we do not have their ovens, nor their flour, nor their years of experience, but that is no reason to deny ourselves the pleasure of making a very good sourdough bread. So often the same is said concerning French bread and Bouillabaisse. The fact that I live in Southwestern United States does not prevent me from enjoying delicious fish stew with home made sourdough bread. Try my Bouillabaisse at the end of this chapter.

Let's dispel the mysterious aura created about sourdoughs and enjoy them. There are many different kinds of starters. To avoid confusion and to use materials readily available, I have chosen three which will be explained fully. For all these starters and breads, I encourage you to use the finest hard wheat flour you can obtain. Each of the starters may be used interchangeably in all the recipes. I have my favorite starter, and I am certain you will find yours.

TECHNIQUES FOR SOURDOUGH STARTERS AND BREADS

A starter-sponge is the basis for all sourdough breads. Making a sponge is a fascinating process. Once the starter is successfully made, it can be kept going for years.

Always store a starter in a stone crock, plastic, or glass container. *Never use metal of any kind.* Two-quart stone crocks with lids are available in many different kinds of stores. They are quite handsome, and just the right size. Since they are inexpensive, purchase two or three as you will find many uses for these lovely crocks. Feed stores are one of the best sources of supply.

A lid should never be sealed too tightly in storing a starter as gasses form while in the refrigerator, and they have been known to explode if too well contained. Label the crock with the kind of starter and beginning date. Under the lid, place a doubled square of cheese cloth. If you cannot use the starter frequently, stir it thoroughly once a week with a spatula which also helps clean the sides of the jar. Most starters will eventually form a whey or clear liquid on the top. (This is what the miners drank!) Pour off part of this liquid before stirring which will help keep your starter thicker and spongier. If you are gone as long as a month, the starter will not be hurt — just pour off the whey and stir thoroughly. Six months absence with no attention would be quite different. You may need to start all over, something easily done. I keep four starters in an auxiliary refrigerator — one brought to me by a daughter-in-law from a hundred year old sponge! It is a delight to open the door and smell that lovely, yeasty aroma.

After you try the recipes and find how easy it is to make and replenish a starter, you will have no qualms about using or giving away some of your sponge.

COMPARISON OF SOURDOUGH WITH REGULAR YEAST DOUGH

1. Sourdough has a spreading quality. This texture has a slightly different feeling and appearance than a regular yeast dough.

2. The doughs generally are stickier. As you knead, flour may be added in small quantities, but do not expect to completely eliminate this sticky quality.

3. Sourdough is slower rising and again has a spreading tendency rather than the puffy fashion of regular yeast dough.

4. A denser texture is characteristic. As a result, sourdoughs never rise as high as other breads unless commercial yeast is added.

5. Some of my recipes have yeast added to quicken the rising action. If you prefer to eliminate the regular yeast, the rising time will take an extra hour.

6. Sourdough breads have a sturdiness (that third dimension) that regular breads sometimes lack. They all make excellent crisp toast and

good sandwiches.

7. If you wish to give away some of your starter-sponge, measure a cup into a container. Give the recipe for replenishing to the receiver.

WILD YEAST STARTER

This is my favorite. No commercial yeast is used so you are creating something special from the wild yeast in the air. The starter becomes a lovely, thick, and creamy sponge. Do try this one.

Pour 2 cups of milk (either whole or enriched skim) into a 2 quart crock, glass, or plastic container, (no metal). Cover with a square of doubled cheese cloth, and set in a warm, protected spot — a sunny window is perfect. Leave it there 24 hours. Stir in 2 cups of flour (preferably unbleached white), beating until smooth. Replace cheese cloth and set back in the protected spot. If the weather is warm, the starter will begin working within one day or overnight, but if you have a cooler temperature, the action may take 3 to 4 days. Be patient. When it begins to bubble, allow it to "work" about 2 days. Stir once each day with a rubber spatula. When the sponge is thick, bubbly and has a lovely, fresh sour aroma, place a lid over the cheese cloth, label the jar, and refrigerate.

TO REPLENISH

Each time the starter is used, add 1 cup of warm milk and 1 cup of flour. Beat with a wire whisk until smooth, cover with the cheesecloth and leave overnight in a protected, warm spot. The next morning, stir the sponge with a rubber spatula and replace in the refrigerator. If this process is followed each time the starter is used, there will be no danger of losing it.

SOURDOUGH STARTER WITH YEAST

A good, standard starter easy to cope with and produces excellent breads.

1 package dry or compressed yeast
2 cups warm water
2½ cups white flour

1 tablespoon sugar
Square of cheese cloth
2 quart container

Pour warm water in a 2 quart container (crock, glass, or plastic, but never metal). Sprinkle in the yeast, stirring with a fork until dissolved. Beat in the flour and sugar with a wire whisk until smooth. Cover container with a square of cheese cloth, double thickness. Place in a warm, protected spot and leave until the sponge begins to bubble, rises, and falls back. This process will take about 8 to 10 hours. Stir with a rubber spatula. Replace the cheese cloth and allow to bubble quietly about 2 days. The action depends upon the warmth of the weather and room. It is necessary to let the sponge "work" to attain thick texture and a fresh, sour aroma. At the end of 2 days, stir again with a rubber spatula, label the jar, place a lid over the cheese cloth, and store in the refrigerator. The starter is now ready to use.

TO REPLENISH

Each time the starter is used, add equal amounts of warm water and flour with 1 teaspoon of sugar. Stir with a wire whisk until free of lumps, cover with the cheese cloth and allow to bubble overnight. Replace the lid and store in refrigerator.

POTATO STARTER

This is amazingly easy, gives good results, and is especially adaptable for my Potato Sourdough bread on page 54.

1 quart of peeled,
   diced potatoes
1 quart of water
2 teaspoons salt

¼ cup sugar
1 package dry or
   compressed yeast
¼ cup potato water

Combine potatoes and water in a large saucepan. Bring to a boil and cook uncovered until tender. Put potatoes through a sieve or ricer (do not blend or use a mixer) into a large mixing bowl. The potatoes must be free of lumps. Add the water in which they were cooked, reserving ¼ cup. Stir in salt and sugar. Cool to lukewarm. Dissolve yeast in the ¼ cup of potato water and add to the lukewarm potato mixture. Cover with a large piece of doubled cheesecloth or a thin teacloth. Place in a warm, protected spot. The mixture will bubble, rise quite high, and fall back. This may be done overnight or started in the morning. When the sponge has settled and is bubbling lightly, stir and pour into a 2 quart crock (no metal). Label, lay a piece of cheese cloth over the top and a lid. Refrigerate.

TO REPLENISH

When starter is diminished to a cup, repeat the recipe, leaving out the yeast. This starter also may be kept going indefinitely.

SOURDOUGH FRENCH BREAD

There are many recipes for Sourdough French bread, short and long methods, with soda and without. I have worked out the following procedure through long testing. You will find it uncomplicated and excellent in texture and flavor.

1½ cups warm water
1½ cups sourdough starter
3 cups white flour, preferably
*   unbleached*
1 tablespoon sugar
2 teaspoons salt

½ teaspoon baking soda
3 to 4 cups flour
Cornmeal
Melted butter

• • •

The Sponge: In a large mixing bowl, combine the warm water, starter, 3 cups of unbleached white flour, sugar, and salt. Beat with a rubber spatula until smooth. Cover with plastic wrap and a towel. Place in a protected, warm spot overnight.

The next morning combine baking soda with 1 cup of flour and beat into the sponge. Add enough more flour to make a soft dough that pulls away from sides of the bowl. Turn out on a lightly floured surface. To obtain the desired texture, it is important to knead at least 15 minutes. The dough will not be hurt by short rests. If you have a heavy mixer with a dough hook, let the machine knead 10 minutes at Number 1 position and finish by hand 3 to 5 minutes. Knead until smooth and resilient, adding just enough more flour to control the stickiness. Round into a ball and place in a warm, greased bowl, turning to coat the top. Cover loosely with plastic wrap and a towel. Put in a cozy, protected spot to double in bulk, about 2 to 2½ hours.

Punch down and knead lightly on a floured board. Cover and let rest 10 minutes. Shape in 2 loaves, round or long (refer to French Bread, page 67). If preferred, place in 2 greased loaf pans, 8½x4½x2½". Place free standing loaves on a greased baking sheet, sprinkled lightly with cornmeal. Cover and allow to double, about 1½ hours. Preheat oven to 400°. To bake the free standing loaves: place a shallow pan on the bottom shelf of the oven and fill with boiling water. Close the door to trap the steam. With a sharp razor, slash the loaves — tic, tac, toe for the round loaf and long diagonal slashes for the long shape. Brush with cool water and place in preheated, steamy oven. Bake 40 minutes. Cool on wire rack.

Eliminate the boiling water for pan loaves. When loaves have reached tops of pans, slash three times, brush with melted butter and bake 40 to 45 minutes or until golden brown.

FAMILY HONEY LOAVES

A sturdy, evenly textured basic white sourdough bread that is great for a family in
making sandwiches, cinnamon bread, and
crisp toast.

1½ cups sourdough starter	1½ cups warm milk
1½ cups warm water	½ cup melted butter or margarine
1 tablespoon honey	½ cup honey
3 cups flour	2 teaspoons salt
• • •	7 to 8 cups flour
1 package dry or compressed yeast	

The Sponge: In the evening combine the first 4 ingredients in a large
mixing bowl. Beat with a rubber spatula until smooth. Cover with plastic
wrap, a big towel, and place in a warm, protected spot overnight.

This bread may be finished the next morning, although if a more
sour flavor is desired, put it together in early afternoon. Sprinkle yeast
over the warm milk, stirring with a fork until dissolved. Add the yeast
mixture, melted butter, honey, and salt to the sourdough sponge. Stir
until smooth. Slowly beat in enough flour to make a soft dough (refer to
Techniques, page 11). Turn out on a lightly floured surface and
knead 10 to 15 minutes, adding flour in small quantities as needed. Place
dough in a warm, greased bowl turning to coat the top. Cover loosely
with plastic wrap and towel. Let double in bulk, about 2 hours.

Turn out on a floured surface, knead lightly, cover, and allow to
rest 10 minutes. Shape in 4 loaves (8½x4½x2½") or 3 large ones (9x5x3").
Place in greased loaf pans, cover with a towel, and let rise to tops of
pans, about 1 hour. With a sharp razor make 3 diagonal slashes across
each loaf. Brush with melted butter and bake in a preheated 350° oven
50 to 55 minutes. Cool on wire racks.

NOTE
Family Honey Loaves can be made without commercial yeast. The
rising after all ingredients are combined will take about 3 hours. The
pan rising will be 2½ hours. A beautiful bread made by either method.

DOUBLE CINNAMON SWIRL

This recipe is especially good with Family Honey Loaves or Potato
Sourdough. It can also be used with any of the white breads in the
first chapter. Your friends will wonder how you did all those lovely
swirls. Here is the secret.

Cut off ¼ portion of dough before the pan molding. Cover with a towel and let rest 10 to 15 minutes. Mix 4 tablespoons of sugar with 1 tablespoon cinnamon. Roll dough in a long rectangle, 8x14″. Sprinkle half the cinnamon-sugar mixture over the oblong to within ½″ of edges. Starting with the narrow end, roll dough tightly jelly roll fashion. Seal the side and let rest 10 minutes. Place seam side down and roll again into a rectangle, pressing out bubbles on the sides. (Do not be disturbed if dough breaks.) If the dough resists, let it rest again for a few minutes. Better yet, make 2 loaves at one time so that while working on one, the other can rest. Sprinkle remaining sugar-mixture over the dough. Roll tightly again, beginning with the narrow end. Seal the ends and side by pinching. Place the loaf seam side down in a greased bread pan, 8½x4½x2½″. Cover with a towel and allow to double in bulk, about 1 hour. Bake in a preheated 350° oven 50 minutes. Turn out on wire rack to cool.

POTATO SOURDOUGH BREAD

Use the Potato Starter to make this bread. The double combination of potatoes makes an exceptionally tasteful bread. My youngest son maintains that it makes superior garlic toast!

1½ cups sourdough starter
1½ cups warm water
1 cup instant potatoes
2 cups flour
¼ cup sugar

• • •
1 package dry or compressed yeast
1 cup warm water

1 cup dry skim milk
2 teaspoons salt
¼ cup sugar
⅓ cup melted butter or
    margarine
8 to 9 cups flour
Melted butter

The Sponge: In the evening combine the starter with 1½ cups warm water, stirring until smooth. Sprinkle the instant potatoes over this mixture. Add 2 cups of flour and the ¼ cup of sugar, beating until smooth. Cover with plastic wrap and a towel. Place in a warm, protected spot overnight.

The next morning, stir down the sponge. Sprinkle yeast over the cup of warm water, stirring with a fork until dissolved. Add yeast mixture, dry skim milk, salt, sugar, and butter to the sponge. Beat with a rubber spatula until smooth. Begin adding flour, stirring until dough leaves sides of the bowl. Turn out on a lightly floured surface and knead 10 minutes or until smooth and bouncy (refer to Techniques, page 11). If dough is sticky, add small amounts of flour as you knead. Round into a ball and place in a warm, greased bowl turning once to coat the top. Cover loosely with plastic wrap and a towel. Place in a protected spot to double, about 1½ hours.

Punch down and turn out on a floured board. Cover and let rest 10 minutes. Form into 4 loaves (8½x4½x2½″) or 3 large loaves (9x5x3″).

Place in greased loaf pans, cover, and allow to curve over the tops of pans, about 1½ hours. Score with a sharp razor in a crisscross fashion. Brush with melted butter. Bake in a preheated 375° oven; 45 minutes for smaller loaves and 50 for the larger ones. If loaves become too brown, cover the last 10 minutes with foil. Cool on wire racks.

SOURDOUGH CRACKED WHEAT OR STEEL CUT OATMEAL

This wonderfully nourishing and crunchy sourdough bread may be made with either cracked wheat or steel cut oatmeal (available in health food stores). Both produce delicious and similar results.

2 cups cracked wheat or steel cut oatmeal
2 cups boiling water
¼ cup honey, brown sugar or molasses
1½ cups sourdough starter
2 cups white flour
3½ cups whole wheat flour

3½ cups white flour
1 package dry or compressed yeast
1 cup warm milk
½ cup melted butter or margarine
2 teaspoons salt
½ cup honey, brown sugar or molasses

The Sponge: Measure the steel cut oatmeal or cracked wheat into a large mixing bowl. Add boiling water and ¼ cup of honey, brown sugar or molasses, stirring until well blended. Cool to lukewarm. When the cereal mixture is cooled, add the sourdough starter and 2 cups of white flour, beating until smooth. Cover with plastic wrap and a clean towel. Let stand overnight in a warm, protected spot.

The next morning, combine the whole wheat and white flours. Sprinkle yeast over the warm milk, stirring with a fork until dissolved. Stir down the starter sponge with a rubber spatula. Add the yeast mixture, butter, salt, and choice of sugar, blending thoroughly. Add sufficient flour mixture to make a soft, workable dough. Turn out on a floured surface. Knead 8 to 10 minutes, adding more flour if necessary. Place dough in a warm, greased bowl, turning to coat the top. Cover loosely with plastic wrap and towel. Let double in bulk, about 2 hours.

Punch down and knead lightly. Cover and let rest 10 minutes. Shape in 4 loaves and place in greased pans, 8½x4½x2½″. Cover with a towel and let rise to tops of pans, 45 minutes to an hour. Bake in a preheated 350° oven 45 to 50 minutes. Cool on racks. Brush with melted butter if desired.

SOURDOUGH RYE

A lusty bread with an old world flavor that many people enjoy. An easy bread to handle; follow molding directions for French breads, page 67.

1½ cups sourdough starter
1½ cups warm water
3 cups rye flour

• • •

1 package dry or compressed yeast
¼ cup warm water
2 teaspoons salt

1 tablespoon caraway seeds
2 teaspoons anise seeds
¼ cup molasses
½ cup melted butter or margarine
3 to 4 cups white flour
1 egg white beaten with
  1 tablespoon water

The Sponge: In the evening combine the starter, warm water, and rye flour in a large mixing bowl. Beat with a rubber spatula until smooth. Cover with plastic wrap and towel. Place in a warm, protected spot and let stand overnight.

The next morning at your convenience, stir the starter. Add the yeast dissolved in the ¼ cup of warm water, salt, seeds, molasses, and butter. (Seeds may be eliminated, if desired.) Stir in enough white flour to make a soft, workable dough. Turn out on a lightly floured surface and knead 8 to 10 minutes. If dough is sticky, add small amounts of white flour to obtain correct texture. When dough is smooth and bouncy, place in a warm, greased bowl, turning to coat the top. Cover loosely with plastic wrap and towel. Allow to double, about 2 hours. Punch the dough down and shape in 3 loaves — round or long. Place on greased baking sheets sprinkled with cornmeal. Cover with a towel and let rise 1 hour. Slash with a sharp razor in diagonal cuts for long loaves or a cross for the round. Brush with egg glaze. Bake in a preheated 375° oven 30 minutes. Cool on wire racks.

SOURDOUGH WHEAT GERM BREAD

I have created this bread for the new defatted wheat germ. The bread looks like whole wheat and has a wonderful nutty flavor.

1 cup sourdough starter
1 cup warm water
¼ cup brown sugar
2 cups unbleached white flour

• • •

1 package dry or compressed yeast
1 cup warm milk

2 teaspoons salt
¼ cup brown sugar
¼ cup melted butter or margarine
1 cup defatted wheat germ*
4 to 5 cups unbleached white flour

The Sponge: In the evening, combine the first four ingredients in a large mixing bowl. Beat with a rubber spatula until smooth. Cover with plastic wrap and a towel. Set in a warm, protected spot overnight.

The next morning at your leisure, stir down the sponge. Dissolve yeast in the warm milk (refer to Ingredients, page 7). Add yeast mixture to the sponge with salt, sugar, melted butter, and wheat germ. Gradually add enough flour to make a soft dough. Turn out on a lightly floured surface and knead 10 minutes, or until smooth and elastic. Round in a ball; place in a greased, warm bowl turning once to coat the top. Cover loosely with plastic wrap and towel. Allow to double in bulk, about 1½ hours.

Remove dough to a floured board, knead lightly, cover, and let rest 10 minutes. Divide in 3 portions and form in loaves. Place in greased 8½x4½x2½″ pans. Cover and let rise to tops of pans, about 1 hour. Score 3 times with a sharp razor and brush with melted butter. Bake in preheated 350° oven 40 to 45 minutes. Cool on wire racks.

*NOTE
If defatted wheat germ is not available in your community, use the regular toasted wheat germ.

SALT RISING BREAD

"Take a pint of milk warm from the cow, if possible. Put in a teaspoon of salt and thicken it with flour to consistency of batter cakes. Set this in a warm place to rise and make your biscuit or bread with it and some new milk" — La Cuisine Creole, 1885.

The following recipe for this old, pioneer bread is a little easier to make now with a few modern tricks that Great-Grandma did not have. A great family recipe given to me by a good friend.

⅔ cup cornmeal, white or
   yellow
1¼ cups hot, scalded milk
• • •
3 cups warm milk
1½ tablespoons salt
1 tablespoon sugar
5 tablespoons shortening
7 to 8 cups flour
Heating pad

The Sponge: Select a 1 quart container, preferably a stone crock. Use no metal bowl. Combine the 1¼ cups of hot milk and cornmeal in the crock, stirring until a smooth batter. Place the container on a heating pad turned low. Cover with a heavy towel and leave overnight.

The next morning check to see if the sponge is bubbling and has a good, strong aroma. If not, allow to set another hour or two. If the sponge is dry, your heating pad is too hot. Place a heavy towel between the crock and pad — you will have to do some experimenting as heating pads do differ in quality of heat. In a large mixing bowl, combine the 3 cups of warm milk, salt, sugar, and shortening, stirring until well blended. Add the sponge mixture and beat thoroughly. Stir in 4 cups of the flour until mixture is smooth. Place the mixing bowl on the heating pad (turned to low), cover with a towel, and allow to rise about 1½ hours. By then, there should be a light, lovely sponge. Stir in enough more flour to make a soft, workable dough. Turn out on a floured surface and knead until smooth and resilient, about 10 to 15 minutes. Divide into 3 portions and place in well greased pans, 8½x4½x2½″. Place pans in an oven preheated to 150°. Allow to remain at this temperature until the dough has reached tops of the pans, about 2 hours. Turn the heat to 250° for 15 minutes. Raise the heat again to 350° and bake 35 minutes. Brush tops with melted butter while hot. Cool loaves on wire racks.

SOURDOUGH ENGLISH MUFFINS

Keep a supply of these muffins in your freezer. They are delicious, split, toasted, and served with poached eggs topped with grated cheese.

1 cup sourdough starter
1 cup warm milk
2 cups flour
• • •
1 to 2 cups flour

1 teaspoon salt
½ teaspoon baking soda
2 tablespoons sugar
White cornmeal

The Sponge: In the evening, combine the starter, warm milk, and 2 cups of flour in a large mixing bowl. Beat with a rubber spatula until smooth. Cover with plastic wrap and a towel. Place in a warm, protected spot overnight.

The next morning, mix 1 cup of flour with the salt, baking soda, and sugar. Stir into the sponge with sufficient flour to make a soft, workable dough. Turn out on a lightly floured surface and knead until smooth, about 5 minutes. Cover with a towel and let rest 10 minutes. Roll dough out to ¾″ thickness. Cover again and allow to rest 10 minutes. Cut muffins with a 3″ biscuit cutter or a 7 ounce clean tuna fish can with both ends removed. If the dough pulls back, let it rest again (refer to Techniques, page 14). Place muffins on waxed paper lightly sprinkled with cornmeal. Sprinkle cornmeal over tops of muffins. Cover and allow to rise 1 hour. Bake on an ungreased preheated griddle at medium to medium-low heat 20 to 30 minutes, turning 3 times. Watch that they do not burn! The muffins will be better if allowed to cool, then split and toasted.

SOURDOUGH CORNBREAD

A lusciously moist bread on the inside, with a brown, crispy crust that is good served with any of the soups at the end of this chapter.

2 cups cornmeal
3 tablespoons sugar
1 teaspoon salt
1 teaspoon baking powder

¼ teaspoon baking soda
2 cups sourdough starter
2 eggs
¼ cup melted butter or
margarine

Preheat oven to 425°. Combine the cornmeal, sugar, salt, baking powder, and soda in a mixing bowl, stirring until all ingredients are blended. In a separate bowl, mix the starter, eggs, and butter until smooth. Add starter mixture to the cornmeal mixture, beating quickly until free of lumps. Grease an 8x12″ pan thoroughly. Spread cornmeal mixture evenly in prepared pan. Bake in preheated oven 30 to 35 minutes. Serve immediately.

SOURDOUGH WHOLE GRAIN MUFFINS

Hot, moist, healthful, muffins served with a chicken salad and a cold soup — what could be better for a summer dinner! Makes 12 large muffins. Recipe doubles easily, but do not double the baking soda.

1 cup rye flour
1 cup whole wheat flour
½ teaspoon salt
1 teaspoon baking soda
1 cup sourdough starter

¾ cup buttermilk
2 eggs
¼ cup melted butter or margarine
2 tablespoons molasses

Preheat oven to 425°. Combine the flours, salt, and soda in a mixing bowl. Make a well in the center. In a separate container, blend together the starter, buttermilk, eggs, butter, and molasses until smooth. Add all at once to the flour mixture. Stir quickly until the dry ingredients are just moistened. Grease muffin tins thoroughly and fill ¾ full. Bake in preheated oven about 25 minutes. Serve immediately. If there are any muffins left, split and toast for breakfast the next morning.

VARIATIONS
1. Add ½ cup diced pitted prunes or dates to the muffin mixture.
2. Blend in ½ cup white raisins and 2 teaspoons grated orange peel.

SOURDOUGH BISCUITS

You have heard of biscuits melting in your mouth — these do! The recipe is best when made with the Wild Yeast Starter, page 50.

2 to 3 cups flour
1 teaspoon salt
2 teaspoons baking powder

1 tablespoon sugar
2 cups sourdough starter
½ cup melted butter or margarine

Preheat oven to 425°. Combine 2 cups of flour with the salt, baking powder, and sugar. Measure the starter into a mixing bowl. Add melted butter and flour mixture. Stir with a rubber spatula until well mixed. Add enough more flour to make a soft, workable dough and remove to a floured surface. Knead lightly. Roll dough about ½" thick. Cut with desired size biscuit cutter. Place on a well greased baking sheet and brush rolls with melted butter. Bake in a preheated oven 15 to 20 minutes or until golden brown.

SOURDOUGH PANCAKES

Start the sponge in the evening; add remaining ingredients the next morning and you are ready to serve a substantial breakfast to family and guests.

1 cup sourdough starter
½ cup milk
1 cup flour
• • •
1 cup flour
½ teaspoon baking soda

1 teaspoon baking powder
1 teaspoon salt
2 eggs, beaten
½ cup milk
¼ cup melted butter or margarine

The Sponge: The night before, combine the starter, ½ cup of milk, and 1 cup of flour. Stir until smooth. Cover with plastic wrap and a towel. Set in a protected spot overnight.

The next morning, mix 1 cup of flour with soda, baking powder, and salt. In a separate bowl, combine beaten eggs with milk and butter. Stir the flour and egg mixtures into the starter sponge, beating until smooth. Cook pancakes on hot, greased griddle, turning once.

OKLAHOMA BOUILLABAISSE

Many communities now have excellent fresh fish flown from all the coasts. Most super-markets handle good frozen fish as well as fresh. In Tulsa we are lucky enough to have all this plus eight man-made lakes surrounding our city stocked with crappie, white bass, and catfish. With all this abundance offered, one can make a fine Bouillabaisse.

1 large onion, finely chopped
3 cloves garlic, minced
1 medium size green pepper, chopped
1 leek, chopped (optional)
3 large ribs of celery, finely chopped
2 cups fresh mushrooms, cleaned
*   and sliced*
⅛ teaspoon saffron
¼ cup oil
1 teaspoon thyme
½ teaspoon each of savory and
*   rosemary*
1 bay leaf

1 teaspoon sweet basil
Grindings of black pepper
4 or 5 drops Tabasco
1 one-pound can tomatoes
1 large fresh tomato, peeled
*   and chopped*
¼ cup finely chopped parsley
2 cups fish stock or 1 bottle
*   of clam juice*
2 cups water
3 cups white wine
4 to 5 pounds fish
Salt

Suggestions for fish:
1. Strongly flavored fish — haddock, halibut, mackeral, seabass or cod
2. Delicate — sole, flounder, whiting or red snapper
3. Shell fish — shrimp, lobster, crabmeat, scallops
4. Fresh local fish

When you purchase the variety of fish you prefer, have it all deboned. Keep all the trimmings — shells, heads, and skin to make a fish stock, page 6.

THE SOUP

In a large soup pot, sauté onions, garlic, green pepper, leek, celery, mushrooms, and saffron in the oil until tender. Add the thyme, savory, rosemary, bay leaf, basil, black pepper, tabasco, tomatoes, parsley, clam juice or fish stock, water, and wine. Bring to a boil, lower heat and simmer uncovered 30 minutes. Dice fish in large pieces, removing any tiny bones. Discard shells and tendons from shell fish. Add all fish to the soup. Bring back to a boil, lower heat, cover, and simmer 15 minutes. Remove the lid and taste for salt and herb seasonings. Adjust. Simmer 15 more minutes or until all fish is done. Toast thick slices of Sourdough French bread and serve in the middle of each bowl. Ten generous servings. Bouillabaisse freezes well.

SPANISH BEAN SOUP

A hearty, full meal soup coming from the Spanish section of Tampa, Florida. Pass a pitcher of sherry for this hot steaming soup — magnificent with Sourdough, French, or Cuban bread.

1 ham bone with meat
1 beef bone
2 large onions, finely chopped
2 cloves garlic, minced
2 bay leaves
2 quarts of water
4 slices bacon
Grindings of black pepper

1 pinch saffron
3 potatoes, diced
2 one pound cans of chick peas
   (Garbanzos)
Salt to taste
2 Spanish Chorizo sausages
   (if not available, substitute
   a spicy Italian sausage)

Combine the ham and beef bones, onions, garlic, and bay leaves in a soup pot. Add 2 quarts of water, using more if needed to cover ingredients. Bring to a boil and simmer uncovered 2 hours. Meanwhile, sauté the bacon, drain, break into pieces and set aside. Remove bones from the soup pot, strip meat, and dice. Add meat back to the soup with a few grindings of black pepper, saffron, diced potatoes, bacon, and chick peas. Bring back to a boil, lower heat and simmer until the potatoes are done. Remove bay leaves, taste for salt and adjust. Slice the sausage and add before serving.

OYSTER STEW

For those who love oysters, there is nothing quite so heart warming as a big bowl of steaming stew. A recent trip to Eastern Canada introduced me to Lobster Stew done in the same manner. So try substituting 2 cups of cooked Lobster in place of the oysters — magnificent!

4 cups milk or half light cream
   and half milk
2 cups fresh oysters and liquid
2 tablespoons butter

Salt to taste
Grindings of black pepper
Butter

Measure milk into a large saucepan and slowly bring just to a boil. Meanwhile, drain the oysters, reserving the liquid. Heat liquid to the boiling point.

In a separate saucepan, melt the 2 tablespoons butter. Add the oysters and heat until the edges curl and they become plumped. Do not let them cook any longer as they will toughen quickly. Add the oyster liquid and hot milk to the oysters. Taste for salt and adjust. Add a few grindings of black pepper. Serve in large warm bowls with a tablespoon of butter added to each serving. Serves 4.

BRUNSWICK STEW

One of the best American soup-stews we have inherited. The recipe can serve 10 to 12 hearty appetites and is excellent with French, sourdough, or any of the dark breads.

5 to 6 pound chicken, baking hen or parts of chicken	2 cups fresh or frozen lima beans
½ cup flour	4 medium tomatoes, peeled and quartered
Oil	2 medium onions, thinly sliced
Celery leaves	4 medium potatoes, diced
3 sprigs of parsley	4 cups fresh or frozen corn
1 small onion, quartered	Salt
3 to 4 quarts of water	Grindings of black pepper
• • •	1 teaspoon sugar
2 cups fresh or frozen okra, sliced	

Cut chicken in pieces for frying. Wash and dry well. Flour lightly and sprinkle with salt and pepper. Sauté in oil or shortening until a golden brown. Transfer chicken to a large soup kettle. Add a few celery leaves, parsley, and quartered onion. Measure in sufficient water to cover ingredients. Bring to a boil uncovered and skim. Lower heat to simmer. Cover and cook slowly about 1½ hours, or until chicken is ready to fall off the bone. Remove chicken and debone. Discard the bones and parsley. Skim off as much fat as possible. Dice chicken and return to soup kettle. Add the okra, lima beans, tomatoes, and onions. Bring to a simmer and cook slowly uncovered 1 hour. Add diced potatoes and corn. Simmer 1 more hour, stirring occasionally. Taste and adjust for salt. Add grindings of black pepper and sugar. Serve in large warm soup bowls.

NOTE
If you prefer a thicker stew, combine ¼ cup of flour with some of the chicken broth whisking until smooth. Stir into the soup.

SHRIMP AND CRAB GUMBO

A pungent soup reminiscent of charming New Orleans where the Creole-French food is unique in our country.

6 tablespoons flour
½ cup shortening or oil
3 large onions, finely chopped
6 cloves garlic, minced
1 small can tomato paste
1 green pepper, chopped
4 bay leaves
1 teaspoon thyme
¼ cup finely chopped parsley
1 medium (No. 2) can tomatoes

½ teaspoon Tabasco sauce
Grindings of black pepper
2½ quarts hot water
1-1½ pounds frozen or sliced
    fresh okra
2 pounds peeled raw shrimp
½ pound crabmeat, fresh or
    frozen
Salt
Cooked rice

In a large soup pot, make a roux (refer to Glossary) of the flour and shortening, cooking and stirring until a dark, golden brown, about 30 minutes. A rich roux is most important to the flavor of this soup so have patience. Add the onions and garlic, sautéing until soft. Stir in the tomato paste. Add green pepper, bay leaves, thyme, parsley, tomatoes, Tabasco sauce, and a few grindings of black pepper. Bring to a simmer and cook slowly until the mixture is a rich, dark color — about 1 hour. Pour the hot water into the soup slowly; add the okra and blend well. When the soup returns to simmer, add the shrimp and crabmeat. Taste for seasoning, adding salt at this time. Cover the soup pot and simmer over low heat 1 hour. Remove bay leaves. Serve in large soup bowls with a mound of cooked rice in the center. With hot bread and a fresh fruit salad, you will have a nourishing and delightful meal.

CLASSIC FRENCH BREADS

SOUPS:

French Onion
Watercress
Vichyssoise
Cream of Mushroom

FRENCH BREAD

French bakers do the majority of bread making in France and are required by law to use just the ingredients you will find in this recipe. We lack their specially equipped ovens and years of experience, but with some American ingenuity we can produce a very fine French bread.

2½ cups warm water
2 packages dry or compressed yeast
1 tablespoon salt

6 to 7 cups unbleached
white flour
Cornmeal

Measure warm water in a mixing bowl. Add yeast, stirring with a fork until dissolved. Stir in the salt and 3 cups of flour. Beat vigorously with a rubber spatula until the batter is smooth. Gradually add enough flour to make a soft, workable dough. Remove dough to a floured board. Knead, adding more flour if necessary, 10 to 12 minutes or until smooth and elastic with bubbles underneath the skin (refer to Techniques, page 11). Place dough in a large, warm, greased bowl, turning to coat the top. It is best to use a bowl with vertical sides rather than one that flares out. Cover loosely with plastic wrap and towel. Set bowl in a protected spot and let dough *triple* in bulk, about 2½ hours. Punch down, knead dough lightly in the bowl, recover and allow to double, about 45 minutes to 1 hour. Turn out on a floured surface, knead lightly, and divide in 3 portions. Cover and let rest 15 minutes. Grease baking sheets and sprinkle lightly with cornmeal. Heavy French baking sheets need not be greased.

THREE METHODS OF FORMING FRENCH LOAVES

1. Press one portion of dough into an oval. If dough pulls back, cover and let rest a few more minutes. With the side of your hand, make an indentation down the center of the oval. Fold dough over and pinch sides together. Turn dough, seam side down and press again into an oval. Again, make an indentation down the center. Fold dough over and pinch sides together. The dough should now begin to have an elongated shape. Roll back and forth to a length that will fit your baking sheet. Place on prepared pan, seam side down. With the tips of your fingers, tuck in sides and ends to smooth out the long, slender shape. Repeat with remaining dough. Cover and allow to double in bulk, about 1 to 1½ hours.

MAKE AN INDENTATION

PRESS INTO OVAL

FOLD DOUGH OVER
PINCH SIDES TOGETHER

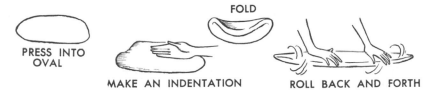

PRESS INTO OVAL

MAKE AN INDENTATION

FOLD

ROLL BACK AND FORTH

2. Roll a portion of dough into a rectangle, 9x16″. Roll tightly, jelly roll style from the long side. Pinch side and ends to seal. Roll back and forth, smoothing outwards into desired length. Place on prepared baking pan seam side down, tucking in sides and ends with finger tips. Cover and let rise 1 to 1½ hours.

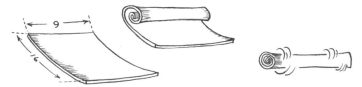

3. Round loaf: With your hands, begin rounding a portion of dough into a ball. Smooth dough by pulling tightly with one hand across the top to underneath the ball. Keep turning in a circle with the other hand until you have a round, satiny loaf. Scoop up with dough scraper and place on prepared baking sheet. Cover and let rise until doubled, about 1 hour.

TWO METHODS OF BAKING

1. Preheat oven to 450°. You will need: a razor, cold water, soft pastry brush and an atomizer containing water. Hold razor at a flat angle and make 3 long, diagonal slashes ¼ to ½″ deep in each loaf. Make a cross or 2 straight slashes on round loaves. Brush with cold water. Place loaves on middle shelf in hot oven and quickly spray water over all to create steam. Set timer for 5 minutes. Spray again. Repeat spraying 2 more times at 5 minute intervals. Bake 10 more minutes. Cool on wire racks.

2.   Preheat oven to 450°. You will need: a razor, soft pastry brush and an egg wash. Beat 1 egg white with 1 tablespoon of water until frothy. Slash loaves as directed in Method Number 1. Bake loaves on middle shelf 15 minutes. Remove and brush thoroughly with the egg wash. Return to oven and bake 10 more minutes. Cool on wire racks.

French bread freezes exceptionally well. Wrap according to directions in FREEZING, page 14. To recrisp: preheat oven to 375°. Heat frozen loaves wrapped in aluminum foil 35 minutes. If room temperature, bake 20 minutes.

VARIATIONS WITH FRENCH BREAD

WHOLE WHEAT FRENCH
Substitute 2 cups of whole wheat flour for white and add 2 tablespoons of wheat germ in the French Bread recipe, page 66. Beat in the whole wheat flour first, then add sufficient white flour to make a workable dough. Shape and cook as directed. Using such simple ingredients allows the full flavor of the whole wheat to permeate the bread besides producing an unusually crisp crust.

HARD ROLLS
Divide French Bread dough in thirds after the second rising. Cover 2 portions of dough with a towel. Cut ⅓ of dough in 16 pieces. Cup hand over one piece on working board and quickly rotate until a smooth bun is formed. Cover and allow to double, 1 to 1½ hours. Brush with egg wash made by beating 1 egg white with 1 tablespoon water until frothy. Sprinkle with poppy or sesame seed, if desired. Bake in preheated 425° oven about 20 minutes or until golden brown.

BREAD STICKS
Divide French Bread dough in thirds after the second rising. Cover dough that you are not working on with a towel. Roll one portion in a rectangle, 7x16″. Cut in strips ¼″ wide from narrow side. Each portion of dough will make about 22 sticks. Double each strip over and roll lightly with floured hands until smooth. Place on greased baking sheet. Repeat directions with remaining dough. Cover and allow to rise 30 minutes. Brush with 1 egg white beaten with 1 tablespoon water. Sprinkle with coarse salt or seeds of your choice. Bake in preheated 375° oven 15 to 20 minutes or until golden and crisp. Cool on wire racks.

BRIOCHE

This tenderest of breads is beautiful to taste and exciting to mold in many fancy shapes. The classical loaves will be described in this chapter; others will be discussed under PARTY IDEAS.

2 packages dry or compressed
*   yeast*
½ cup water
2 tablespoons sugar
4½ cups sifted flour
2 teaspoons salt

6 eggs
1½ cups butter or margarine,
*   room temperature*
1 egg beaten with 1
*   tablespoon water*

Combine yeast, water, and sugar, stirring with a fork until dissolved. Set aside. Resift flour with the salt into a large mixing bowl. Make a well in the flour mixture. Add the eggs and yeast mixture. Beat thoroughly with a rubber spatula. If you own a heavy electric mixer, use the flat beater — excellent for beating brioche dough. Beat several minutes until batter is smooth and light. Brioche dough requires hard beating to incorporate ingredients and as much air as possible. Begin to add the butter, one or two tablespoons at a time, beating after each addition until completely combined into the dough. If you do not have a heavy mixer, try this "slapping" method which is much better than using either a spatula or wooden spoon. With each addition of butter, vigorously slap and lift dough against side of bowl with one hand and hold the bowl steady with the other. If bowl slips, place on a wet tea towel. The dough will become stringy and fall from your hands in great globs. It is a most effective method and easier to do than it might sound. If you tire, rest your arms on the bowl for a few minutes. When all butter is combined, place dough in a greased bowl. Cover with plastic wrap and towel. Allow to double in bulk, about 2 hours. Punch down, recover and place in refrigerator overnight. At your leisure the next day, make any of the following breads.

BRIOCHE A TETE

The recipe for brioche can be made in two charming loaves with a topknot. They may be served hot or cold, and sliced in pie shaped wedges with your favorite jam. You may cut off the topknot, hollow out the loaf, fill with your best creamed seafood, chicken or a pâté and then replace the jaunty top. Don't throw away the insides! Toast in a slow oven (250°) until crisp. Cool and whirl in a blender for some of the best breadcrumbs you've ever tasted. Keep the crumbs in a jar in the refrigerator.

Brush 2 large brioche pans heavily with soft butter. Remove dough from refrigerator and divide in half. Return one portion to refrigerator. Place the other piece on a floured board. Cut off ¼ of dough and set aside. Roll the larger portion into a smooth ball, using flour on your hands if dough becomes sticky. Place the ball of dough in prepared brioche pan. With your first 3 fingers, make a conical shape hole in the dough, 2″ across the top, 1″ at the bottom and about 2″ deep. Roll the small portion of dough into a ball. Mold into a pear shape, using flour on hands when necessary. Insert the pointed piece of dough into the conical hole. Set aside uncovered to double in bulk, about 2½ to 3 hours. Repeat directions with second portion of dough.

With a light pastry or feather brush, paint egg wash over tops of breads. Avoid too much glaze seeping down where the head joins the main part of dough. Allow to set 2 to 3 minutes and lightly brush with egg wash again. With kitchen scissors, make 4 slanting clips under the head and into the large ball of dough. Place brioche pans on a baking sheet to avoid butter bubbling on bottom of oven. Bake in preheated 450° oven 15 minutes. Lower heat to 350° and continue baking 35 more minutes. If loaves become too brown, cover with foil during the last 15 minutes of baking (refer to Techniques, page 14). Cool on wire racks.

PETITE BRIOCHE

Twenty fun little muffins all in different styles as some tops will stand straight and others tip in a variety of directions. Brioche muffin tins are the best but custard cups or medium size muffin tins can be substituted.

Brush 20 small brioche molds with soft butter. Remove ¼ of dough from refrigerator at a time. Divide in 5 portions. Molding muffins: Cut ¼ dough off each portion. With floured hands roll the large piece in a round ball. Set in a prepared mold. Form the smaller portion of dough into a pear-shaped knob. Indent the ball of dough with one finger. Insert the pear-shaped dough point side down into the hole. Press gently to set firmly. Work quickly and keep your hands floured. If dough becomes too soft, chill for a few minutes. Repeat directions with remaining dough. Place brioche tins on a baking sheet. Set aside uncovered to double, about 2 hours. Brush lightly with egg glaze, let set 2 minutes and brush again. Bake in preheated 475° oven 10 minutes. Reduce heat to 375° and bake 10 to 15 minutes, until puffed and golden brown. Cool on wire racks.

PAN LOAVES

The brioche recipe will make 2 large loaves, 9x5x3" or three smaller loaves, 8½x4½x2½". Grease pans thoroughly with melted butter. Divide dough and mold into loaves with your hands. Pat and shape into the loaf pans. Brioche dough is so rich and soft that it is easily shaped. Set aside uncovered to double, about 2 hours. Brush with egg wash. Bake in a preheated 375° oven 40 minutes for smaller loaves and 45 for larger size. Check with a cake tester for doneness. Cover with foil the last 15 minutes if bread becomes too brown. Cool on wire racks.

BRIOCHE EN COURONNE

Here is the lovely, adaptable Crown Brioche that may be used simply as a bread or fill the center with a favorite creamed dish. The recipe for brioche dough may be made into one large ring or 2 smaller ones. Shape the chilled dough into a round loaf on a greased baking sheet. Insert 2 fingers in the center and make a hole. Gently pull the center wider to about 5" in diameter for the large loaf and 4" for the two smaller ones. Shape and tuck under any ragged pieces of dough to form into a doughnut shape. Cut gashes around the center top with kitchen shears about 1½" apart. Set aside to rise uncovered, until doubled, about 2 hours. Brush lightly with egg wash. Bake in 375° oven 45 minutes for large loaf and 35 for smaller ones. Remove to wire racks.

BRIOCHE BRAIDS

Divide the brioche dough in 2 portions. Return one piece to the refrigerator. Cut one portion into 3 equal pieces. With floured hands, roll into smooth ropes, 18″ in length. Cross the 3 pieces in the center and braid loosely out to each end. Place on a greased baking sheet and tuck the ends under. Repeat directions with second portion of dough. Cover and allow to double in size, about 1½ to 2 hours. Brush with egg glaze. If desired, sprinkle the braids lightly with granulated sugar. Bake in a preheated 375° oven about 35 minutes or until golden brown. Remove to wire racks and cool. Serve a braid heated for dinner or sliced and toasted for breakfast.

CRUSTY FRENCH ROLLS

A delicate texture inside with a lovely, golden crust outside make these easily produced rolls a delight for a dinner party.

1½ cups warm water
2 packages dry or compressed yeast
2 tablespoons sugar
1½ teaspoons salt
3 tablespoons melted butter or
margarine

5 cups flour, approximately
3 egg whites, beaten stiff
1 egg white beaten with 1
tablespoon water
Cornmeal

Measure water into a mixing bowl. Add yeast, stirring until dissolved. Blend in the sugar, salt, and butter. Stir in 2 cups of the flour until batter is smooth. With a rubber spatula, fold beaten egg whites into dough mixture. Add enough more flour to form a soft, workable dough. Turn out on a floured board and knead until smooth and resilient, about 10 minutes. Place dough in a warm, greased bowl, turning to coat the top. Cover loosely with plastic wrap and a towel. Allow to *triple* in bulk, about 1½ hours. Punch down, knead in the bowl, recover, and let rise until doubled, about 1 hour. Knead lightly on a floured board, cover and let rest 10 minutes. This recipe will make 16 large or 32 smaller rolls. To form: divide dough into desired number of pieces. Place one portion on a floured board; cup your hand over it. Rotate quickly in a circular motion until a smooth bun is formed. Repeat with remaining dough. Place on greased baking sheets lightly sprinkled with cornmeal. Cover and let double, about 45 minutes. Brush with egg wash. Bake in preheated 425° oven 15 to 20 minutes. Cool on wire racks.

CROISSANTS

Making the true, flaky, rich croissant is time consuming but an exceedingly fascinating process that can be a challenge to your expertise. The delightful part is that they may be made one day and baked the next, or completed in a single day.

¾ pound cold butter
⅓ cup flour
2 packages dry or compressed yeast
¼ cup warm water
1¼ cups cold milk

1 tablespoon sugar
2 teaspoons salt
4 cups flour, approximately
1 egg beaten with 1
   tablespoon milk

Slice butter in pieces into a mixing bowl and add the ⅓ cup flour. Cut with a pastry blender until well mixed. Mark a rectangle, 8x14″ on 2 sheets of waxed paper. Place butter mixture between the two sheets. Roll mixture into size of marked rectangle. Fold paper on all sides and refrigerate until thoroughly chilled.

Sprinkle yeast into the warm water, stirring with a fork until dissolved. In a mixing bowl, combine cold milk, sugar, and salt. Add yeast mixture. Beat in 2 cups of flour until smooth. Stir in sufficient more flour to make a soft, workable dough. Turn out on a lightly floured board and knead about 5 minutes. Cover and let dough rest 30 minutes. Roll dough in a rectangle 10x16″. Remove chilled butter from refrigerator and pull off waxed paper. Place rectangle of butter on left hand side of prepared dough. Fold right side of dough over and press edges to seal.

1.   Roll into a rectangle ⅛″ thick (about 12x22″). Fold top third of dough toward the center; fold bottom third on top as an envelope. This makes 3 layers. Slip in a plastic bag and chill 30 minutes.

2.   Remove dough to a floured board so that open end faces you. Roll out again to ⅛″ thickness. (Always roll in a rectangle.) Fold in thirds as before. If dough becomes sticky, scatter more flour on your board and rolling pin.

3.   Turn dough so open end faces you. Roll out again, fold as before, place in plastic bag and chill 30 minutes.

4.   Remove dough and go through the rolling and folding process 2 more times. If butter begins to ooze out at any time, chill a few minutes. Cut dough in half for ease of handling. Place each portion in a plastic bag and chill 1 hour.

5. Remove one portion of dough. Place on floured board and roll into a square, ¼" thick. Cut into squares either 4x4" or 5x5". Divide each square into triangles. Starting from widest side, roll each triangle up loosely and stretch lightly. Place croissants on greased baking sheets, point side down, 1½" apart. Curve ends into a crescent.

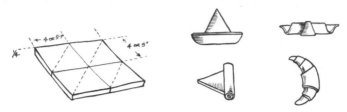

6. Cover and let rise until double, about 2½ hours. Brush rolls with egg wash. Bake in preheated 375° oven about 20 minutes or until golden. Cool on wire racks 10 minutes before serving.

7. If using baked croissants the following day, reheat in a 350° oven 8 to 10 minutes.

8. Serving and baking the next day: after forming rolls, cover securely and refrigerate overnight.. Remove 3 hours before serving. Let rise and bake as directed. Croissants freeze well. Recrisp in 350° oven about 15 minutes.

FRENCH ONION SOUP

The secrets to an excellent Onion Soup are use of purple onions, if available, a long slow cooking of those onions, and a rich beef broth. 10 to 12 servings.

3 tablespoons butter	Salt
2 tablespoons oil	3 tablespoons cognac
8 packed cups thinly sliced onions,	Grated Swiss or Parmesan
preferably purple	cheese
8 cups boiling beef broth	Toasted slices French bread
½ cup dry white wine	Melted butter
Grindings of black pepper	

Melt butter and oil in a large soup pot. Stir in the onions until well coated. Cover pot and cook at low heat 15 minutes. Uncover and raise heat to medium. Cook 40 minutes, stirring frequently until onions turn clear and golden. Do not allow to brown. Add the boiling broth and wine. Simmer partially covered 40 minutes. Skim if necessary. Taste for salt and add a few grindings of black pepper. The soup may be prepared ahead or frozen at this point.

About 20 minutes before serving, add cognac to the hot soup. Pour soup into a tureen or individual oven proof soup bowls. Brush French toast with butter. Place bread on top of soup in the tureen or bowls. Sprinkle with either the Swiss or Parmesan cheese. If soup is boiling hot, slide under the broiler until cheese is bubbling and lightly brown. If soup is just warm, bake 15 to 20 minutes in preheated 350° oven. Turn to broil a few minutes to brown cheese. Serve immediately.

WATERCRESS SOUP

American produce is becoming more luxuriant and available. When watercress appears in April and May, make this soup to freeze for a lovely winter dinner.

¼ cup butter	6 cups hot chicken broth
½ cup chopped onion	3 egg yolks
4 cups packed watercress,	1 cup heavy cream
coarsely chopped	Salt
¼ cup flour	White pepper

Melt butter in a saucepan; sauté onion until golden and tender, about 10 minutes. Do not allow to discolor. Add the watercress, stir thoroughly, cover pan and cook over moderately low heat 5 minutes. Remove lid. Whisk in the flour and stir until smooth and bubbling. Take saucepan off the burner. Add the hot chicken broth, stirring rapidly to keep smooth. Return to heat, bring to a simmer and cook for 10 minutes, stirring occasionally. Whirl soup through a blender and return to a clean saucepan. (The soup may now be frozen and finished when ready to serve.)

Combine the egg yolks and cream in a small bowl. Stir in ½ cup of hot soup. Pour egg mixture slowly into the soup, stirring constantly. Reheat slowly but do not allow to boil. Taste for salt and adjust. Add a dash or two of white pepper, if desired. Serves six to eight.

VICHYSSOISE

No other soup is quite like this beautiful classic originated by M. Diat. My version is equally good hot or cold.

4 cups sliced leeks or combination	*Nutmeg*
of leeks and yellow onions	*Salt*
½ cup butter	*White pepper*
4 cups diced potatoes	*Chives for garnish*
1½ quarts chicken broth	
1 cup heavy cream	

Clean leeks thoroughly and slice, using only the white portion. (Peel and chop onions, if used.) In a large saucepan, sauté leeks in butter until tender, about 10 to 15 minutes. Do not allow to discolor. Add diced potatoes and broth. Bring to a simmer and cook until vegetables are soft. Rub through a strainer or purée in an electric blender. Return to a clean saucepan. Slowly add cream, stirring constantly. Season with nutmeg, pepper, and salt to taste. Stir until well heated but do not allow to boil. Pour into a container and chill thoroughly. Serve in chilled cream soup bowls with chives for a garnish or more nutmeg if preferred. If soup becomes too thick, thin with broth or cream.

CREAM OF MUSHROOM SOUP

A classic soup that should be in every serious cook's repertoire. I have designed this soup in two parts so that it may be served as a bouillon or as a cream soup.

PART 1. THE BOUILLON

½ cup chopped onion
3 tablespoons butter or margarine
9 cups chicken broth, canned, cubes
   or your own make
3 parsley sprigs

1 bay leaf
¼ teaspoon thyme
Stems from 1½ lbs.
   mushrooms
Cheese cloth

In a large saucepan, sauté onion in butter until tender, about 10 minutes. Do not allow to discolor. Add chicken broth, parsley, bay leaf, thyme, and mushroom stems. Bring to a simmer and cook uncovered 35 minutes. Strain the broth through wet cheese cloth placed in a colander over a large bowl. I have used this flavorful broth many times for a buffet party as guests love a hot, delicious bouillon. If you make a dish that uses fresh mushrooms, this broth is an excellent way to use the stems. Freeze broth for future use.

PART 2. THE CREAMED SOUP

1½ lbs. mushrooms, cleaned and
   thinly sliced
2 tablespoons butter or margarine
2 teaspoons lemon juice
¼ cup butter or margarine
¼ cup flour

Strained broth
2 cups hot milk
3 egg yolks
½ cup dry sherry
Salt
Grindings of black pepper

In a skillet, sauté mushrooms with 2 tablespoons of butter for 3 minutes, stirring constantly. Add the lemon juice, cover skillet and cook over low heat 5 minutes. Set aside. In a large saucepan, melt the ¼ cup of butter. Whisk in the flour until smooth and bubbly. Blend in the strained broth and hot milk, stirring until thickened. Add sauteed mushrooms with any cooking juice in the skillet.

Whip egg yolks and sherry together. Stir in a small amount of hot soup. Slowly blend egg mixture into the soup. Taste and adjust for salt. Add a few grindings of black pepper. Heat but do not allow to boil. Present in warmed cream soup bowls with slices of toasted home made miniature bread as an accompaniment. Serves 8 to 10.

WHOLESOME DARK BREADS

SOUPS:

Black Bean Soup
Hot Russian Borscht
Sue's Lamb and Barley
Mulligawtawney

HINTS FOR WORKING WITH WHOLE GRAIN FLOURS

The whole grain flours you will be working with in this chapter are rye, buckwheat, cornmeal, whole wheat, and unbleached white. (Refer to Wheat and Flours, page 94). All the following recipes use mixtures of flours. The rye, buckwheat, cornmeal, and similar flours do not have sufficient gluten to produce the gases necessary to raise breads as we like them, so white flour is included to make a lighter loaf. Heavier grains produce a dense bread.

Never sift any of the whole grain flours; it is unnecessary and you will lose part of the grains. In reading these recipes you will observe that frequently the whole grain flour is beaten into the liquids first. White flour is added to finish making a workable dough. Always stir in the white flour gradually to prevent producing a heavy, dry dough. Since these flours do form a heavier dough, the rising process will be slower. So have patience; buy good stone ground flours and they will create a delicious flavor — nutty, healthful, and sustaining. There is great satisfaction in making these particular breads and the men in your family will especially relish them.

TOPPINGS

For most breads in this chapter, a topping is suggested to give a special finishing touch. Here is a list of various types and what they produce. The toppings may be interchanged. If you particularly like one, use it on other breads.

1. Egg white beaten with 1 tablespoon of water: gives a shiny, hard finish.

2. Whole egg beaten with 1 tablespoon water: produces a golden shiny finish that is softer than the egg white.

3. Postum or Instant Coffee mixed with a small amount of water: both are used to make a darker finish.

4. Cornstarch and water: Combine 1 teaspoon cornstarch with ½ cup water in a small saucepan. Bring to a boil, stirring constantly and cook 3 minutes. Brush this topping on a bread 5 minutes before it is done and place back in the oven to finish baking. It produces a lovely soft-shiny appearance.

5. Brush loaves with cold water just before baking, spray oven with cold water. Spray oven again in 5 minutes. Produces a crisp crust.

6. Melted butter or margarine may be brushed on a loaf just before baking. This makes a crisp, brown crust.

Postum, Instant Coffee, and bitter chocolate are used in dough to make them darker. If you have access to caramel, use several drops while mixing the dough. Commercial bakers utilize caramel to produce the very dark, black breads.

A LIGHT RYE

An easily made flexible rye bread. You may use your choice of seasonings or leave it unadorned.

2 cups water
½ cup molasses or brown sugar
1 teaspoon salt
2 teaspoons caraway seeds
1 teaspoon anise seeds
2 tablespoons melted butter or margarine

1 package dry or compressed yeast
2 cups white flour
3½ cups rye flour, approximately
1 egg white beaten with 1 tablespoon water

Combine water, sugar, salt, seeds, and butter in a saucepan; bring to a boil and let bubble 3 minutes. Cool to lukewarm. Transfer water mixture to a large mixing bowl. Sprinkle in the yeast, stirring with a fork until dissolved. Beat in the white flour until mixture is a smooth batter. Cover with a towel and allow to rise until doubled and bubbly, about 1½ hours. Stir down the sponge. Gradually add enough rye flour to make a soft, workable dough. Turn out on a lightly floured board. Knead until smooth and elastic (refer to Techniques, page 11), about 10 minutes. Place dough in a warm, greased bowl, turning to coat the top. Cover loosely with plastic wrap and a towel. Let rise until doubled, about 1 hour. Punch down, knead lightly, divide in 2 portions, cover and let rest 15 minutes. Mold into round or long French loaves. Place French shaped loaves on greased baking sheets and round breads in 8″ cake pans. Cover and allow to double, 45 minutes to 1 hour. Slash long loaves diagonally and round loaves with a cross. Brush with egg glaze. Bake in a preheated 375° oven 35 minutes. Cool on wire racks.

LOAF PANS

Divide dough in 2 portions. Shape and place in greased 8½x4½x2½″ pans. Cover and let rise to tops of pans, about 1 hour. Slash each loaf 3 times and bake in 375° oven 40 minutes. Cool on wire racks.

A DARK RYE

A dark color with a smooth, fine texture characterizes this rye bread. The recipe was given to me several years ago by a young, Swedish American Field Service student who lived in our home for a year.

2½ cups warm milk
2 packages dry or compressed
    yeast
¾ cup dark molasses
⅓ cup melted butter or margarine
2 teaspoons salt
3 teaspoons fennel seed,
    lightly crushed

6 cups rye flour, approximately
2 cups white flour
1 egg beaten with 1 tablespoon
    water
Caraway or anise seeds

Measure warm milk into a large mixing bowl. Sprinkle in the yeast, stirring with a fork until dissolved. Blend in the molasses, butter, salt, and fennel. Beat in 4 cups of rye flour until batter is smooth. Stir in the 2 cups of white flour. Gradually add enough more rye flour to make a soft dough. Turn out on a lightly floured surface (using white flour) and knead until smooth and elastic, about 10 minutes. Place in a warm, greased bowl, turning to coat the top (refer to Techniques, page 12). Cover loosely with plastic wrap and a towel. Allow to double in bulk, about 1½ hours.

Punch the dough down, knead lightly, cover and let rest 15 minutes. Divide in 3 portions. Shape into round or French loaves. Place round loaves in 8″ greased cake tins; French loaves on a baking sheet. Cover and allow to double, about 1 hour. Slash French loaves diagonally and round loaves tic-tac-toe. Brush with egg wash. Sprinkle with caraway or anise seeds, if desired. Bake in preheated 375° oven 30 minutes. Cool on wire racks.

NOTE

If a crisper crust is desired, brush loaves before baking with cold water. Spray hot oven with cold water. After 5 minutes of baking, spray loaves again with water. Proceed as directed.

SWEDISH LIMPE

This is the popular Rye Bread flavored with orange so favored in Sweden. A firm bread good for making sandwiches or toast.

2 tablespoons orange peel,
    finely chopped
2 packages dry or compressed
    yeast
2½ cups warm water
½ cup brown sugar, lightly packed
1½ teaspoons salt

¼ cup melted butter or margarine
3 cups rye flour
4 cups white flour,
    approximately
1 egg beaten with 1 tablespoon
    water
Caraway or anise seed (optional)

Remove orange peel with a potato peeler, avoiding any white portion. Chop finely and set aside. Sprinkle yeast over warm water in a large mixing bowl. Stir with a fork until dissolved. Blend in the brown sugar, salt, butter, orange peel, and rye flour. Beat until smooth. Add enough white flour to make a soft dough. Turn out on a lightly floured board.

Knead 10 minutes or until smooth and resilient, adding small amounts of white flour if necessary. Place in warm, greased bowl, turning to coat the top. Cover loosely with plastic wrap and a towel. Place in a draft free spot and allow to double in bulk, about 1½ hours. Remove to a floured surface and knead lightly. Cover and let rest 10 minutes.

Form dough in 2 large or 3 smaller loaves — either round or French. Place on greased baking sheets. Cover and allow to double in bulk, about 45 minutes to 1 hour. Slash with a sharp razor, diagonal for French loaves and a cross for the rounds. Brush with egg wash. Sprinkle with caraway or anise seed if desired. Bake large loaves in preheated 350° oven 45 minutes and 30 for smaller breads. Cool on wire racks.

RYE BUTTERMILK BREAD

An unusually tasteful and nourishing recipe using buttermilk, which always seems to give breads a special quality.

2 packages dry or compressed yeast	3 cups stone ground rye flour
½ cup warm water	3 cups unbleached white
2 cups warm buttermilk	flour, approximately
½ cup molasses or brown sugar	1 egg white beaten with 1
⅓ cup melted butter or margarine	tablespoon water
2 teaspoons salt	
1 tablespoon caraway or anise seed	

Sprinkle yeast over the warm water, stirring with a fork until dissolved. Set aside. In a large mixing bowl, combine the warm buttermilk (do not be disturbed if milk curdles), molasses, butter, salt, and choice of seeds. Blend well and add the yeast mixture. Beat in the rye flour until smooth. Gradually add enough white flour to make a soft dough. Turn out on a lightly floured board and knead until smooth and resilient, about 10 minutes. Place in a warm, greased bowl, turning to coat the top. Cover loosely with plastic wrap and a towel. Allow to double in bulk, about 1½ hours. Remove to a floured board and knead lightly. Cover and let rest 10 minutes.

Divide dough in 3 portions; shape into round or French breads (refer to French bread, page 67). Place long loaves on greased baking sheets. Cover and allow to double in bulk, about 1 hour. Slash with a sharp razor, diagonally. Brush with egg wash. Bake in preheated 350° oven 35 minutes. If bread becomes too brown, cover with aluminum foil the last 10 minutes. Place round loaves in greased 8" cake pans and proceed as directed. Three pan loaves (8½x4½x2½") may also be formed. Slash 3 times, brush with egg wash and bake 40 minutes in 350° oven. Remove to wire racks.

RYE BREAD WITH BEER

A slight tang makes this a perfect bread for cheese and cold meats. Try a toasted cheese sandwich — delicious!

2 packages dry or compressed yeast
¼ cup warm water
1¾ cups beer (10 oz. can)
¼ cup melted butter or margarine
¼ cup molasses
1 teaspoon salt
1 tablespoon fennel or anise seeds

1 tablespoon orange peel,
   chopped (optional)
3½ cups rye flour
2 to 3 cups white flour
1 egg beaten with 1
   tablespoon water

Sprinkle yeast over the warm water, stirring until dissolved. Set aside. Heat beer with butter until warm. Transfer beer mixture to a large mixing bowl. Add the molasses, salt, seeds, orange peel (if desired), and yeast mixture. Blend well. Beat in the rye flour until smooth. Add enough white flour to make a soft dough. Remove to a lightly floured board and knead until smooth and bouncy, about 10 minutes. Place in a warm, greased bowl, turning to coat the top. Cover loosely with plastic wrap and a towel. Allow to double in bulk, about 1 to 1½ hours. Punch the dough down and knead lightly. Cover and allow to rest 10 minutes. Shape in 2 round loaves. Place on a greased baking sheet. Cover and let double, about 1 hour. With a sharp razor, slash a cross on breads. Brush with egg wash. Bake in a preheated 350° oven 40 to 45 minutes (refer to Techniques, page 14). Remove from pans and cool on wire racks.

PUMPERNICKEL

A German gentleman named Pumper Nickel created this robust, popular bread by combining whole grain flours and cereal. Don't be afraid of making this bread — the biggest trouble is gathering all the ingredients together.

2½ cups boiling water
2 tablespoons molasses
2 tablespoons instant coffee
2 tablespoons melted butter or oil
2 teaspoons caraway seeds
1 tablespoon salt
2 packages dry or compressed yeast

2 cups rye flour
1 cup whole bran cereal
½ cup yellow cornmeal
1 cup mashed potatoes
4 cups unbleached white
   flour, approximately

In a large mixing bowl, combine water, molasses, coffee, butter or oil, seeds, and salt. Stir until thoroughly mixed. Cool to lukewarm. Sprinkle in the yeast and beat with a fork until dissolved. Set aside.

In a separate bowl, combine the rye flour, bran cereal, cornmeal, and 1 cup of the white flour. Add to the yeast mixture. Beat with a rubber spatula until smooth. Stir in the cup of mashed potatoes (refer to Ingredients, page 9). Add enough more white flour to make a soft dough. Turn out on a lightly floured surface and knead until smooth and resilient, about 10 minutes. The dough will be sticky. Brush your hands and kneading board with white flour as needed, but do not expect to eliminate the stickiness completely or your bread will become heavy. Place dough in a warm, greased bowl turning to coat the top. Cover loosely with plastic wrap and a towel. Let rise until doubled in bulk, about 1½ hours. Turn out on a board and divide in 2 portions. Shape into round loaves. Place in greased 8" cake tins. Cover and let double, about 1 hour. Slash a cross on each loaf. Bake in preheated 350° oven 50 minutes. Remove from pans and cool on wire racks.

BLACK PEASANT BREAD

A pungent, dark, and sustaining bread that is excellent served with Black Bean soup and a good sharp cheese.

2 packages dry or compressed yeast
2 cups warm water
½ cup molasses
1 tablespoon salt
¼ cup melted butter or margarine
1 square bitter chocolate, melted
1 teaspoon fennel seeds, lightly crushed

1½ tablespoons caraway seeds
1 cup whole bran cereal
1 cup buckwheat flour
1 cup whole wheat flour
2 cups rye flour
2 to 3 cups unbleached white flour

In a large mixing bowl, sprinkle yeast over the warm water. Stir with a fork until dissolved. To the yeast mixture, add the molasses, salt, butter, chocolate, and seeds. Blend thoroughly. With a rubber spatula beat in the cereal, buckwheat, whole wheat, and rye flours until smooth. Gradually add enough white flour to make a soft dough. Knead on a lightly floured board until smooth and resilient, about 10 minutes. As with most heavy, dark breads, the dough tends to be sticky. Do not attempt to eradicate the stickiness or you will have a heavy, dry bread. Place dough in a warm, greased bowl turning to coat the top. Cover loosely with plastic wrap and a towel. Allow to double in bulk, about

1½ hours.

Turn out on a floured surface and divide in 2 portions. Mold in round loaves and place on a greased baking sheet. Cover and allow to double, about 45 minutes. Bake in a preheated 350° oven 45 minutes. Remove and brush with cornstarch topping*. Return to oven and bake 5 more minutes. Turn loaves out on wire racks to cool. (Refer to Techniques, page 14).

*TOPPING

Combine ½ cup water with 1 teaspoon cornstarch in a small saucepan. Bring to a boil, stirring constantly and cook 2 minutes.

FENNEL CAKES

Try these round, flat loaves split or cut in pie shaped wedges toasted and served with drip beef. Superb flavor and quickly made.

3 cups warm water	*⅓ cup molasses*
2 packages dry or compressed yeast	*4 cups rye flour*
¼ cup melted butter or margarine	*3 cups white flour,*
1 teaspoon salt	*approximately*
1 tablespoon fennel seeds, lightly crushed	*Melted butter*

Measure the warm water into a large mixing bowl. Add yeast, stirring with a fork until dissolved. Blend in the butter, salt, fennel, and molasses. Beat in the rye flour until mixture is smooth. Gradually add enough white flour to make a workable dough (refer to Techniques, page 11). Turn out on a floured surface and knead until smooth and bouncy. Divide dough in 4 portions. Cover with a towel and let rest 15 minutes. Roll each portion into a round cake about 8 or 9 inches in diameter. With a 1½″ biscuit cutter, cut a hole in the center of each cake. Place loaves on greased baking sheets. Prick each cake with a fork. The leftover dough may be molded into a small bun or miniature loaf. Cover and let rise 60 minutes. Bake in a preheated 425° oven 15 to 20 minutes or until brown. Remove loaves to racks and brush with melted butter if desired.

RYE ROLLS

A versatile, delicious roll easily changed into hamburger buns. Note two additional ingredients described at end of the recipe.

1½ cups warm water
1 package dry or compressed yeast
1 teaspoon salt
2 tablespoons molasses
2 tablespoons melted butter or margarine
2 cups white flour

2 cups rye flour
Caraway, anise, poppy,
   or sesame seeds
1 egg beaten with 1
   tablespoon water

Measure warm water into a mixing bowl. Add yeast, stirring with a fork until dissolved (refer to Ingredients, page 7). Blend in salt, molasses, and butter. Combine the white and rye flours. Add enough flour mixture to the yeast mixture to make a soft dough. Turn out on a lightly floured surface and knead until smooth and elastic, about 10 minutes. If dough is sticky, add small amounts of white flour while kneading. Round into a ball. Place in a warm, greased bowl, turning to coat the top. Cover loosely with plastic wrap and a towel. Allow to double in bulk, about 1½ hours. Punch the dough down, knead lightly, cover and let rest 10 minutes. Divide dough in 16 portions. Form round rolls and place on greased baking sheets. Cover, and let rise 30 minutes. Make a slash lengthwise on top of each roll. Brush with egg wash and sprinkle with choice of seeds. Bake in preheated 375° oven 25 minutes or until golden brown. Cool rolls on wire racks or serve immediately.

HAMBURGER BUNS

Blend 2 more tablespoons melted butter and 2 beaten eggs into the yeast mixture. Proceed as described. You will need about ½ to 1 more cup of rye flour. After the first rising, roll dough ¼ to ½" thick. Cut buns with a 3½" biscuit cutter or form round rolls and press flat. Place on greased baking sheets. Let rise covered 30 minutes. Brush with egg wash and sprinkle with desired seeds. Bake in preheated 400° oven 15 minutes.

SWEDISH RYE RUSKS

A delicious dry toast for munching at parties or in front of television. Much healthier and less calories than potato chips!

Rind of 2 oranges
2 packages dry or compressed yeast
2½ cups warm milk
½ cup melted butter or margarine
½ cup molasses

⅓ cup sugar
¼ teaspoon salt
2 cups rye flour
6 cups white flour,
   approximately

Remove rind from oranges with a potato peeler, avoiding any white portion. Chop rind finely with a sharp knife and set aside.

In a large mixing bowl, sprinkle yeast over the warm milk, stirring with a fork until dissolved. Blend in the butter, molasses, sugar, salt, and prepared orange rind. Beat in the rye flour until smooth. Gradually add enough white flour to make a workable dough (refer to Ingredients, page 8). Turn out on a floured surface and knead until smooth and satiny, about 10 minutes. Place in a warm, greased bowl, turning to coat the top. Cover loosely with plastic wrap and a towel. Let double in bulk, about 1½ hours.

Punch down and divide dough in 6 portions. Roll each part into a loaf 18″ long. Place loaves on 2 greased baking sheets. Cover and let rise 45 minutes. Bake in a preheated 375° oven 20 minutes. Remove loaves to towels. Brush with warm water and allow to cool. When cold, slice loaves in half lengthwise. Cut each length in 1 to 1½″ slices. Place on clean baking sheets. Dry in a slow 250° oven until light brown, about 2 hours. Turn off heat, open oven door slightly and leave rusks until oven cools.

RYE BREADSTICKS

Place these breadsticks in a crockery jar for a soup party. Your guests will inhale them!

1 package dry or compressed yeast
1 cup warm water
1 egg
3 tablespoons melted butter or margarine

1 tablespoon sugar
1½ teaspoons salt
1 cup rye flour
2 teaspoons caraway seeds
2½ to 3 cups white flour

1 egg white beaten with 1
*   tablespoon water*
Anise seeds
Coarse salt
Sesame seeds

Sprinkle yeast over the warm water, stirring with a fork until dissolved. Beat the egg in a mixing bowl. Blend in the butter, sugar, and salt. Add the yeast mixture, rye flour, and caraway seeds. Beat until smooth. Stir in enough white flour to make a soft dough. Turn out on a lightly floured board and knead until smooth and resilient, about 5 to 8 minutes. Place in a warm, greased bowl. Cover loosely with plastic wrap and a towel. Allow to double in bulk, approximately 1½ hours.

Punch the dough down. Turn out on a floured board and knead lightly. Cover and let rest 10 minutes (refer to Techniques, page 13). Divide dough in 2 parts. Roll each portion in a rectangle 8x18″. With a dough scraper or sharp knife, cut each oblong in 24 sticks. For easier manipulation, fold each strip double and roll between the hands or on the table to desired length. Place sticks on a greased baking sheet ¾″ apart. Cover and allow to double, about 45 minutes. Brush with egg wash. Sprinkle with seeds of your choice or the coarse salt. If salt is used as a topping, eliminate ½ teaspoon salt from recipe. Bake in preheated 400° oven 15 to 18 minutes or until golden brown. Cool sticks on wire racks.

OLD FASHIONED BUCKWHEAT PANCAKES

The method of making these pancakes is similar to Sourdough. The batter will keep well in the refrigerator for several weeks.

4 cups warm water (or 2 cups milk and 2 cups water)
1 package dry or compressed yeast
4 cups buckwheat flour*
1 teaspoon salt

3 tablespoons brown sugar or molasses
½ teaspoon baking soda
1 tablespoon oil or melted margarine

Measure warm water into a large crock. Sprinkle in the yeast, stirring with a fork until dissolved. Beat in the flour until mixture is smooth. Cover with a towel and let stand overnight. The next morning, add the salt, sugar, soda, and oil. Mix thoroughly. Use a ¼ cup to measure size of pancakes. Bake on a lightly greased, hot griddle until golden brown, turning once. The batter that is left may be stored, covered, in the refrigerator until ready to use again.

To Replenish: Stir in equal amounts of liquid (warm water or milk) and buckwheat flour to remaining batter. Beat with a rubber spatula until smooth, cover and allow to stand overnight. When ready to cook, add ½ teaspoon salt, 2 tablespoons brown sugar or molasses, ½ teaspoon soda, and 1 tablespoon melted margarine or oil. These ingredients will be sufficient for an additional 3 cups of flour and liquid.

*NOTE
Optional — you may substitute 1 cup white flour for 1 cup buckwheat.

BLACK BEAN SOUP

A pungent, aromatic soup that satisfies one's inner being. Men especially enjoy the good, strong flavor. Excellent to use after a football game with a hot black bread.

2 cups black beans	¾ cup celery, chopped
3 quarts water	3 medium tomatoes, chopped
1 ham bone	1 bay leaf
½ pound ham, diced	1 tablespoon salt
3 tablespoons oil	½ teaspoon ground chili peppers
3 cloves garlic, peeled and	2 teaspoons paprika
minced	3 tablespoons butter
3 medium onions, chopped	3 tablespoons flour
1 large carrot, chopped	¼ to ½ cup dry sherry
1 green pepper, chopped	Thin slices of lemon or lime

Wash the beans thoroughly; cover with water and soak overnight. The next morning, drain the beans and wash again. In a 6 quart soup kettle, combine the beans, water, ham bone, and ham. Bring to a boil, skim, and reduce heat to simmer. Cover and let bubble lightly about 2½ to 3 hours.

Meanwhile, heat the oil in a large skillet. Saute the garlic, onions, carrot, green pepper, and celery 15 to 20 minutes or until tender but not brown. Add to the bean mixture with the tomatoes, bay leaf, salt, chili peppers, and paprika. Cover and simmer for 1 to 1½ hours. Remove the ham bone and discard. Purée the soup in a blender. Return soup to a clean kettle. Knead the butter and flour together with a wooden spoon. Add a little hot soup and mix well. Stir into the soup kettle. Taste and adjust for salt and chili pepper. If desired, the soup may be refrigerated or frozen at this point.

PRESENTATION
Heat soup to boiling. Stir in the sherry. Serve in large, warm soup bowls. Garnish with slices of lemon or lime. Pass the sherry pitcher for an additional fillip! Serves 12.

NOTE
If you prefer a thinner soup, omit the flour and butter. The soup will become thicker when chilled. Thin with a small amount of beef bouillon when reheating, if necessary.

HOT RUSSIAN BORSCHT

Here is another excellent full meal soup. Serve with hot peasant or pumpernickel bread accompanied with a good yogurt or cream cheese.

2½ cups peeled beets, cut in strips | 1 tablespoon lemon juice
2 cups canned tomatoes | 2 tablespoons sugar
4 cups water | Salt
1 small onion, finely diced | 4 eggs
¾ pound beef — rump, round, or breast

Place the strips of beets in a small soup pot. Strain the tomatoes through a fine sieve over the beets. Do not allow any seeds through the sieve. Add the water, onion, and meat cut in small pieces. Bring to a boil and skim. Lower heat to a simmer and cook partially covered 30 minutes. Add the lemon juice, sugar, and taste for salt. Bring back to simmer and let bubble lightly 30 more minutes, or until meat is very tender. Whisk the eggs thoroughly in a small bowl. Slowly add 1 cup of the hot borscht, stirring constantly. Gradually add the egg mixture to the soup. Serve at once. Six servings.

SUE'S LAMB AND BARLEY SOUP

One of the very best vegetable soups — served hot with a pumpernickel or rye bread leaves one with a feeling of great contentment. The soup is quite adaptable to beef in place of lamb.

PART I

1 lamb breast | ⅛ teaspoon Cayenne pepper
1½ pounds lamb shoulder, boned | Bouquet Garni
   or 2 lamb shanks | ½ teaspoon thyme
2 quarts water | 12 peppercorns, crushed
1 can beef bouillon, diluted | 1 large bay leaf
   to make 2 cups | 3 large cloves garlic, smashed
¾ cup pearl barley | 3 sprigs parsley
2 teaspoons salt

Remove as much fat from meat as possible and discard. Place meat in a soup kettle with the water and diluted bouillon. Add the barley, salt, and Cayenne pepper. Combine the ingredients for the Bouquet Garni in a small piece of cheese cloth and tie firmly with a piece of string. Drop into the soup kettle. Bring soup to a boil and skim well. Lower heat to simmer, cover, and cook for 2 hours. Remove meat from broth, cover, and refrigerate. Discard Bouquet Garni. Cool broth, then refrigerate. When cooled, remove fat and discard.

PART II

1 large carrot, diced
1 small turnip, diced
¾ cup chopped onion
1 large tomato, seeded and chopped
    or an 8¾ oz. can tomatoes

½ cup frozen peas
Chopped fresh mint

Bring broth to a boil; add the carrot, turnip, onion, and tomatoes. Allow vegetables to simmer until tender. Meanwhile, dice the refrigerated lamb. Fifteen minutes before serving add the frozen peas and meat. Taste for seasoning and adjust. When all ingredients are hot, serve in large bowls topped with fresh mint. Serves 8 generously.

If beef is preferred, use 3½ pounds of good stewing meat and include either a knuckle or marrow bone for flavor. Proceed as directed.

MULLIGAWTAWNEY

An East Indian curried soup that is a substantial meal. With a fruit salad and one of the dark breads, dinner will be complete.

2½ pound chicken or parts of chicken
2 quarts chicken broth, canned or
    your own make
1 carrot, sliced
1 onion, quartered
1 large rib celery, chopped
3 sprigs parsley
1 bay leaf

6 tablespoons butter or margarine
1 medium onion, finely chopped

2 cloves garlic, finely minced
¼ cup flour
1 tablespoon curry powder
2 cups canned garbanzos
    with liquid (10 oz.)
1 raw apple, peeled and
    finely chopped
Salt
Hot cooked rice
Thinly sliced lemon

In a soup kettle, combine the first seven ingredients. Bring to a boil and skim. Lower heat to simmer, cover, and allow to cook until chicken is done, about 1 hour. Remove chicken, debone, dice, and set aside. Discard bones. Strain broth through a fine sieve into a large bowl. Rinse out the soup pot, dry, and return to the burner. Melt butter in the soup pot. Add chopped onion and garlic. Sauté, stirring occasionally until tender, about 10 minutes. With a wooden spoon, stir in the flour and curry powder. Cook 3 to 4 minutes, stirring constantly. Slowly add chicken broth, beating with a wire whisk to avoid lumping. Whirl the garbanzos and liquid in a blender. Add to the soup with the reserved, diced chicken. Bring ingredients to a simmer and stir in the chopped apple. Taste for salt and adjust. Cook slowly for 10 minutes.

Ladle soup in large, warm soup bowls. Serve hot cooked rice in the center of each bowl with sliced lemon on the side. Serves 6 to 8.

HEALTH BREADS

SOUPS:

Herbed Vegetable Soup

Minted Yogurt

Lamb Barley Mushroom

Cream of Herb

Lentil

WHEAT AND FLOURS

A graceful shaft of wheat is used on pottery, embroidered in wall hangings, added to dried arrangements, and found on ancient tomb drawings. Man first experimented with wild cereal grasses over 10,000 years ago, finally cultivating wheat. Now there is an amazing variety of wheat producing many different kinds of flour.

Wheat is a grass, and on each stalk is a spear of kernels. Each tiny kernel has an amazing construction. The outer shell is a hard coat of bran. Inside the kernel, at one end, is the germ or embryo section which contains high quality protein, Vitamins B and E, as well as minerals and crude fiber. No wonder it has sustained man for centuries! The majority of the kernel is made up of carbohydrate, but the important section is the germ, with a protein content varying from 8 to 17 per cent. Wheat and rye are the only grain cereals that contain gluten, a sticky substance when combined with yeast produces bubbles which makes dough rise. Protein is the catalyst in gluten that gives energy to make bread. Thus, the higher the content of protein, the more superior the bread.

What happens to all these components, and especially to the protein, when a kernel goes through the large commercial flour mills?

1. The wheat is sifted to remove dirt.

2. Heat and moisture are applied to soften the outer bran covering.

3. The mills have enormous steel rollers. The first grinding begins to break the outer coating of bran.

4. The bran, and what is called the "middlings", are expelled and most is sold as cattle feed. The remainder is put through another series of rollers and ground into a fine white dust. The germ of the wheat in all this fast milling is rubbed into a clump and thrown off.

5. At this point, chemical enrichment is introduced along with preservatives to supplement the loss of the germ. Because wheat germ has a rich oil that deteriorates easily, both flour and bread become more perishable when it is retained.

Since the Egyptian era, people have preferred white, white flour. Privileged upper classes have always demanded white bread. It is a fundamental part of man's nature to want what the aristocracy has. Through enactment of laws the majority of people have desired, our flour is bleached and degermed. This, plus our enormous surge in population in the past hundred years, has necessitated a fast method of producing large amounts of bread.

Stone ground flours are milled quite differently. The germ is ground into the flour through a slow, cool process. If you ever have a chance to see a stone grinding mill, observe that one large round granite stone is stationary and another stone revolves against it very slowly. As a result the wheat germ is dispersed throughout the flour.

Seldom are white flours stone ground, but they are easily obtainable unbleached with no chemical added. Stone ground wheats, ryes, and a variety of flours may be purchased in health food stores, specialty shops, mills, and a few supermarkets. The term *Buhr* is on many brands of stone ground flours. Buhr is a French granite that millers consider the finest stone for grinding. Water ground flour simply means the milling is powered by water.

The confusing term "Graham" flour often appears. A man by the name of Sylvester Graham, who lived in the middle of the 19th century, was the forerunner of health food agencies of today. He was a most colorful individual, had a great deal of publicity, and believed completely in the use of whole wheat. As a result, Graham flour became the term for whole wheat flour. A few contemporary mills now produce a "Graham flour" composed of unbleached white flour with finely ground bran and wheat germ added.

In color, wheat ranges from red to white. It can be grown from Alaska to the tropics. There are hard and soft wheats; winter and spring wheats. Spring wheat is sown when winter ends and harvested in 12 to 20 weeks. Winter wheat is sown in late fall and harvested four to six weeks earlier than spring wheat. The quality depends on the climate, season, soil, and variety grown. The hard spring wheat from dry climates produces a higher content of protein.

Most all purpose flours are bleached with chemicals added for enrichment. Unbleached all purpose white flour has no chemicals nor preservatives added. However, it is refined and has no germ. Since it is made of the finest wheat, the protein content is high, creating excellent breads.

Stone ground whole wheat and rye flours retain all their components and no preservatives are added. Breads from these flours have a delicious, nutty flavor, but being heavier in texture, are harder to handle. Whole wheat flour processed by fast milling is a softer, finer flour to which chemicals have been added.

Specialty flours, such as millet, peanut, soy, legume, oatmeal, and many others are very high in protein but dense in texture. All these are beneficial and pleasurable added in small quantities to breads for further enrichment.

Our abundance of flours gives an extensive choice. Any flour on the market will make a most acceptable bread. Certainly the stone ground flours give more nutrition, but they are not easily available in many areas. If you are concerned about this problem, there are solutions.

1. Sources of supply for health food products, including many kinds of flours, are listed at the end of my book.

2. Any bread recipe can be supplemented with healthful ingredients to enhance the nutrition.

3. For sugar — use honey, blackstrap molasses, raw, or brown sugar.

4. To any of my bread recipes, you may add 3 tablespoons of wheat germ and the flavor will not be affected.

5. Study the Cornell Bread recipe to see how special ingredients are added for a complete food. Be careful in adding the high, dense protein flours such as millet and soy. Use only ½ to 1 cup which will give you the nutrient value as well as flavor.

6. Most health food devotees prefer the whole wheat and ryes. If you especially want a white bread, use the unbleached white flour, adding wheat germ, honey, and powdered milk.

7. Home made butter, oils, and special margarines can solve the fat problem.

8. Home made yogurt, buttermilk, powdered dry milk and good whole milk are excellent for liquids.

9. If you are concerned about the quality of yeast, make the Wild Yeast Starter in Chapter III.

Any recipe in my book can easily be turned into a health food product. Learn to work with what is available to you. Through your own ingenuity you can add the nutrition that you desire.

STONE GROUND WHITE BREAD

In the state of Missouri (sources of supply) there is a flour mill that grinds an unusually good white blended flour which is called stone ground white flour. This flour makes some of the best bread you will ever taste. At end of the recipe there are suggestions to simulate this flour.

½ cup warm water
1 teaspoon organic honey
½ teaspoon ginger
2 packages dry or compressed
    yeast
• • •
3 cups warm water
⅓ cup organic honey

1 cup dry skim milk
4 cups unbleached stone ground
    white flour*
2 teaspoons salt
⅓ cup melted butter or margarine
5 cups unbleached stone ground
    white flour, approximately

Combine the first four ingredients, (refer to page 7) stirring with a fork until dissolved. Set aside until bubbling. In a large mixing bowl, blend the 3 cups water, honey, dry milk, and 4 cups of flour. Beat until smooth and add the yeast mixture. Cover with a towel and allow to double in bulk, about 45 minutes.

When the sponge becomes bubbly, stir down. Add the salt and butter. Slowly beat in enough more flour to make a soft dough. Turn out on a lightly floured board and knead until smooth and elastic, about 10 minutes (refer to Techniques, page 11). Round into a ball and place in a warm, greased bowl, turning to coat the top. Cover loosely with plastic wrap and a towel. Allow to double in bulk, about 1 hour. Remove to a floured surface and knead lightly. Cover and let rest 10 minutes. Form into 4 loaves. Place in greased pans, 8½x4½x2½". Cover and let rise to tops of pans, approximately 45 minutes. Bake in a preheated 375° oven 35 to 40 minutes. Turn loaves out on wire racks to cool. Brush tops with melted butter if desired.

*NOTE

To simulate the stone ground white flour — add 1 cup toasted wheat germ or 1 cup of Graham flour to the recipe. This is an excellent bread to manipulate. Try making any of the health food swirls on page 107.

BLACKSTRAP-YOGURT BRAID

A robust loaf of bread that creates a pungent aroma. If you do not make your own yogurt, be certain to purchase a brand without a lot of additives.

2 packages dry or compressed yeast
1½ cups warm water
3 tablespoons safflower oil
¼ cup Blackstrap molasses
1½ teaspoons salt
1 cup yogurt*

2 cups rye flour
2 cups stone ground whole wheat flour
1 to 2 cups white unbleached flour
Toasted wheat germ

Sprinkle yeast over the warm water in a large mixing bowl. Stir with a fork until dissolved. Add the oil, molasses, salt, and yogurt. Blend well with a wire whisk to remove any lumps. Beat in the 2 cups of rye flour until smooth. Add the whole wheat flour and enough white flour to make a soft, workable dough. Turn out on a lightly floured board. Knead about 10 minutes, or until smooth and elastic. Cover with a towel and lest rest 10 minutes (refer to Techniques, page 13). Divide the dough in 3 parts. Roll each portion into 22" lengths. Braid the lengths together, starting from the center and working out to each end. Place the braid on a large, greased baking sheet. Cover and allow to rise for 1 hour. Brush with melted margarine and dust with toasted wheat germ. Bake in a preheated 350° oven 40 to 45 minutes. Remove braid on a wire rack to cool. If desired the dough may be divided in 2 loaves and baked in greased 8½x4½x2½" pans for 35 to 40 minutes.

* Do not allow but one rising. A second rising where yogurt is used produces a bitter flavor.

A COMPLETE RYE

Many people are allergic to wheat. Rye flour does not have as much gluten as wheat, but enough to make a very satisfactory bread. It is a heavy, dense bread with a fine flavor and adaptable to a variety of seasonings.

3 packages dry or compressed yeast
2½ cups warm water
½ cup dry instant potatoes
½ cup light molasses
6 to 7 cups stone ground rye flour

¼ cup melted butter or margarine
2½ teaspoons salt
2 large eggs, beaten
1 tablespoon caraway seeds*

The Sponge: Combine the yeast and warm water in a large mixing bowl (refer to Ingredients, page 7). Stir with a fork until dissolved. Sprinkle in the instant potatoes. Add the molasses and stir until well blended. Beat in 2 cups of rye flour until smooth. Cover with a towel. Set aside to double, about 1 hour.

When the sponge is bubbly, add the melted butter or margarine, salt, beaten eggs, and seeds. Gradually stir in enough flour to make a soft dough. Be careful not to add too much flour; it is better to have a slightly sticky dough. Turn out on a lightly floured surface. Knead until smooth and bouncy, about 10 minutes. Round into a ball and place in a warm, greased bowl, turning to coat the top. Cover loosely with plastic wrap and a towel. Set in a protected spot to rise until doubled, about 1 hour. Turn out on a floured surface and knead lightly. Cover and let rest 10 to 15 minutes. Cut in 2 portions and mold into loaves. Place in well greased loaf pans, 8½x4½x2½″. Brush with melted butter. Cover and let rise to tops of pans, about 30 minutes. Bake in a preheated 350° oven 10 minutes. Lower heat to 300° and bake 50 minutes. Turn loaves out on wire racks to cool.

VARIATIONS

1. Round the 2 portions of dough in balls and place on greased cake pans. Cover and allow to rise as recipe specifies. Just before baking, slash a cross on the loaves and brush with melted butter.

*2. Add 2 teaspoons of anise seed instead of, or in addition to the caraway. Omit seeds if you do not care for them.

3. A delicious addition is 2 tablespoons finely chopped orange peel. Remove peel from an orange with a potato peeler, avoiding any white portion. Chop finely and add when mixing ingredients. Try this bread with melted cheese — delightful.

GRANOLA WHOLE WHEAT CASSEROLE BREAD

A quick, healthful batter bread that can be whipped together in two hours — excellent served hot out of the oven or toasted for breakfast.

2 packages dry or compressed yeast
2½ cups warm water
6 tablespoons light molasses
¼ cup melted butter or margarine
2 teaspoons salt

2 eggs
2 cups stone ground whole wheat flour

4 cups unbleached white flour
2 cups granola
1 cup raisins (optional)

Sprinkle yeast over the warm water in a large mixing bowl. Stir with a fork until dissolved. Blend in the molasses, butter, salt, and eggs. Beat in the whole wheat flour until batter is smooth. Add 2 cups of white flour and beat vigorously with a rubber spatula or an electric mixer for 2 minutes. Add the remaining flour and beat another 2 minutes. Stir in the granola and raisins. Pour in two 1½ quart greased casseroles. Cover and let rise until double (just below rim of bowl), about 50 to 60 minutes. Bake in a preheated 375° oven 50 minutes. If top becomes too brown, cover with foil the last 15 minutes. Cool loaves on a wire rack or serve immediately.

SOY-WHEAT GERM BREAD

Soy flour is a high protein, dense flour. It should be added to a recipe in small quantities and the flour should never be packed when measuring. A healthful and flavorful bread.

2 packages dry or compressed yeast	4 to 5 cups unbleached
2 cups warm water	white flour
¼ cup natural sugar	¼ cup soy flour
1 cup dry skim milk	¼ cup wheat germ
2 teaspoons salt	Melted margarine
¼ cup light oil or melted margarine	Wheat Germ

Combine yeast, water, and sugar in a large mixing bowl. Stir with a fork until dissolved. Blend in the dry milk, salt, and margarine. Mix 2 cups of flour with the soy flour and wheat germ. Add to the yeast mixture and beat until smooth. Gradually add sufficient flour to make a soft workable dough. Turn out on a lightly floured board and knead until smooth and elastic. Round dough in a ball and place in a warm, greased bowl, turning to coat the top. Cover loosely with plastic wrap and a towel. Set aside to double in bulk, about 1 hour. Punch down the dough, knead lightly in the bowl, recover, and allow to double again, about 30 minutes.

Turn dough out on a floured board, knead for 1 minute, cover and let rest 10 minutes. Divide dough in 2 portions. Shape into loaves and place in greased pans, 9x5x3". Cover and let rise until doubled, 30 to 45 minutes. Brush tops with melted butter and sprinkle with wheat germ. Bake in a preheated 375° oven about 45 minutes. If loaves become too brown, cover with foil the last 15 minutes. Turn loaves out on wire racks to cool.

SOY-OATMEAL BREAD

A combination of oats, soy flour, and molasses produces **three** enriched brown and crusty loaves which in turn make heavenly toast.

2 cups oats
2 cups boiling water
½ cup molasses
2 packages dry or compressed yeast
½ cup warm milk
5 to 6 cups unbleached white flour

1 cup soy flour
1 teaspoon salt
¼ cup melted butter or
    margarine

Combine oats and boiling water in a large mixing bowl. Stir in **the** molasses. Set mixture aside to cool.

The Sponge: Sprinkle yeast over the warm milk, stirring with a **fork** until dissolved. Combine 1½ cups of the white flour with the soy **flour** and salt. Stir the butter, yeast, and flour mixtures into the cooled **oat** mixture. Beat until smooth. Cover with a towel and set aside **to double** in bulk, about 45 minutes.

Stir down the sponge. Gradually add sufficient more white flour **to** make a soft, workable dough. Turn out on a lightly floured board **and** knead until smooth and elastic, about 8 minutes. Place in a **warm,** greased bowl, turning to coat the top. Allow to double in bulk, **about** 1 hour. Punch the dough down, place on a floured board, knead **lightly,** cover, and let rest 10 minutes. Divide in 3 portions and shape in loaves. Place in greased loaf pans, 8½x4½x2½″. Cover and let rise to tops of pans, about 45 minutes. Bake in a preheated 375° oven 40 minutes. **Turn loaves** out on wire racks to cool.

MILLET-SESAME BREAD

A combination of healthful ingredients that **make** a light unusually aromatic bread. Even those who **are** not health food devotees will enjoy these golden loaves.

2 packages dry or compressed yeast
2½ cups warm water
1 cup dry skim milk
¼ cup safflower oil
⅓ cup brown sugar
½ cup toasted sesame seeds
1 cup millet flour

1½ teaspoons salt
¼ cup wheat germ

4 to 5 cups unbleached
    white flour

Sprinkle yeast over the warm water in a large mixing bowl. Stir with a fork until dissolved. Add the dry milk, oil, brown sugar, sesame seeds, millet flour, salt, and wheat germ. Stir with a wooden spoon or a whisk until well blended. Add 2 cups of flour, the yeast mixture, and beat until smooth. Stir in enough more flour to make a soft, workable dough. Turn out on a lightly floured surface. Knead until smooth and resilient, about 10 minutes. Place in a warm, greased bowl, turning to coat the top. Cover loosely with plastic wrap and a towel. Allow to double in bulk, about 1½ hours. Punch down and knead lightly on a floured surface. Cover and allow to rest 10 minutes. Divide in 3 portions. Shape in loaves and place in greased bread pans, 8½x4½x2½". Cover with a towel and let rise to tops of pans, about 45 minutes. Bake in a preheated 350° oven 35 to 40 minutes. Turn out on racks to cool. Brush loaves while hot with melted butter if desired.

MARY'S MIXTURE

A health bread my family has enjoyed for many years. A good toasting bread and adaptable to the swirls on page 107.

2 packages dry or compressed yeast
1 cup warm water
1 cup unbleached white flour

• • •

2 cups warm water
⅓ cup light molasses
¼ cup melted butter or margarine
2 teaspoons salt

½ cup toasted wheat germ
1 cup stone ground rye flour
1 cup stone ground whole
    wheat flour
3 to 4 cups unbleached white
    flour
Melted butter

The Sponge: Sprinkle yeast over the 1 cup of warm water in a large mixing bowl. Stir with a fork until dissolved. Beat in 1 cup of white flour until smooth. Cover with a towel and set aside to double, about 45 minutes.

Stir down the sponge. Add the 2 cups of warm water, molasses, margarine or butter, salt, and wheat germ. Measure in the rye and whole wheat flours, beating vigorously with a rubber spatula. Stir in enough white flour to make a soft dough (refer to Techniques, page 11). Turn out on a lightly floured board. Knead until smooth and elastic, about 10 minutes. Place in a warm, greased bowl, turning to coat the top. Cover loosely with plastic wrap and a towel. Allow to double, about 1½ hours. Punch the dough down, turn out on a lightly floured surface, and knead lightly. Cover with a towel and let rest 10 minutes. Mold into 3 loaves and place in greased loaf pans, 8½x4½x2½". Cover with a towel and let rise to tops of pans, about 30 minutes. Bake in a preheated 375° oven 40 to 45 minutes. Cool loaves on wire racks. Brush with melted butter while hot if a soft crust is desired.

GRANOLA BREAD

Granola is a happy combination of wholesome ingredients that has become exceedingly popular in the health food world. This recipe makes two elegant loaves that may be frosted and served in healthful splendor for a brunch.

2 packages dry or compressed yeast
½ cup warm water
1 cup warm milk
¼ cup melted butter or margarine
¼ cup organic honey
1 teaspoon salt

1 egg
1 cup Granola*
3 tablespoons wheat germ
Grated rind of 1 lemon
4 to 4½ cups unbleached
*   white flour*

Sprinkle yeast over the warm water, stirring with a fork until dissolved. Set aside. In a large mixing bowl, combine the warm milk, butter, honey, salt, and egg. Blend well. Add the Granola, wheat germ, grated lemon rind, and yeast mixture. Stir in 2 cups of flour and beat until smooth. Add enough more flour to make a soft, workable dough. Turn out on a lightly floured surface and knead until smooth and elastic, about 10 minutes. Place in a warm, greased bowl, turning to coat the top (refer to Techniques, page 12). Cover loosely with plastic wrap and towel. Allow to double in bulk, about 1½ hours. Remove to a floured board and knead lightly. Cover and allow to rest 10 minutes. Divide in 2 portions. Mold into loaves and place in well greased pans, 8½x4½x2½″.

For a variation make pretty, round loaves. Form each portion into a ball. Pat into two greased 1 quart soufflé bowls. Cover and let rise to tops of pans or bowls, about 30 minutes. Bake in a preheated 350° oven 30 to 35 minutes. Cool loaves on wire racks. Dribble lemon Confectioner's Icing (page 268) over the cooled loaves.

*NOTE
Granola, Bircher Muesli, and special health food cereals may be purchased in health food stores, specialty shops, and your local super market. Try making Granola at home; it is quite easy and better than most products on the market. Following is an excellent recipe.

GRANOLA

The great difficulty with home made Granola is to stop nibbling. It is a wonderful combination of crunchy ingredients. Besides putting Granola in breads, try it as a cereal, on top of cereals. topping for ice cream or yogurt, and even mixed with peanut butter. Much better than dipping into popcorn and all those other dehydrated products. All ingredients are easily available.

5½ cups natural rolled oats
1 cup untoasted sesame seeds
1 cup untoasted sunflower seeds
1 cup wheat germ, untoasted
1 cup coconut (optional)
1 cup nuts, preferably slivered
   almonds

1 cup dry skim milk
• • •
1 cup safflower oil
1 cup organic honey
1½ teaspoons vanilla flavoring
1 cup raisins or currants
   (optional)

In a very large bowl, mix together the first seven ingredients. In a separate bowl, stir together the oil, honey, and vanilla flavoring. Pour the oil mixture over the oat mixture and stir until all is well blended — best to use your hands and get right with it. Spread on 2 baking sheets. Bake in a preheated 225° oven for 1 hour or longer, until nicely browned. Stir with a wooden spoon every 15 minutes or the ingredients will stick together and brown unevenly. Remove from oven and set baking sheets on wire racks to cool. Stir several times during the cooling process to keep the Granola from massing together. When cooled add the raisins or currants. Store in jars or plastic containers and label.

MULTI-GRAIN BREAD

Multi-grain, or 7 grain flour is a combination of seven different hearty, unadulterated flours available in health food stores. I have made this a simple, easy bread so that the flour of this delicious combination is not disturbed.

2 packages dry or compressed yeast
2 cups warm water
¼ cup light oil
½ cup honey or brown sugar

2 teaspoons salt
3 cups multigrain flour*
4 cups unbleached white flour
   approximately

Sprinkle yeast over the warm water in a large mixing bowl. Stir with a fork until dissolved. Add the oil, honey or sugar, and salt, blending well with a wooden spoon or rubber spatula. Beat in 3 cups of multigrain flour until very smooth. Gradually add enough white flour to make a soft dough. Turn out on a lightly floured board and knead 10 minutes or until smooth and bouncy. Place in a warm, greased bowl, turning to coat the top. Cover loosely with plastic wrap and towel. Allow to double in bulk, about 2 hours (refer to Techniques, page 12).
   Punch down and turn out on a floured surface. Knead lightly, cover and let rest 10 minutes. Divide into 3 portions. Mold in loaves and place in greased pans, 8½x4½x2½″. Cover and let rise to tops of pans, approximately 45 minutes to an hour. Bake in a preheated 350° oven 40 to 45 minutes. Cool loaves on wire racks. Brush with melted butter while hot, if desired.

*VARIATION

Eliminate the white flour and use only the multigrain. Proceed as directed. Multigrain is a flour designed and sold through El Molino Mills.

GLUTEN BREAD

Gluten flour produces a dough rather like a soft rubber ball — very bouncy and fun to handle. The wheat germ and soy flour have been added for flavor, as bread with just gluten flour is rather tasteless.

2 cakes dry or compressed yeast
2 cups warm water
3½ cups gluten flour

1 cup soy flour
¾ cup toasted wheat germ
1 teaspoon salt

In a large mixing bowl, sprinkle yeast over the warm water. Stir with a fork until dissolved. In a separate bowl, combine the gluten flour, soy, wheat germ, and salt. Combining the flours helps avoid lumps. Add enough of the combined flour mixture to the yeast mixture to make a soft dough. Turn out on a lightly floured board and knead 10 to 15 minutes, until smooth and resilient. (If there is any flour mixture left, place in a jar, cap, and label to use for the next batch of bread.) When kneading is finished, cover dough with a towel and let rest 10 minutes. Divide in 2 portions. Mold into loaves and place in greased 8½x4½x2½" pans. Cover and let rise just to tops of pans, about 45 minutes. Do not allow to over rise as huge bubbles will form under the crust while cooking. Bake in a preheated 375° oven 40 to 45 minutes. Cool loaves on wire racks.

EXPLANATION OF CORNELL BREAD

Recipes for Cornell breads are in many cook books and appear frequently in magazines. My students were curious concerning the derivation of the name. I wrote to Cornell University and received a most gracious reply.

Cornell bread was developed by a Dr. McCay during the 1940's while he worked with the State Hospitals of New York State. Much bread was consumed by patients so he felt it necessary to develop a really nutritious product. Later, a recipe was developed for commercial bakeries and was given the name of Cornell Formula Bread. Cornell University had nothing to do with development of this bread even though the name has been retained.

When you read the recipes, you will see that both the white and whole wheat loaves are full of high protein. One could easily exist on just this bread and milk for quite a while.

CORNELL WHITE BREAD

Try this bread. You will be amazed and delighted at the easy handling of the dough and the pleasant texture of the bread.

2 packages dry or compressed yeast
3 cups warm water
2 tablespoons honey
3 cups unbleached white flour
½ cup soy flour
3 tablespoons wheat germ

¾ cup dry skim milk
2 teaspoons salt
2 tablespoons light oil
3 to 4 cups unbleached white
    flour

Sprinkle yeast over the warm water in a large mixing bowl. Add the honey and stir until dissolved. In a separate bowl, blend the 3 cups of white flour, soy flour, wheat germ, and dry milk. Beat the flour mixture into the yeast mixture until smooth. Add the salt, oil, and enough of the remaining flour to make a soft workable dough. Turn out on a lightly floured board and knead until smooth and elastic, about 10 minutes. Add small amounts of flour if needed to cut the stickiness (refer to Techniques, page 11). Place in a warm, greased bowl, turning to coat the top. Cover with plastic wrap and a towel. Allow to double in bulk, about 1½ hours. Punch down the dough and allow to rise a second time until doubled, approximately 30 minutes. Turn out on a floured surface and divide in 3 portions. Cover and let rest 10 minutes. Shape into 3 loaves and place in greased loaf pans, 8½x4½x2½". Cover and let rise to tops of pans, about 45 minutes. Bake in a preheated 350° oven 45 to 50 minutes. If loaves become too brown, cover with foil the last 15 minutes. Cool on wire racks. Brush loaves with melted butter while hot if desired.

CORNELL WHOLE WHEAT BREAD

2 packages dry or compressed yeast
3 cups warm water
¼ cup light molasses
¼ cup brown sugar
5½ to 6 cups stone ground whole
    wheat flour

½ cup soy flour
¾ cup dry skim milk
3 tablespoons wheat germ
2 tablespoons Brewer's yeast
1 tablespoon salt
3 tablespoons oil

Combine the yeast, water, molasses, and brown sugar in a large mixing bowl. Stir until ingredients are dissolved. In a separate bowl, combine 4 cups of flour with soy flour, dry milk, wheat germ, Brewer's yeast, and salt. Stir the flour mixture into the yeast mixture. Beat with a rubber spatula or in an electric mixer until smooth. Add the oil. Stir in enough more flour to make a heavy batter and beat vigorously until smooth. Pour in 2 greased pans, 8½x4½x2½″. Cover and let rise 30 to 45 minutes. Bake in a preheated 375° oven 50 minutes (refer to Techniques, page 14). Turn out on wire racks to cool.

VARIATIONS

Several additions may be made to this nutritious bread. If you desire a higher, lighter loaf, add one or two eggs with the final beating. One cup of rinsed, dried raisins or currants make a delicious loaf. Chopped dried fruit also make a tasteful breakfast bread.

HEALTH BREAD SWIRLS

Everyone likes a bit of sweet bread occasionally despite the caloric content and devotion to health foods. Here are three delicious and nourishing swirls that may be made with several breads in this chapter. The loaves may be dribbled with frosting for a party or left plain. All make excellent toast.

The breads best adaptable and amount of dough necessary are as follows:

MARY'S MIXTURE — ⅓ of dough at end of first rising
MULTIGRAIN — ⅓ of dough at end of first rising
STONE GROUND WHITE BREAD — ¼ to ⅓ of dough at end of second rising
CORNELL WHITE BREAD — ⅓ of dough at end of first rising

GRANOLA SWIRL

Roll any of the suggested doughs into a rectangle about ¼″ thick. Sprinkle a cup or more of Granola over the dough leaving ½″ free edge. Roll tightly jelly roll style, pinch sides and ends. Place in a greased 9x5x3″ loaf pan. Pierce with a toothpick in 6 places to release air. Cover and let rise until just curved over top of pan. Bake in a preheated 350° oven 40 to 45 minutes. Cool on a wire rack.

CINNAMON SWIRL

Combine ½ cup natural sugar and 1 tablespoon of cinnamon. Roll selection of dough into a rectangle about ¼″ thick. Brush with melted butter or margarine. Sprinkle the cinnamon mixture over the rectangle leaving ¼″ free edge. If desired sprinkle with ½ cup raisins, rinsed in hot water and dried. Roll tightly jelly roll style, pinching side and edges. Place in greased 9x5x3″ pan. Pierce in 6 places with a toothpick to release air. Cover and allow to double in bulk. Bake in a preheated 350° oven about 35 minutes. Turn out on wire rack to cool.

ANNIE'S HALVAH SWIRL

This is an idea presented to me by one of my daughters-in-law born and raised in Beirut. The experiment proved to be most delicious. Halvah is ground sesame seed (made somewhat similar to peanut butter) and is available in many kinds of stores. Combine and mix thoroughly 6 tablespoons of Halvah and 4 tablespoons of light molasses. Roll out your choice of dough into a rectangle ¼" thick. With a rubber spatula, spread the Halvah mixture thickly over the dough leaving ½" free edge. Roll tightly, pinching side and ends. Place in a 9x5x3" greased loaf pan. Pierce with a toothpick 6 times to release air. Cover and let rise to top of pan. Bake in a preheated 350° oven about 40 minutes. Cool on wire rack. If there is any Halvah mixture left, use it on hot toast — yummy!

HERBED VEGETABLE SOUP

The title of this recipe tells the whole story — full of fresh vegetables and herbs. A soup you can make to suit your own taste by adding other vegetables you particularly enjoy and the choice of beans and pasta you like.

2 carrots, scraped and diced
2 zucchini, washed and sliced
2 yellow squash, washed and sliced
1 cup coarsely cut celery
1 box frozen cut or 2 cups of fresh
    green beans
1 box frozen cut asparagus
3 cloves garlic, peeled and minced
1 can plain white beans, black eyed
    peas, or garbanzos

3 sprigs parsley
3 or 4 sprigs fresh basil or
    1 teaspoon dried
8 cups chicken stock, canned,
    cubes, or homemade

½ cup small pasta, optional
Grindings of black pepper
Salt
Parmesan cheese

Combine the first 12 ingredients in a large soup pot. Bring to a boil, lower to simmer, and cook uncovered about 30 to 40 minutes, or until vegetables are tender. If a thicker soup is desired, add the small pasta after the first 15 minutes of simmering. Season with black pepper and salt to taste. Serve Parmesan cheese as a garnish with a hot health bread as an accompaniment.

MINTED YOGURT SOUP

Many people shy away from yogurt because of the sour flavor. When combined with other ingredients, this healthful food gives a wonderfully piquant flavor. Try this soup — you will be surprised and delighted with the result. Serves 6.

½ cup uncooked rice
1 tablespoon flour
2 teaspoons dried mint, crushed
1 egg, slightly beaten

4 cups rich chicken broth
1 cup plain yogurt
Salt

Combine the rice, flour, and mint in a saucepan. Mix in the beaten egg. Add the broth and yogurt. Bring soup to a boil, stirring constantly, Reduce heat and let simmer uncovered 25 to 30 minutes. Taste for salt and adjust. If the soup is too thick, thin with additional broth or water. Serve either hot or cold with a dollop of yogurt on top.

LAMB BARLEY MUSHROOM SOUP

Another full meal soup that utilizes good leftovers. If you are able to obtain organically grown vegetables, the soup will certainly be even more enhanced in fresh flavor.

1 onion, chopped
1 carrot, chopped
2 large ribs of celery, chopped
2 cloves of garlic, minced
2 tablespoons margarine or oil
2 tablespoons flour
8 cups lamb broth*

1 teaspoon thyme
3 ounces of dried or 1 cup
*   fresh mushrooms, sliced*
½ cup barley
Grindings of black pepper
Salt

Sauté onion, carrot, celery, and garlic in the margarine or oil until wilted, about 10 minutes. Add the flour and stir until smooth, cooking about 2 or 3 minutes. Set aside. If using dried mushrooms, soak in water to cover 20 minutes. Drain, squeeze out the water and dice. Measure the lamb broth into a large soup pot. Add the sautéed vegetables, thyme, and mushrooms. Bring to a boil and skim. Add the barley, lower heat to simmer, and cook uncovered 1 to 1½ hours. Add any left over lamb. Stir in a few grindings of black pepper and salt to taste. Bring to a boil and serve steaming hot in warm soup bowls.

*Save any lamb bones and freeze. When you have accumulated about 4 pounds, make a broth as follows: Cover bones with water in a soup pot. Add 1 onion stuck with a clove, 1 carrot, 1 rib of celery, and 6 peppercorns. Bring to a boil, skim, and allow to simmer uncovered 2 to 3 hours. Strain through a fine sieve or wet cheesecloth. Strip off any meat and add to Barley Soup. If you can obtain fresh lamb bones, the broth will be even better.

 # CREAM OF HERB SOUP

Fresh herbs are a delight to use. Even though you are a big city apartment dweller, you can grow many herbs in pots. Try basil first as it is the easiest. Buy a packet of seeds, a large clay pot, use ordinary dirt, place in a sunny spot, water consistently and soon there will be all the basil you could want.

3 tablespoons butter or margarine
1 cup chopped green onions
1 cup chopped spinach, frozen
*   or fresh*
¼ cup chopped fresh basil or
*   ½ cup watercress*
¼ cup chopped parsley
5 cups chicken broth

1 teaspoon natural sugar
1 cup half and half cream
Salt
Grindings of black pepper
2 tablespoons soft butter
*   or margarine*
2 tablespoons flour

Melt the butter or margarine in a large saucepan. Sauté onions until tender, about 10 minutes. Add the spinach, basil or watercress, and parsley. Cover and simmer 10 minutes. Add the chicken broth and sugar. Recover and simmer 30 minutes. Remove cover and slowly stir in the cream. Blend together the 2 tablespoons of butter and flour. Whisk in some hot soup, beating until smooth. Add mixture to the soup, stirring constantly. Bring just to a boil and remove from burner. Serve in warm soup bowls with chopped parsley or chives as a garnish.

LENTIL SOUP

Here is a soup that may be used for your family as a main course. It will use the last bit of the ham you cooked for Sunday dinner. Eight generous servings.

2 cups lentils, rinsed thoroughly
Meaty ham hock or left over
   ham bone
2 medium onions, peeled and
   sliced
2 carrots, scraped and chopped
1½ cups celery, coarsely chopped
1 medium potato, peeled and
   chopped (about 1 cup)
3 cloves garlic, peeled and minced

3 sprigs parsley
2 bay leaves
2 sprigs fresh basil or 1
   teaspoon dried basil or thyme
¼ teaspoon Cayenne pepper
3 quarts water
Grindings black pepper
Salt

In a large soup pot, combine the lentils, ham, onions, carrots, celery, potato, garlic, parsley, bay leaves, basil or thyme, Cayenne, and enough water to cover. Bring to a rapid boil, skim, cover and lower heat to a simmer. Allow to slowly bubble 3 to 4 hours. Remove the bay leaf, parsley, and fresh basil, if used. Add black pepper and adjust for salt. Strip meat from ham bone; discard the bone and return meat to soup pot. Bring back to a boil. Serve in large soup bowls with a hearty bread for a nourishing and satisfying meal.

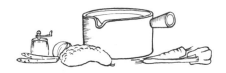

DINNER ROLLS, BUNS, BAGELS AND MUFFINS

SOUPS:

Fresh Cream of Asparagus

Cream of Corn

Chilled Cucumber

Avocado

Creamy Canadian Cheese

MARY'S DINNER ROLLS

Here is the roll you have been looking for — light and golden with melt-in-the-mouth goodness that is adaptable to any occasion or molding. All the mixing may be done one day and finished the following day.

2 packages dry or compressed
   yeast
¼ cup warm water
1½ cups warm milk
¾ cup melted butter or margarine
2 eggs, lightly beaten
⅓ cup sugar

1 teaspoon salt
1 teaspoon powdered cardamom
5 to 5½ cups flour
Melted butter
1 egg yolk mixed with 1
   teaspoon water

Sprinkle yeast over the warm water, stirring with a fork until dissolved. Set aside. In a large mixing bowl, combine milk, butter, eggs, sugar, salt, and cardamom. Stir until thoroughly blended. Add the yeast mixture. Gradually add enough flour to make a soft dough. Beat thoroughly until mixture is smooth and elastic. If you have a heavy mixer, use the flat beater for this purpose. Cover with plastic wrap and a towel. Refrigerate overnight. The next morning you may prepare rolls on baking sheets, cover, and return to the refrigerator until time for rising and baking. Or you may take the dough out 2 hours before serving and form the rolls. This dough is so adaptable that it may also be mixed early in the morning and refrigerated until evening.

FINAL PREPARATION

Turn the chilled dough out on a floured board and knead lightly. Divide in half and return one portion to refrigerator. The dough is ready to form in rolls of your choice, page 124. Place rolls on greased baking sheets or muffin tins. Repeat with remaining dough. Cover and allow to rise until doubled, about 1 to 1½ hours. Brush rolls with either the melted butter or egg glaze. Bake in a preheated 350° oven 10 to 15 minutes or until a golden brown. Serve immediately.

CRUSTY BUTTERMILK ROLLS

Light and airy as a feather are these golden, crusted buns. Makes 48 medium size rolls.

1 package dry or compressed yeast
¼ cup warm water
2 cups warm buttermilk
½ cup melted butter or margarine
4 to 5 cups flour

½ teaspoon baking soda
1 teaspoon salt
3 tablespoons sugar
Melted butter

Sprinkle yeast over the warm water, stirring with a fork until dissolved (refer to Ingredients, page 7). Set aside. Combine the buttermilk and butter. Do not be disturbed if buttermilk curdles.

In a large mixing bowl, combine 4 cups of the flour, soda, salt, and sugar. Make a well in dry ingredients. Add yeast and milk mixtures, stirring with a rubber spatula so that you can scrape down the sides of the bowl. Turn dough out on a lightly floured surface and knead about 8 minutes or until smooth and satiny. Brush hands and board with flour if necessary to cut stickiness. Place dough in a warm, greased bowl, turning to coat the top. Cover with plastic wrap and towel. Allow to double in bulk, about 1 to 1½ hours. Remove to a floured board and knead lightly. Cover, and let rest 15 minutes. Roll out to ¼" thickness. Cut into rounds with a biscuit cutter (about 1½" in diameter or larger if desired). If dough resists, allow to rest another 5 minutes. Place on a buttered baking sheet. Cover rolls and let rise until doubled, about 1 hour. Brush with melted butter. Bake in a preheated 400° oven 15 to 20 minutes or until golden brown. Serve immediately.

BESS'S CREOLE ROLLS

A delicate roll beginning with a sponge similar to a sourdough. With the combination of potatoes and sourdough effect, the resulting dough makes an unusually tasteful dinner roll.

1 cup mashed potatoes
  instant or regular
1 cup potato water
  (refer to page 9)
¾ cup sugar
1 package dry or compressed yeast
1 cup warm water
• • •
1 cup potato sponge

1 package dry or
  compressed yeast
2 tablespoons warm water
1 tablespoon sugar
1 egg
¼ cup melted butter
1 teaspoon salt
2½ to 3 cups flour
Melted butter

The Sponge: Combine mashed potatoes, potato water, and sugar in a 1 quart crockery or glass container. Stir until sugar is dissolved. Cool to lukewarm. Sprinkle yeast over warm water, stirring with a fork until dissolved. Add to the potato mixture. Cover with a towel and allow to stand 3 hours. Stir down, cover with a lid and store in refrigerator.

When ready to make rolls, remove sponge from refrigerator. Stir well. Measure out 1 cup potato mixture into a small bowl and let stand 1 hour. Return remaining sponge to refrigerator. Combine the yeast, 2

115

tablespoons water, and 1 tablespoon sugar. Stir with a fork until dissolved. Set aside. Beat the egg in a mixing bowl. Add the butter, salt, 1 cup of sponge, and yeast mixture. Blend well. Beat in 2 cups of flour until smooth. Add sufficient flour to make a soft dough that pulls away from sides of the bowl. Turn out on a lightly floured board and knead 5 minutes. Add more flour if dough is very sticky. Cover and let rest 10 minutes. Shape in desired rolls, refer to page 124, and place on greased pans. Brush with melted butter. Cover, and let rise until doubled, about 1½ to 2 hours. Bake in a preheated 375° oven 15 to 20 minutes.

CORN ROLLS

Try these amazingly light cornmeal rolls. The dough is especially adaptable to small pan rolls that may be cooked and frozen in foil cake pans for future use.

⅓ cup cornmeal　　　　　　　*1 package dry or compressed yeast*
½ cup sugar　　　　　　　　　*¼ cup warm water*
1 teaspoon salt　　　　　　　　*2 eggs, lightly beaten*
½ cup butter or margarine　　　*4 to 5 cups flour*
2 cups milk　　　　　　　　　*Melted butter*

Combine cornmeal, sugar, salt, butter, and milk in a heavy saucepan. Cook over medium heat until thick, stirring constantly. Transfer to a mixing bowl. Set aside and cool to lukewarm. Stir occasionally to prevent a crust forming on top.

Sprinkle yeast over warm water, stirring with a fork until dissolved. Blend into the cooled cornmeal mixture with beaten eggs. Stir thoroughly until free of any lumps. Cover and set aside to rise until light and bubbly, about 1½ hours.

Stir down the sponge with a rubber spatula. Gradually add sufficient flour to make a soft, workable dough. Turn out on a floured board and knead until smooth and elastic, about 10 minutes, (refer to Techniques, page 11). Place in a warm, greased bowl, turning to coat the top. Allow to double in bulk, about 1 hour. Punch down the dough. Turn out on a floured surface. Roll out to ½" thickness. Cut rolls with a small biscuit cutter, form in Parker House rolls, or pinch portions off and roll into small balls. Place on greased baking sheet or round cake tins ¼" apart. If desired, form part of dough in a loaf and place in greased pan, 8½x4½x2½". Brush rolls with butter, cover and let double 45 minutes to 1 hour. Allow the loaf pan 1 hour. Bake rolls in preheated 375° oven 15 to 20 minutes. Bake pan bread 30 to 35 minutes. Serve immediately or cool on wire racks.

MARGUERITE'S ICE BOX ROLLS

You will enjoy serving these golden, light, easy to make rolls. The dough keeps well in the refrigerator for a week.

2 packages dry or compressed yeast
2 cups warm water
5½ to 6 cups flour
½ cup sugar
¼ teaspoon baking soda

2 teaspoons salt
⅔ cup melted butter or
    margarine
1 egg, lightly beaten

Sprinkle yeast over the warm water in a large mixing bowl. Stir with a fork until dissolved. In a separate bowl, mix 2 cups of the flour with sugar, baking soda, and salt. Blend butter and egg into the yeast mixture. Beat in the flour mixture until batter is smooth. Gradually add sufficient flour to make a soft workable dough. Turn out on a lightly floured surface and knead until smooth and satiny, about 10 minutes. Round into a ball and place in a warm, greased bowl, turning to coat the top. Cover loosely with plastic wrap and a towel. Let double in bulk, about 1 hour. Punch down, recover, and place in refrigerator until ready to use. If dough rises in refrigerator, punch down and cover.

Remove desired amount of dough about 2 hours before serving. Form into rolls, page 124. Place on greased pans, cover, and allow to rise 1½ hours. Bake in a 375° oven 15 to 20 minutes or until golden brown. Serve immediately.

POTATO REFRIGERATOR ROLLS

Instant dry potatoes are quicker and work as well as regular potatoes (refer to Ingredients, page 9). These high rising rolls are particularly great for the clover leaf shape.

1 cup mashed potatoes
1 package dry or compressed yeast
½ cup warm water
⅔ cup melted butter or margarine
½ cup sugar

1 teaspoon salt
2 eggs, beaten
1 cup warm milk
6 to 7 cups flour
Melted butter or margarine

If using instant dry potatoes, use only boiling water for mixing. Beat regular, cooked potatoes with just enough hot water to make a smooth consistency. Set mashed potatoes aside to cool.

Sprinkle yeast over the warm water, stirring with a fork until dissolved. Set aside. In a large mixing bowl, combine cooled potatoes, butter, sugar, salt, and eggs. Beat well with a rubber spatula until smooth. Stir in the yeast mixture and 2 cups of flour. Gradually add enough more flour to make a soft dough. Turn out on a lightly floured board and knead until smooth and elastic, about 10 minutes. Place dough in a warm, greased bowl, turning to coat the top. Cover loosely with plastic wrap and towel. Allow to double in bulk, about 1½ hours. Knead lightly in the bowl. Recover tightly and store in refrigerator until ready to use. Two hours before baking, cut off desired amount of dough. Form in rolls, page 124, place on greased baking sheets or muffin tins. Brush with melted butter, cover and let double, about 1 to 1½ hours. Bake in a preheated 400° oven 15 to 20 minutes or until light and golden. Serve immediately.

BRAN-HONEY REFRIGERATOR ROLLS

A light, healthful dinner roll flavored with honey and toasted wheat germ. Just the right thing to have when your health food oriented friends come for dinner.

1 cup butter or margarine
1 cup boiling water
½ cup honey
1 cup All Bran or Bran Buds
1½ teaspoons salt
2 packages dry or compressed yeast

1 cup warm water
2 eggs, well beaten
¼ cup toasted wheat germ
*5 to 6 cups unbleached white
    flour*
Melted butter

In a large mixing bowl, combine butter, boiling water, honey, bran, and salt. Stir until well blended. Set aside until lukewarm. Sprinkle yeast over the 1 cup of warm water, stirring with a fork until dissolved. Add the yeast mixture, eggs, and wheat germ to the cooled bran mixture. Beat in 3 cups of flour until batter is smooth. Gradually add sufficient flour to form a soft dough that pulls away from sides of the bowl. Turn out on a lightly floured board and knead until smooth, about 5 minutes. Place in a greased bowl, turning to coat the top. Cover tightly with plastic wrap and towel. Store in refrigerator until ready to use. The dough will keep for several days. Two hours before serving, remove dough from refrigerator. Mold rolls in desired shapes, refer to page 124. Place on greased baking sheets or muffin tins. Cover and allow to double in bulk. Brush tops with melted butter. Bake in a preheated 400° oven 15 to 20 minutes. Makes 36 small rolls.

FREEZER DINNER ROLLS

Since frozen doughs were introduced on the market, there has been more interest in home made rolls and breads made in this fashion. Any plain dough may be frozen for a short length of time — not more than four weeks. The following rolls are easily molded and may be stored in a freezer for one month.

2 packages dry or compressed yeast
1 cup warm water
¾ cup warm milk
⅓ cup melted butter or margarine
½ cup sugar

1½ teaspoons salt
2 eggs, lightly beaten
6 to 7 cups flour
Melted butter or margarine

Combine yeast and warm water in a large mixing bowl. Stir with a fork until dissolved. Blend in the milk, butter, sugar, salt, and eggs. Beat in 2 cups of the flour until batter is smooth. Gradually add sufficient flour to make a soft workable dough. Turn out on a lightly floured board and knead until smooth and elastic. Cover with plastic wrap and a towel. Allow to rest on the board for 30 minutes. Punch the dough down and shape in desired rolls, page 124. You will find this dough very relaxed and easily molded into any desired shapes. Place formed rolls on greased baking sheets. Cover well with plastic wrap. Place in freezer until firm. Remove and transfer rolls to plastic bags or wrap in foil for easier storage.

When ready to bake, remove rolls and place on greased baking sheets. Cover and let rise until doubled, about 2 to 2½ hours. Brush with melted butter. Bake in a preheated 350° oven 15 to 20 minutes or until golden brown. Serve immediately.

WHOLE WHEAT DINNER ROLLS

Whole wheat dough will form into any kind of roll you wish. Once the dough has relaxed, the shaping is easy and the finshed roll just as light as though made with all white flour.

2 packages dry or compressed
  yeast
¼ cup warm water
1¾ cup warm milk
⅓ cup sugar or honey
2 teaspoons salt

¼ cup melted butter or margarine
2 eggs, lightly beaten
3½ cups whole wheat flour
3 cups white flour, approximately
Melted butter

Sprinkle yeast over water, stirring with a fork until dissolved. In a large bowl, combine milk, sugar, salt, butter, and eggs until all ingredients are well blended. Add the yeast mixture. Beat in the whole wheat flour with a rubber spatula until smooth. Add sufficient white flour to make a soft, workable dough that leaves sides of the bowl. Turn out on a lightly floured board. Knead until smooth and resilient, about 10 minutes. Round in a ball and place in a warm, greased bowl, turning to coat the top (refer to Techniques, page 12). Cover loosely with plastic wrap and a towel. Set aside in a protected area to double in bulk, about 1½ hours. Punch down the dough, knead lightly, cover, and let rest 10 to 15 minutes. Form in desired rolls, page 124. Place on greased baking sheet or muffin tins. Brush with melted butter. Cover and let double, about 45 minutes to 1 hour. Bake in a preheated 400° oven 20 minutes. Serve immediately.

WHOLE WHEAT REFRIGERATOR ROLLS

The full, hearty flavor of whole wheat plus the convenience of refrigeration, make these rolls a double favorite. Carefully covered, the dough will keep a week.

2 packages dry or compressed yeast	1½ teaspoons salt
3 cups warm milk	½ teaspoon soda
⅓ cup sugar	1½ teaspoons baking powder
½ cup melted butter or margarine	¼ cup wheat germ
4 cups white flour	Melted butter
4 cups whole wheat flour	

Combine yeast and milk in a large mixing bowl. Stir with a fork until dissolved. Blend in the sugar and butter. In a separate bowl, measure the white and whole wheat flours, salt, soda, baking powder, and wheat germ. Mix ingredients thoroughly. Beat 2 cups of the flour mixture into yeast mixture until smooth. Gradually add enough of the remaining flour mixture, stirring until dough pulls away from sides of the bowl. Place dough in a warm, greased bowl, turning to coat the top. Cover with plastic wrap and a towel. Place dough in refrigerator. The dough will keep one week.

When ready to use, remove dough 2½ hours before serving. Cut off desired amount and return remaining dough to refrigerator. Knead dough lightly, adding white flour if necessary. Shape in desired rolls as shown on page 124. Place in greased pans and brush with melted butter. Cover and allow to double, about 1½ to 2 hours. Bake in a preheated 400° oven 20 minutes, or until light and browned. Serve immediately.

HAMBURGER BUNS

Family and friends will love a patio party with your very own home-made hamburger buns. Don't forget — these buns freeze well so they can be made in any quantity ahead for a party, leaving you free to do other chores.

2 packages dry or compressed yeast
2 cups warm water
¾ cup light oil
½ cup sugar

1 tablespoon salt
3 eggs, lightly beaten
8 to 9 cups flour

In a large mixing bowl, combine yeast and warm water. Stir with a fork until dissolved. Blend in the oil, sugar, salt, and eggs. Beat in 4 cups of flour until batter is smooth. Gradually add sufficient flour to make a soft workable dough. Turn out on a lightly floured board and knead until smooth and elastic, 8 to 10 minutes. Round into a ball and place in a warm, greased bowl, turning to coat the top. Cover loosely with plastic wrap and a towel. Set aside in a protected area to double in bulk, about 1 hour.

Punch the dough down, cover and let rest 10 minutes. Divide into 24 pieces. Cup hand over a portion of dough and rotate quickly until a smooth ball is formed. Repeat with remaining portions. Place on greased baking sheets and press to a 3″ circle. When all the buns are formed, press again to flatten a bit more. Cover and let rise until double, 30 to 45 minutes. Brush with desired topping described at end of recipe. Bake in preheated 375° oven 10 to 15 minutes or until golden brown. Cool on wire racks.

TOPPINGS

Combine 1 egg beaten with 1 tablespoon water. Brush tops of buns with egg glaze. Sprinkle with either sesame, poppy, anise, caraway, coarse salt, or leave plain. In place of the egg wash, brush buns with half and half cream. This produces a lovely golden color.

VARIATION

Add ½ cup toasted wheat germ when mixing in the first 4 cups of flour. Proceed as directed. Brush formed buns with egg glaze as described and sprinkle with wheat germ as a topping.

DINAH'S BAGELS

The popular bagel, Viennese in origin, proved to be exciting for testing. Such fun to find I could twirl the dough around a finger to form the classical shape.

2 cups hot water
¼ cup instant dry potatoes
2 packages dry or compressed yeast
1 tablespoon salt
1 tablespoon sugar

¼ cup light oil
4 eggs, lightly beaten
7 to 8 cups flour
2 to 3 quarts boiling water
2 tablespoons sugar

Combine hot water and instant potatoes in a large mixing bowl. Beat with a whisk until dissolved. Cool to lukewarm. Sprinkle yeast over the potato water, stirring until dissolved. Blend in the salt, sugar, oil, and eggs. Beat in 3 cups of flour until mixture is smooth. Gradually add sufficient flour to make a soft, workable dough that pulls away from sides of the bowl. Turn out on a lightly floured board and knead until smooth and elastic, about 10 minutes. Use additional small portions of flour to cut stickiness, but do not allow dough to become dry (refer to Techniques, page 11). Place in a warm, greased bowl, turning to coat the top. Cover loosely with plastic wrap and a towel. Set aside in a protected area until doubled in bulk, about 1½ hours. Punch down, turn out on a floured surface and knead lightly. Cover and let rest 15 minutes.

Fill a deep skillet with the boiling water and add the sugar. Preheat oven to 450°. Grease 2 baking sheets. Divide relaxed dough in 2 portions. Cover one piece and set aside. Cut the other portion in 12 pieces. Cup hand over a piece of dough and rotate rapidly until a bun is formed. Stick a floured forefinger through center of bun. Whirl around your finger until a good hole is formed — this is great fun and works beautifully. Repeat with remaining dough. Drop bagels one at a time in the boiling water. Cook no more than 3 at once. As they rise to the surface, turn them over and let bubble 5 minutes. Remove with a slotted spoon and place on greased baking sheets. Bake in preheated oven 15 minutes, or until a light golden color. Cool on wire racks. Repeat with remaining dough.

ANGEL BISCUITS

A wonderful little refrigerator roll that has swept the country the last few years. With the assistance of a good Texas friend, here is my version that makes 4 dozen 1½″ biscuits.

5 cups unsifted flour
¼ cup sugar
3 teaspoons baking powder
1 teaspoon soda
1½ teaspoons salt
1 cup margarine

1 package dry or compressed
  yeast
2 tablespoons warm water
2 cups buttermilk
Melted margarine

Sift flour, sugar, baking powder, soda, and salt together in a large mixing bowl. Cut in the margarine with a pastry blender until mixture is crumbly. Sprinkle yeast over warm water in a small bowl. Stir with a fork until dissolved. Blend yeast mixture into the buttermilk. Make a well in the dry ingredients and add buttermilk mixture. Stir with a rubber spatula until well mixed. Knead lightly in the bowl. Brush a clean bowl with melted margarine. Round dough in a ball and place in greased bowl, turning to coat the top. Cover with plastic wrap and a towel. Place in refrigerator. The dough will keep several weeks.

Cut off amount you wish to bake. Roll dough out on a lightly floured board ½" thick. Cut with a 1 or 1½" biscuit cutter. Place on greased baking sheet or cake tins. Brush tops with melted margarine and let rise 1½ to 2 hours. Bake in a preheated 400° oven 15 minutes or until lightly brown. Serve immediately.

ENGLISH MUFFINS

English muffins are always best if allowed to cool, then split and toasted. It was always a special breakfast treat in our family to have these muffins with cream cheese and strawberry jam.

1 package dry or compressed yeast
½ cup warm potato water
2 tablespoons sugar
1½ cups warm milk
1 cup sieved, cooked potato (do not pack)

¼ cup light oil
1 teaspoon salt
6 cups flour, approximately
White cornmeal

Combine yeast, potato water (reserved when cooking potato), and sugar in a small bowl. Stir with a fork until dissolved. Blend the milk, sieved potato, oil, and salt in a mixing bowl. Add the yeast mixture and 2 cups of flour. Beat until smooth. Stir in sufficient flour to make a soft, workable dough. Turn out on a lightly floured surface and knead until smooth and elastic, about 8 minutes. Place in a warm, greased bowl, turning to coat the top. Cover loosely with plastic wrap and a towel. Let double in bulk, about 1½ hours.

Turn out on a floured board and knead lightly. Cover and let rest 15 minutes. Roll dough ½" thick. Cut with floured 3" biscuit cutter or use a cleaned tuna fish can. If dough pulls back, cover and let rest again. Place muffins on waxed paper sprinkled with white cornmeal. Sprinkle tops of rolls with cornmeal. Cover and let double, about 1 hour. Heat an ungreased griddle to medium high heat. Turn heat to low and cook muffins about 30 minutes, turning occasionally. Do not allow to burn! Cool muffins, split, and toast.

SHAPING OF ROLLS

CLOVER LEAF 1

Grease medium size muffin tins. Cut or pinch off 1″ balls of dough. Roll with hands until smooth. Arrange 3 balls to a cup.

CLOVER LEAF 2

Form a 1″ ball and place in a muffin tin. Pinch off tiny portions of dough and roll into balls. Place 5 tiny balls around the large ball.

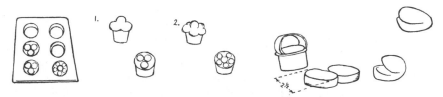

PARKER HOUSE

Cut off a piece of dough and roll ¼″ thick. Cut in 2½″ circles. With the dull edge of a knife, make a crease just to one side of center. Brush with melted butter. Fold large side over and press edges securely. Place on greased baking sheets 1″ apart.

FANTANS

Roll a portion of dough in a 9x15″ rectangle, ¼″ thick. Brush with melted butter. Cut in 6 strips 1½″ wide. Stack the strips evenly. Cut in 1″ pieces. Place cut side down in greased muffin tins.

BUTTERHORNS AND CRESCENTS

Roll a piece of dough in an 8 or 9″ circle, ¼″ thick. Brush with melted butter. With a dough scraper, cut in 8 pie shape wedges. Roll each toward the point. Place on greased baking sheet point side down. Leave the butterhorns straight. Curve the crescents in shape of a quarter moon.

SNAILS

Roll a portion of dough in a rope ½″ thick and 10″ long. Hold one end and wind rope around, tuck outside end underneath, and place on greased baking sheet.

FIGURE EIGHTS WITH DOUGHNUT CUTTER

Roll a portion of dough ¼" thick. Cut with a doughnut cutter. Punch out the center. Twist ring of dough into a figure 8. Place on greased baking sheet.

BOWKNOTS

Roll a portion of dough in a smooth rope ½" in diameter and 10" long. Grasp one end and make a loop. Ease the other end through the hole. Place on greased baking sheet 1½" apart.

BRAIDS

Roll 3 smooth ropes ½" thick. Braid ropes. Cut in 3½" lengths. Pinch ends together and place on greased baking sheets.

FOUR LEAF CLOVERS

Roll portions of dough in 2¼" balls. Place in greased muffin cups. With scissors, clip top of balls in half and then across to make fourths. There will be four little points sticking up. Brush carefully with melted butter.

DINNER ROLLS

Shape dough in 2" balls. With floured hands roll each ball in a 4" long roll. Taper the ends. Place on greased pan 2" apart.

PAN ROLLS

Shape dough in 2" smooth balls. Dip in melted butter and place in a round greased cake tin. Allow balls to just touch one another.

BUTTERFLY ROLLS

Roll a portion of dough in a rectangle ¼" thick and 6" wide. Brush with melted butter. Roll jelly roll style from the long side. Cut in 2" widths. Place on greased baking sheet. Make a depression down center of each roll with a small wooden handle.

  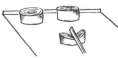

FRESH CREAM OF ASPARAGUS SOUP

We are most fortunate in our country in obtaining wonderful fresh vegetables. Asparagus is one of the finest — so when the season arrives, try this delicious soup.

1½ pounds fresh asparagus	*2 cups hot half and half cream*
1 quart water	*Salt*
¼ cup butter or margarine	*Ground Nutmeg*
¼ cup flour	

Clean asparagus thoroughly with a brush under running water. Cut tips off and set aside. Break off any hard stalk and discard. Cut the remainder in small pieces. Place asparagus pieces in a saucepan with the quart of water. Bring to a boil, lower heat to simmer, and cook uncovered 40 minutes, or until vegetable is tender.

Drain asparagus and reserve the stock. Purée the asparagus in a blender, using a small amount of the reserved stock. Cook the asparagus tips in the remaining stock 5 to 10 minutes or until just tender. In a separate pan, make a roux of the butter and flour (refer to glossary). Add the hot cream all at once, stirring vigorously with a whisk until smooth and thick. Blend in puréed asparagus, cooked tips, and reserved stock. Stir and cook over low heat until smooth and just bubbling. Taste for salt and adjust. Serve in warm soup bowls with a light dusting of nutmeg. Serves six.

CREAM OF CORN SOUP

A lovely, smooth, and golden soup with the good flavor of rich creamed corn. Ideal for a luncheon to serve with finger sandwiches. Serves six to eight.

½ cup chopped onion	*Pinch or two of white pepper*
3 tablespoons butter	*1 cup light cream*
3 tablespoons flour	*Salt*
2 cups hot chicken broth	*Finely chopped parsley*
2 cans (1 lb., 1 oz. size) creamed corn	

Sauté onion in butter until golden, but do not allow to brown, about 10 minutes. Whisk in the flour until smooth. Add the hot chicken broth all at once, stirring rapidly until thick. Blend in the creamed corn, add pepper, and cook over moderate heat until thick and creamy. Put soup through a blender and pour into a clean saucepan. Return to heat and slowly add the cream. Taste for salt and adjust. Bring to a boil, stirring constantly. Serve in cream soup bowls sprinkled lightly with chopped parsley.

CHILLED CUCUMBER SOUP

When summer arrives bringing especially tasteful cucumbers, whirl this soup together just before dinner. If you can obtain fresh basil, the soup will be even more refreshing.

1 large cucumber, peeled and chopped
   (about 1½ cups)
2 tablespoons chopped celery leaves
1 tablespoon fresh basil or ½ teaspoon dried
½ cup cold chicken broth

¾ cup sour cream
Salt
White pepper

Combine cucumber, celery leaves, basil, chicken broth, and sour cream in a blender. Whirl until smooth. Remove lid, taste, and adjust for salt. Add a pinch or two of white pepper. Whirl again and serve in chilled cups. Serves 4.

AVOCADO SOUP

One of the prettiest and simplest soups to make; a lovely, creamy rich green color that tastes as good as it looks. Serves 6.

2 cups ripe mashed avocado
2½ cups chicken broth
1 cup light cream
1½ tablespoons lemon juice

Salt
White pepper (optional)
2 to 3 tablespoons dry sherry
Avocado cubes

Mash ripe avocados with a silver fork and transfer to a blender. Add 2½ cups chicken broth and whirl until smooth. Pour in a saucepan; stir in the cream and lemon juice. Over moderate heat, bring just to a boil, stirring constantly. Taste for salt and adjust. Add a few grindings of white pepper if desired. (I prefer the unadulterated taste of the soup without either the pepper or sherry.) Add either gradually to suit your taste. Serve garnished with tiny cubes of avocado.

CREAMY CANADIAN CHEESE SOUP

A delicious and quite satisfying soup that is particularly attractive served for a winter luncheon.

½ cup carrot, finely chopped
½ cup onion, finely chopped
½ cup celery, finely chopped
½ cup butter or margarine
⅓ cup flour
4 cups hot chicken broth
2 cups hot milk

3 cups tightly packed grated
   cheddar cheese
Salt
Grindings of black pepper
Chopped fresh parsley or chives
Dry Sherry

In a large saucepan, sauté the carrots, onion, and celery in butter until tender but not brown, about 10 minutes. Whisk in the flour. Cook 2 minutes, stirring constantly. Add the hot broth all at once, beating vigorously to avoid lumping. Blend in the hot milk. Stir with a spoon until mixture thickens. Add the cheese, lower heat, and simmer, stirring occasionally until cheese is melted. Taste for salt, adjust, and add a few grindings of black pepper. Serve in warm soup bowls, topped with fresh parsley or chives. Pass a pitcher of sherry for optional addition. Serves 8 to 10.

SWEET ROLLS

SOUPS:

Shrimp Bisque
Cream of Broccoli
Boula Boula
Butternut Squash

TIPS FOR WORKING WITH SWEET DOUGHS

A sweet dough full of eggs, sugar, butter, and milk mixes together easily, is slower to rise, and the texture delightful to feel. Here are suggestions for your orientation.

1. Do not fear handling the rich, fancy doughs. The kneading is a great pleasure as the addition of eggs, butter, and sugar make the dough silky to touch. You will experience more ease of handling than with a bread dough. Eggs do have a drying effect, so be careful in the addition of flour. Add flour slowly and only when necessary while kneading. When large amounts of butter and sour cream are used, the dough seems to inhale flour. Less kneading is required for this kind of dough, but the addition of flour must still be watched. If you want a brighter colored dough, add drops of yellow cake coloring while mixing ingredients.

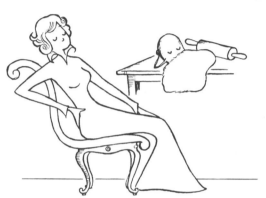

2. Be certain to allow a dough full risings. This helps create the light rolls and cakes you desire. Sweet doughs are slow in rising, so don't hover. Keep yourself busy by preparing the fillings, toppings, and frostings. Relax with a cup of coffee.

3. In many recipes there is much rolling of dough into rectangles, squares, ropes, and circles. *Always let a dough rest* before shaping. If the dough continues to pull back or "resist", cover and allow to rest longer. For example: when rolling a rectangle, pull or press the dough to square a corner — make the dough do what you want. This is the reason for the resting periods; once the dough is relaxed it will follow directions. When working with one piece of dough, cover the remaining dough with plastic wrap or a towel. Don't worry if the waiting dough rises.

4. When butter is brushed over a dough to hold a filling, do so within ½" of edges. Then the butter will not ooze out and make the dough difficult to handle.

5. There will be braiding with the sweet breads, especially the International and Holiday chapters. Roll ropes to specified length by working from the center out. Keep rolling until smooth and even. When ready to braid, cross the ropes in the center and braid out to each end. Pick up braids and turn to your convenience. Always tuck the ends under to seal.

6. Lower temperatures are specified in comparison to regular bread doughs. Sugar burns easily. Always preheat your oven during the last rising period.

7. Another secret to a luscious dough is to frost rolls and cakes while still warm. The icing then has a chance to melt into the bread.

8. Any of the rolls, cakes, and fancy breads may be frozen after they are cooked. They must be thoroughly cooled, wrapped in foil, labeled, and placed in the freezer. Do not frost until ready to serve. Reheat and then dribble with icing.

9. Take your time when working with these beautiful doughs. There are many kinds of formations. Read a recipe carefully and reread before you begin. The more you practice all these fun shapings, the more expert you will become.

10. **Cinnamon-Sugar:** Combine and mix well 1 cup granulated sugar with 2 tablespoons of cinnamon. Make up a large supply as suggested on page 267. When Cinnamon-Sugar is specified in any of the recipes, use this mixture. Great to keep for the children's cinnamon toast.

11. Uncooked sweet rolls or coffee cakes will not freeze well. For better results, they should be baked and wrapped as described in Number 8. Raw dough will become soggy with sugar mixtures if frozen before baking.

BASIC SWEET ROLL DOUGH

A light, adaptable sweet dough that is easy to manipulate and form into the large variety of rolls following this recipe. Be sure to read Tips on Handling Sweet Doughs.

2 packages dry or compressed yeast
1 cup warm water
1 teaspoon salt
2 tablespoons sugar
1 cup flour
   • • •

1½ cups warm milk
½ cup melted butter or
  margarine
¼ cup sugar
3 eggs, beaten
7 to 8 cups flour

The Sponge: In a small mixing bowl, sprinkle yeast over the warm water, stirring with a fork until dissolved. Add salt, the 2 tablespoons of sugar, and 1 cup flour. Beat with a whisk or rubber spatula until smooth. Cover and let stand until light and bubbly, about 30 minutes.

In a large mixing bowl, combine milk, butter, the ¼ cup sugar, and eggs. Stir down the sponge and add to the milk mixture. Beat in 3 cups of flour until batter is smooth. Gradually stir in enough more flour to make a soft, workable dough. Turn out on a lightly floured surface. Knead until smooth and elastic, adding small portions of flour if needed (refer to Ingredients, page 11). Place in a warm, greased bowl, turning to coat the top. Cover loosely with plastic wrap and a towel. Let double in bulk, about 1 hour.

Punch the dough down, knead lightly, cover and allow to rest 15 minutes. Divide dough in desired portions and make rolls of your choice. The roll recipes are designed so that you can make all of one kind or a variety of rolls.

CINNAMON ROLLS

¼ Basic Sweet Roll dough
Melted butter or margarine
Cinnamon-Sugar, page 131
½ cup currants or raisins
   rinsed in hot water and dried

½ cup chopped nuts (optional)
Confectioner's Icing, page 268

Roll dough in an 8x15" rectangle. Brush with melted butter to within ½" of edges. Sprinkle heavily with Cinnamon-Sugar. Scatter raisins and nuts over sugar mixture. Roll tightly from the long side. Use your dough scraper to help in rolling if dough sticks to the board. Pinch side and ends to seal. With a bread knife, slice into 1" rolls. Be sure to slice with slow even strokes to avoid squashing the dough! Place in a greased 9" cake tin ½" apart. Cover and let rise until light and touching, about 30 minutes. Bake in a preheated 350° oven, 25 minutes. Cool on a wire rack. If serving immediately, turn rolls out on a pretty plate and frost with Confectioner's Icing.

 ## FRESH LIME ROLLS AND TWISTS

One day I decided fresh lime could be just as good as lemon in a sweet roll. This is the result — delightfully fragrant with a tangy sweetness.

1 cup granulated sugar
Grated rind 1 large lime
⅛ teaspoon nutmeg

½ Basic Sweet Roll Dough
Melted butter or margarine
Confectioner's Icing*

ROLLS
Combine sugar, grated rind, and nutmeg in a small bowl. Set aside. Divide ½ Basic Sweet Roll Dough in 2 portions. Roll one part into a 9x16" rectangle. Brush with melted butter to within ½" of edges. Sprinkle half the sugar mixture over the rectangle. Roll tightly jelly roll style from the long side. Pinch side and ends. Slice into 1" rolls and place in

greased 9" cake tin. Cover and let rise 30 minutes or until light and touching. Bake in a preheated 350° oven 25 minutes. Turn out on a tray and frost with Confectioner's Icing while warm. Cool on wire rack if not serving immediately.

TWISTS

Roll remaining dough into a rectangle, 9x16". Brush with melted butter to within ½" of edges. Sprinkle remaining sugar mixture over half the oblong, lengthwise. Fold the other half on top and pinch edges to seal. Beginning at narrow end, cut in ½" strips. Twist each piece twice and place on a greased baking sheet. Cover and let rise until doubled, about 45 minutes. Bake in a preheated 375° oven 12 to 15 minutes. Cool on wire racks. Brush while warm with Confectioner's Icing.

*CONFECTIONER'S ICING

Combine 1 cup powdered sugar with 2 tablespoons lime juice. Whisk until creamy and smooth.

COCONUT CRESCENTS

1½ cups coconut	Glaze:
4 tablespoons grated orange rind	¾ cup sugar
1½ cups sugar	½ cup sour cream
Basic Sweet Roll Dough	3 tablespoons orange juice
Melted butter or margarine	¼ cup butter

Combine coconut, grated orange rind, and 1½ cups sugar. Blend well. Divide Basic dough in 4 portions. Roll one piece in a circle 12" in diameter. Brush circle with melted butter to within ¼" of edge. Sprinkle ¼ of coconut mixture over the circle. Slice into 12 pie shape wedges. Roll each piece tightly from long side (as with croissants). Place rolls point side down on a greased 9x13x2" baking sheet 1" apart. Repeat with remaining dough. Cover and let rise until doubled, about 45 minutes. Bake in preheated 350° oven 25 minutes or until golden brown. Remove rolls from oven and place pan on wire rack. Brush glaze over hot rolls. Serve immediately or allow to cool in pan.

GLAZE

While rolls are cooking, prepare the glaze. Combine ¾ cup sugar, sour cream, orange juice, and ¼ cup butter in a small saucepan. Stir and bring to a boil. Cook for 3 minutes.

ALMOND-LEMON ROLLS

One of the yummiest recipes I know and popular with all my classes.

1½ cups sugar	2 cups slivered almonds
½ cup butter or margarine	1½ cups sugar
½ cup light corn syrup	2 teaspoons nutmeg
¼ cup lemon juice	Basic Sweet Roll Dough
3 tablespoons grated lemon rind	Melted butter or margarine

Combine 1½ cups sugar, ½ cup butter, corn syrup, lemon juice, and grated rind in a sauce pan. Bring to a boil and cook 4 minutes, stirring constantly. Grease four 9″ cake tins. Sprinkle almonds over the 4 pans. Pour lemon topping over the almonds. Set aside.

In a small bowl, combine 1½ cups of sugar with the nutmeg. Divide Basic Sweet Roll Dough into 4 portions. Roll each part into a 9x15″ rectangle. Brush with melted butter to ½″ of edge. Sprinkle ¼ of sugar mixture over each oblong. Roll tightly jelly roll style from the long side. Pinch side and ends to seal. Cut into 1″ rolls and place in prepared cake tins. Cover and let rise until light and touching, about 30 minutes. Bake in a preheated 350° oven 25 minutes. Turn out immediately on wire racks so that syrup will run through the rolls. Place foil underneath rack to catch excess syrup. If you wish to freeze these rolls, bake in foil cake tins, allow to cool in pans, wrap in foil, label, and place in plastic bags.

HONEY GLAZED BUNS

Topping

¼ cup butter or margarine	½ Basic Sweet Roll Dough
½ cup brown sugar, packed	Melted butter or margarine
⅓ cup honey	¾ cup Cinnamon-Sugar, page 131

Combine the ¼ cup butter, brown sugar, and honey in a small saucepan. Cook and stir until ingredients are dissolved. Brush two 10″ cake tins with melted butter. Pour half the honey mixture in each pan, spreading evenly. Set aside.

Divide ½ of Basic Sweet Roll Dough in 2 portions. Roll one piece in a 10x15″ rectangle. Brush with melted butter to within ½″ of edges. Sprinkle lightly with Cinnamon-Sugar. Roll tightly jelly roll style from the long side. Pinch edge to seal. Slice in 1″ rolls with a sharp or serrated knife. Arrange in prepared cake tins ½″ apart. Repeat with remaining dough. Cover and let rise until light, about 30 minutes. Bake in a preheated 350° oven 25 minutes. Turn out on wire racks with foil underneath to catch excess syrup. If serving immediately, place rolls on a tray or plate. If desired, these rolls can be made in large muffin tins. Grease cups and place 2 tablespoons of topping in each one. Place a roll in each cup. Proceed as directed.

RUM ROLLS!

A delightful marinade for raisins, a good dough, a touch of orange, and frosting flavored with rum — it is all enough to make your head swim. But they are delicious and great for a holiday season.

1 cup raisins
2 tablespoons light rum
1 teaspoon grated orange rind
¼ Basic Sweet Roll dough
Melted butter
½ cup sugar

1 teaspoon nutmeg
Frosting:
1 cup confectioner's sugar
Grated rind of 1 lemon
2 tablespoons light rum

Combine raisins, rum, and grated orange rind in a small bowl. Stir well and set aside for 1 hour or longer if possible.

Roll ¼ of Basic Sweet Roll Dough in a rectangle, 10x15″. Brush with melted butter to within ½″ of edges. Combine the ½ cup of sugar with nutmeg. Sprinkle over the rectangle. Dry raisins on paper toweling. Scatter raisins over the sugar mixture. Roll tightly jelly roll style from the long side. Seal edges by pinching. Cut 1″ slices with a sharp knife. Brush a 10″ cake tin with melted butter. Place rolls in prepared pan, ½″ apart. Cover and let rise 30 minutes. Bake in a preheated 350° oven 25 minutes. Turn out on a wire rack. Combine and beat until smooth the confectioner's sugar, grated rind, and enough light rum to make a good spreading consistency. Frost the rolls while warm.

MAPLE NUT ROLLS

A flavoring that makes one think of a golden fall in Vermont, a walk in the woods, and back to a roaring fireplace, coffee and maple rolls.

Topping
¼ cup maple syrup
¼ cup brown sugar, lightly packed
¼ cup melted butter
⅓ cup chopped pecans
¼ Basic Sweet Roll Dough

Filling
½ cup brown sugar, lightly packed
½ cup raisins or currants, rinsed in hot water and dried

Combine the ¼ cup of maple syrup, brown sugar, melted butter, and pecans. Stir until well mixed. Lightly brush a 10″ cake tin or square cake pan with melted butter. Pour topping in and spread evenly over bottom of pan. Set aside.

Roll ¼ of Basic Sweet Roll Dough in a rectangle, 10x16″. If dough resists, cover, and allow to rest a few minutes. Brush lightly with maple syrup to within ½″ of edges. Slice 1″ rolls with a sharp or serrated knife. Place rolls in prepared pan ½″ apart. Cover and allow to rise until light and touching, about 30 minutes. Bake in a 350° oven 25 minutes. Turn out immediately on a tray or wire rack. Place foil underneath rack to catch excess syrup. Serve while warm.

 ## ORANGE ZEST ROLLS

If you love the pure flavor of orange, try this simply made roll.

½ Basic Sweet Roll Dough
1 cup granulated sugar
Grated rind of 2 oranges
Melted butter or margarine

1 cup powdered sugar
2 tablespoons fresh orange juice

Divide ½ of Basic Sweet Roll Dough in 2 portions. Roll one piece in a rectangle, 10x15″. Brush with melted butter to within ½″ of edges. Combine the granulated sugar with grated orange rind. Sprinkle ½ of sugar mixture over the rectangle and smooth evenly with your hand. Roll tightly jelly roll style from the long side. Pinch side to seal. Brush two 10″ cake tins with melted butter. Cut rolls in 1″ slices. Place in prepared cake pan ½″ apart. Repeat with remaining dough. Cover and let rise until light, 30 minutes. Bake in a preheated 350° oven 25 minutes. Turn out on wire racks to cool. Combine the powdered sugar and fresh orange juice, beating until smooth. Frost rolls while still warm.

DANISH PASTRY

There is nothing quite so delightful with a cup of hot coffee than a piece of Danish Pastry. They are worth the trouble for those few minutes of melting flavor.

1¼ cups cold butter
⅓ cup flour
2 packages dry or compressed yeast
1 cup warm milk

¼ cup sugar
1 teaspoon salt
1 egg
4 cups flour, approximately

Measure butter and ⅓ cup of flour into a mixing bowl. Work with a pastry blender until well mixed and crumbly. With a knife and ruler, mark a 6x12″ rectangle on 2 sheets of waxed paper. Place butter mixture in the center of one marked rectangle and cover with the other sheet of paper. Roll with a rolling pin until mixture fits in oblong. Work quickly so that butter does not become too soft. Chill thoroughly in refrigerator.

In a large mixing bowl, sprinkle yeast over the warm milk, stirring with a fork until dissolved. Set aside and allow to cool. Blend in the sugar, salt, and egg. Gradually add enough flour to make a soft, workable dough. Knead on a floured surface until smooth and elastic; refer to Techniques, page 11. Cover and let rest 15 minutes.

Preparation of dough

1. Roll dough into a 14″ square. Remove butter mixture from refrigerator and gently peel off wax paper. Place chilled butter on half the dough. Fold other half of dough over butter and seal edges by pinching or pressing with thumb.

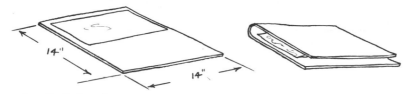

2. Roll dough into a 12x20″ rectangle. Fold dough in thirds (like an envelope). Use plenty of flour on working surface as well as on rolling pin.

3. Turn open side toward you. Roll again into a rectangle. Fold dough into thirds. If butter begins to seep or become too soft, refrigerate 15 to 20 minutes.

4. Repeat rolling action a third time.

5. You now have rolled and folded the dough 3 times. Cut dough into 3 portions for ease in handling. Cover with plastic wrap. Return to refrigerator at least one hour. Remove one portion at a time for molding into any of the following rolls.

FILLINGS FOR DANISH PASTRY

ALMOND PASTE

¼ pound ground almonds
½ cup granulated sugar

1 egg, beaten

Combine almonds and sugar in a small bowl. Gradually add the beaten egg until mixture is smooth.

VANILLA CREAM

1 tablespoon flour
1 tablespoon sugar
½ cup milk

1 egg yolk
½ teaspoon vanilla

In the top of a small double boiler, combine flour and sugar. Slowly add the milk and egg yolk. Cook over boiling water, stirring constantly until thick. Cool, stirring occasionally. Add vanilla flavoring.

COCONUT FILLING

1 cup coconut
2 tablespoons lemon juice

½ cup powdered sugar

Blend all ingredients together in a small mixing bowl.

ALMOND-SUGAR

Combine ½ cup ground almonds with ½ cup granulated sugar. This mixture is used for toppings.

EGG GLAZE

Combine 1 egg with 1 tablespoon of water. Beat thoroughly. Keep a pastry brush available with the egg glaze to coat rolls before baking.

DANISH TWISTS

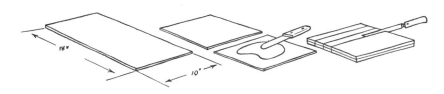

Remove one portion of dough. On a lightly floured board, roll dough into a 10x18″ rectangle. Cut in half, crosswise. Spread half the dough with Almond Paste Filling. Top with remaining dough. Slice filled dough in half to make 2 rectangles. Cut ½" strips crosswise. Twist each strip several times and place on a greased baking sheet about 2" apart. Cover and allow to rise 1 hour. Brush with egg glaze. Sprinkle with Almond-Sugar. Bake in a preheated 375° oven 15 minutes or until golden brown. Cool on wire racks.

COCKSCOMBS

On a lightly floured board, roll one portion of dough into a long strip 5" wide and ¼" thick. Place Almond Paste Filling down the center of strip about ½" wide. Fold dough over and press edges to seal. Cut in 4" lengths. Sprinkle Almond-Sugar on a clean board. Place rolls on sugar mixture. Slash side of each roll 4 times and about ¾" deep. Arrange rolls on greased baking sheets and spread fingers apart. Cover and let rise 15 minutes. Brush with egg glaze. Bake in a preheated 375° oven about 20 minutes. Cool on wire racks.

ENVELOPES

Roll one portion of dough in a rectangle 5" wide and ¼" thick on a lightly floured board. Cut in squares, trimming to make even. Spread with 1 tablespoon Vanilla Cream or a favorite jam. Fold corners into center and press down. Cover and let rise 15 minutes. Bake in preheated 375° oven about 20 minutes. Cool on wire racks.

CRESCENTS

Roll ⅛ portion of dough into a rectangle ¼" thick (5x10") on a floured board. Cut into squares. Cut each square into triangles. Place 1 tablespoon Coconut Filling on each triangle. Roll from the wide side as with croissants. Place point side down on greased baking sheet. Cover and let rise 1 hour. Brush with egg wash. Bake in a preheated 375° oven 15 to 20 minutes or until golden brown. Cool on wire racks.

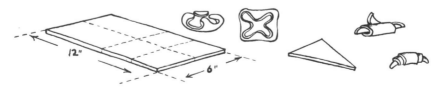

WHOLE WHEAT SWEET DOUGH

A combination of healthful ingredients that creates an exceptionally light whole wheat dough. So, all you health food devotees with a sweet tooth — this is for you!

2½ cups warm water
3 packages dry or compressed yeast
1 cup dry skim milk
¾ cup melted butter or margarine
¾ cup honey
3 eggs, lightly beaten

2 teaspoons salt
3 tablespoons wheat germ
5 cups stone ground whole
  wheat flour
5 cups unbleached white flour

Measure the warm water into a large mixing bowl. Sprinkle in the yeast, stirring with a fork until dissolved. Blend in the dry milk, butter, honey, eggs, salt, and wheat germ. In a separate bowl, combine the 2 flours. Add 3 cups of flour mixture to the yeast mixture. Beat with a rubber spatula until smooth. Gradually stir in enough more flour to make a soft, workable dough that leaves the sides of the bowl. Turn out on a lightly floured board. Knead 10 minutes or until smooth and elastic. Place in a warm, greased bowl, turning to coat the top. Cover loosely with plastic wrap and a towel. Allow to double in bulk, about 1½ hours (refer to Techniques, page 12). Turn out on a floured surface, knead lightly, cover and let rest 10 minutes. The dough is ready to form into rolls or coffee cakes.

ORANGE-HONEY WHOLE WHEAT ROLLS

This combination of honey and orange blends with the whole wheat to make an exceptionally moist and tasteful roll.

½ cup soft butter
½ cup honey
Grated rind of 1 large orange
1½ cups golden raisins, rinsed
  with hot water and dried

½ Whole Wheat Sweet Dough
Confectioner's Icing, page 268

Combine butter, honey, and grated rind in a small bowl. Beat until smooth and creamy. Divide ½ Whole Wheat Dough in 2 portions. Roll one piece into a rectangle 9x16". Spread half the butter filling over the oblong with a rubber spatula to within ½" of edges. Sprinkle half the raisins over the butter mixture. Roll tightly jelly roll style from the long side. Slice into 1" rolls. Place ½" apart in a greased 8x12x2" pan. Cover and let rise 45 minutes. Repeat directions with remaining dough. Bake in preheated 350° oven 25 minutes. Turn out on wire rack to cool. While rolls are still warm, frost with Confectioner's Icing flavored with orange juice.

CINNAMON WHOLE WHEAT ROLLS

Follow directions on page 132 for Cinnamon Rolls. Use ¼ of Whole Wheat Sweet Dough at end of first rising. Brown sugar has an affinity for whole wheat dough. You can substitute brown sugar for white. Proceed as recipe directs.

CARAMEL WHOLE WHEAT ROLLS

Filling:
1 cup brown sugar, packed
2 teaspoons cinnamon
1 cup raisins, rinsed in hot water
  and dried
• • •
½ Whole Wheat Sweet Dough
Melted butter or margarine

Frosting:
¼ cup butter or margarine
½ cup brown sugar, packed
1 teaspoon cinnamon
2 tablespoons milk
1 cup powdered sugar

Combine 1 cup brown sugar and 2 teaspoons cinnamon. Set aside. Divide ½ the Whole Wheat Sweet Dough in 2 portions. Roll one part in a 9x16" rectangle. Brush with melted butter to within ½" of edges. Sprinkle with half the brown sugar mixture. Scatter ½ cup of the raisins over the sugar. Roll tightly jelly roll style from long side. Pinch edge and sides to seal. Slice in 1" rolls. Place in greased 9" cake tin which will hold 10 to 11 rolls. Cover and let rise about 30 minutes, or until light and puffy. Repeat directions with remaining dough. Any rolls left, bake in a small pan for after school snacks. Bake rolls in a preheated 350° oven 25 minutes. Turn out on wire racks. Frost with the following icing while rolls are still warm.

FROSTING
(Make frosting while rolls are rising.) Melt ¼ cup of butter in a small saucepan. Add the ½ cup of brown sugar and bring quickly to a boil, stirring constantly. Stir and cook at a rolling boil about 2 minutes. Remove from burner. Add cinnamon and milk. Bring back to a boil. Set aside until lukewarm. Beat in the powdered sugar until smooth.

WHOLE WHEAT DATE BRAID AND RING

Date Filling:

2 cups chopped dates
1 teaspoon cinnamon
¼ teaspoon nutmeg
Grated rind 1 lemon
1 cup sugar
1 cup water
2 tablespoons butter

½ Whole Wheat Sweet Dough
1 egg mixed with 1 tablespoon
  water
Struesel*
Confectioner's Icing, Page 268

• • •

FILLING

Combine dates, cinnamon, nutmeg, grated rind, sugar, water, and and butter in a saucepan. Bring to a boil and cook until thick, stirring occasionally. Set aside to cool.

BRAID

Divide ½ of the Whole Wheat Sweet Dough in 2 portions. Cover one part and set aside. Roll the other portion into an 8x16" rectangle. Place on a greased baking sheet. With a rubber spatula, spread half the date mixture down the center third of the rectangle. With a sharp knife, cut 1" slits in dough on each side of filling. Fold strips across filling at an angle, alternating from side to side. Cover and allow to rise 30 minutes.

*STREUSEL

While braid is rising, make the following streusel. Combine ½ cup sugar, ¾ cup flour, and ⅓ cup melted butter. Mix together with your hands until mixture is crumbly. This is sufficient for 2 braids.

When the braid has finished rising, brush with egg glaze (beat 1 egg with 1 tablespoon water). Sprinkle half the streusel over the cake. Bake in a preheated 350° oven 25 minutes. Cool on wire rack.

TEA RING

Roll second portion of dough into a 9x16" rectangle. Spread remaining date mixture over the oblong to within ½" of edge. Roll tightly jelly roll style from long side. Pinch seam and place on a greased baking sheet. Make a circle of the dough. Smooth and stretch the ring. Insert the two ends together. Flatten slightly with hands. With kitchen shears, make cuts at 1" intervals and about 1" into the ring. Flatten again with hands. Cover and let rise until almost double, about 45 minutes. Bake in a preheated 350° oven 25 minutes. Cool on wire rack. If serving immediately, frost with Confectioner's Icing while still warm.

SOUR CREAM TWISTS

A chapter on Sweet Rolls is not complete without a sour cream dough. Because of its richness, the dough will not be as high and puffy as others but has a lush flavor. It is most adaptable for the classic Schnecken.

4 cups sifted flour
½ teaspoon salt
1 cup margarine or butter
2 packages dry or compressed yeast
¼ cup warm water
1 cup sour cream

1 whole egg
2 egg yolks
1½ cups sugar
Grated rind of 1 orange
2 teaspoons cinnamon

Measure flour into a mixing bowl. Add salt and cut in the butter with a pastry blender until well mixed.

Sprinkle yeast into the warm water, stirring with a fork until dissolved. Combine the sour cream, egg, and egg yolks, beating lightly until well blended. Add the sour cream and yeast mixtures to the flour. Stir with a rubber spatula or your hands until thoroughly mixed. Leave dough in a bowl, cover with plastic wrap and a towel. Refrigerate at least 2 hours or overnight.

Mix sugar with grated rind or cinnamon. You may also divide the sugar and add cinnamon to one portion and rind to the other.

Cut dough in 6 pieces for ease of handling. Return 5 pieces back to the refrigerator. Sprinkle ¼ cup of sugar mixture on your board. Place dough on sugar mixture, turn over once so both sides are coated and quickly roll into a rectangle 12x17″. Fold into thirds like an envelope. Roll out again. Fold dough lengthwise. (If dough becomes too soft, return to refrigerator 15 minutes.) You now have a long rectangle. Cut into ½″ lengths from the short side. Twist several times and place on ungreased baking sheet. Bake in a preheated 375° oven 15 minutes. Cool on wire racks. Repeat directions with remaining dough.

SCHNECKENS

Topping:
¾ cup soft butter
1 cup brown sugar, packed
1½ tablespoons white corn syrup
Whole pecan meats

Filling:
1½ cups brown sugar
3 teaspoons cinnamon
1 cup currants, rinsed in hot
   water and dried
Sour Cream Twist Dough

Topping
Cream the butter, brown sugar, and syrup until smooth. This will be sufficient for 24 large muffin tins. Brush the topping into each cup. Place 2 or 3 pecans in bottom of cup. Set aside.
Filling
Combine the brown sugar, cinnamon, and currants in a small bowl. Divide Sour Cream Dough in 2 portions. Return one part to the refrigerator. Roll half the dough on a floured board into a rectangle, 12x17″. Sprinkle with half the filling. Roll tightly jelly roll style from long side. Seal side and ends. Cut in 1″ rolls and place in prepared muffin tins. Repeat directions with remaining dough. Working with a rich dough will require extra flour on both your rolling pin and board. Cover and let rise 20 minutes. Bake in a preheated 375° oven 20 minutes. Turn out immediately on racks with foil underneath to catch excess syrup.

KOLACHY

Two bites and these delicious Czechoslovakian rolls are gone. A selection of fillings is described following the basic dough recipe.

1 cup warm water
1 cup warm milk
2 packages dry or compressed yeast
½ cup melted butter or margarine
⅔ cup sugar
1½ teaspoons salt

2 eggs, lightly beaten
¼ teaspoon nutmeg
Grated rind of 1 lemon
1 teaspoon lemon juice
8 to 9 cups flour

Combine water and milk in a large mixing bowl. Sprinkle in the yeast and stir with a fork until dissolved. Blend in the butter, sugar, salt, eggs, nutmeg, lemon rind, and juice. Beat in 3 cups of flour until mixture is smooth. Gradually add sufficient flour to form a soft, workable dough. Turn out on a lightly floured surface and knead until smooth and elastic, about 10 minutes. Place in a warm, greased bowl, turning to coat the top (refer to Techniques, page 12). Cover loosely with plastic wrap and a towel. Allow to double in bulk, about 1 hour. Punch the dough down, turn out on a floured surface, knead lightly, cover and let rest 10 to 15 minutes.

Pinch or cut off pieces of dough the size of a large walnut. Roll roughly into a ball. Place on a greased baking sheet. With thumb, make a depression in the center of each roll. Fill with any of the suggested fillings. Brush dough around the edge with melted butter. Cover and let rise 20 minutes. Bake in a preheated 375° oven 15 to 20 minutes. Remove to wire racks. These little rolls are good hot or cold. If desired, you may frost lightly with Confectioner's Icing, page 268.

KOLACHY FILLINGS

Date Filling: Combine 2 cups pitted, chopped dates, ⅓ cup water, ⅓ cup brown sugar, and 3 tablespoons butter in a small saucepan. Cook, stirring constantly until thick. Add ½ teaspoon vanilla extract. Allow to cool.

Coconut Filling: Combine and mix thoroughly ½ cup packed brown sugar, ½ cup moist, flaky coconut, and 3 tablespoons soft butter.

Poppy Seed Filling: Combine 1 cup poppy seed, ¼ cup butter, ¼ cup honey, ¼ cup sugar, 1½ teaspoons lemon juice, ¼ cup milk, and ½ teaspoon cinnamon in a saucepan. Stir and bring to a simmer. Cook for 5 minutes. Set aside to cool.

Cottage Cheese: Drain 1 cup cottage cheese. Combine with 2 egg yolks, 3 tablespoons sugar, ¼ cup dark or golden raisins, 1 tablespoon soft butter, ¼ cup chopped almonds, and 1 teaspoon grated lemon rind. Mix thoroughly.

Prune Filling: Use Prune Filling for the Prune Swirl on page 155.

Streusel Topping: Combine ½ cup flour, ¼ cup sugar, ¼ cup melted butter, and 1 teaspoon cinnamon. Mix with a fork or your hands until crumbly. Sprinkle on Kolachy indentation just before baking.

Apricot Filling: Use Apricot Filling for the Apricot Tea Ring on page 156.

Preserves or Jams: Choose any thick preserves or jams such as apricot, strawberry, pineapple, rhubarb, peach, or blueberry. Place 1 to 2 tablespoons of preserves in each Kolachy.

Blueberry Filling: Use the Blueberry Filling for Blueberry Braid on page 154.

BLANCHE'S TEA RING

A luscious coffee cake taught me by a great cook. The recipe will make four rings or the Sticky Buns and Crispies on the following pages.

2 packages dry or compressed yeast
¼ cup warm water
2 cups warm milk
½ cup sugar
8 to 8½ cups flour
3 eggs lightly beaten
1 cup melted butter or margarine
1 teaspoon salt
Melted butter or margarine

Filling:
(sufficient for 1 tea ring)
½ cup brown sugar, lightly packed
1 teaspoon cinnamon
¼ teaspoon mace
½ cup chopped nuts
Icing:
1 cup powdered sugar
Grated rind 1 large orange
3 tablespoons water

The Sponge: Combine yeast and water in a small bowl. Stir with a fork until dissolved. In a mixing bowl, blend 1 cup of the milk, ¼ cup sugar, and 2 cups of flour. Add the yeast mixture and beat with a wire whisk until smooth. Cover and set aside 30 minutes or until double and bubbling.

Stir down the sponge. Add remaining milk, ¼ cup sugar, eggs, butter, and salt. Whisk in 2 cups of flour beating mixture smooth. With a rubber spatula, stir in enough flour to make a soft workable dough that leaves sides of the bowl (refer to Techniques, page 11). Turn out on a lightly floured surface and knead until smooth and elastic, about 10 minutes. Place in a warm, greased bowl, turning to coat the top. Cover loosely with plastic wrap and towel. Set aside in a protected spot to double in bulk, about 1 hour.

Combine the brown sugar, cinnamon, mace, and nuts. Punch the dough down, turn out on a floured board, knead lightly, cover and let rest 10 minutes. Cut off ¼ of dough. Roll in a rectangle 10x19″. Brush with melted butter to within ½″ of edges. Sprinkle with sugar mixture. Roll tightly jelly roll style from the long side. Pinch side to seal. Roll with hands to smooth and elongate the roll 1 inch more. Place on a greased baking sheet seam side down. Insert ends and pinch to seal. Press or flatten ring with hands about 1″ high. Slash at 1″ intervals with kitchen shears 1½″ into the ring. Twist each finger of dough and press flat. Cover and let rise 30 minutes. Bake in a preheated 350° oven 20 to 25 miuutes. Remove to a wire rack. Brush with the following Confectioner's Icing while cake is hot.

FROSTING

Combine ½ cup powdered sugar, 1½ tablespoons water and grated rind of 1 orange. This is a thin icing that will melt into the warm tea ring giving it a luscious and tasteful texture.

PHILADELPHIA CINNAMON STICKY BUNS

Each time I taste a Sticky Bun brings memories of the downtown Farmer's Market in Lancaster, Pennsylvania and all the excitement of selling their fresh wares with such fascinating items as cup cheese, head cheese, masses of sausages, beautiful fresh and dried flowers, and huge Sticky Buns!

Topping:
½ cup brown sugar
1 tablespoon melted butter
¼ cup corn syrup
¼ Blanche's Tea Ring Dough
  (at end of second rising)
Melted butter or margarine

Filling:
½ cup brown sugar, lightly
  packed
½ cup currants, rinsed in hot
  water and dried
2 teaspoons cinnamon
Grated rind 1 orange

Combine brown sugar, 1 tablespoon butter, and corn syrup. Stir until smooth. Grease a 10″ cake tin lightly. Pour topping in the pan, spreading evenly over the bottom.

Roll dough in a rectangle, 9x12″. Brush with melted butter to within ½″ of edges. Combine the ½ cup brown sugar, currants, cinnamon, and grated rind. Sprinkle evenly over the rectangle. Roll tightly jelly roll style from the long side. Pinch side to seal. With a sharp knife, slice 1″ rolls and place in prepared cake tin ½″ apart. If there are rolls left, cook in a small pan for the children as a special treat. Cover and let rise 30 minutes. Bake in a preheated 350° oven 25 minutes. Remove from oven and turn out on a tray or plate immediately so that topping will run through the rolls.

CINNAMON PECAN CRISPIES

These are cinnamon rolls that are rolled flat and cooked quickly to produce a crispy, crunchy bun. Be certain to read directions carefully.

¼ Blanche's Tea Ring Dough
  (at end of second rising)
Melted butter or margarine
½ cup Cinnamon-Sugar, page 131

Topping:
½ cup chopped nuts
½ cup Cinnamon-Sugar

At end of the second rising for Blanche's Tea Ring Dough, cut off ¼ portion. Roll in a 12″ square. If dough resists, cover and let rest. Brush lightly with melted butter to within ½″ of edges. Sprinkle with ½ cup Cinnamon-Sugar. Roll tightly jelly roll style. Pinch edge to seal. With a sharp knife cut into 12 slices. Place on a large, greased baking sheet, preferably one without raised edges. Flatten each roll with your hands to 3″ in diameter. The rolls should barely touch. Cover and set aside to rise 30 minutes. Again press each roll with your hands. Brush with melted butter. Combine the chopped nuts and ½ cup Cinnamon-Sugar. Sprinkle tops of rolls with sugar mixture. Cover with a sheet of waxed paper. Roll over the paper with a rolling pin to flatten rolls again. Bake in a preheated 375° oven about 15 minutes. Watch that they do not burn! Remove immediately to wire racks. Good when cooled as well as when hot. Don't forget that you can always double this recipe or make all the Tea Ring Dough into Crispies.

 # SHRIMP BISQUE

At first glance this may look like a complicated recipe, but I have arranged easy directions for this elegant soup in separate sections to make the process inviting for the novice cook.

2 pounds raw shrimp in the shell

Shell, clean, and wash shrimp. Reserve shells for fish stock, page 6.

PART ONE — A MIREPOIX

4 tablespoons butter
2 tablespoons chopped carrots
2 tablespoons chopped celery

2 tablespoons chopped parsley
3 tablespoons warm brandy

Melt butter in a skillet. Sauté carrot, celery, and parsley with the cleaned shrimp 8 minutes. Flame with brandy. (Pour part of warm brandy over ingredients, ignite remaining brandy and pour over the vegetables, shaking skillet to keep the flame going.) Remove the shrimp and reserve.

PART TWO — THE BASE

¼ cup flour
2 cups hot chicken broth
*1 cup hot fish bouillon or clam
    juice*
1 bay leaf

½ teaspoon thyme
1 tablespoon lemon juice
*1 large tomato, peeled and
    chopped*

Transfer the cooked mirepoix to a large saucepan, add the flour, and stir until smooth and bubbly. Add chicken and fish stocks, whisking until smooth. Stir in remaining ingredients, cover and simmer 30 minutes. Discard bay leaf and purée the mixture in a blender. Return to a clean saucepan.

PART THREE — THE COMPLETED SOUP

1 cup half and half cream
½ cup heavy cream
2 egg yolks
Grindings of black pepper

Tabasco
Worcestershire
Salt

Dice the reserved shrimp into small pieces. Slowly add the half and half cream to the hot soup, stirring constantly. Combine the heavy cream and egg yolks. Add a small amount of hot soup to egg mixture. Stir slowly into the soup. Add chopped shrimp, pepper, a dash of Tabasco, and Worcestershire. Taste and adjust for salt. Heat thoroughly, but do not allow to boil. Serves 6 to 8.

CREAM OF BROCCOLI SOUP

One of the most delicious soups I have ever had the pleasure of tasting — and a favorite with all my students. It is equally good made with cauliflower, freezes well and doubles easily.

1 quart fresh broccoli heads, packed
⅔ cup butter
½ cup flour
3 cups warm milk
2 cups hot chicken broth
2 teaspoons salt
¼ teaspoon white pepper
3 tablespoons lemon juice

1 clove garlic, crushed
1 tablespoon Worcestershire
¼ teaspoon Tabasco
• • •
2 cups heavy cream
3 egg yolks
Florets of broccoli

Wash broccoli, trim and dry. Reserve a few florets for topping. In a saucepan cook broccoli in the butter until soft. Blend in the flour and simmer until smooth and bubbling, stirring occasionally. Add the next 8 ingredients. Stir constantly until smooth and thick. Remove from burner and whirl ingredients in a blender, using a little cream if necessary. Strain soup through a fine strainer into a clean saucepan. The soup may be frozen, or made the day before serving at this point and finished later.

Stir in the remaining cream, return to burner, and bring just to a boil. Remove from fire. Beat egg yolks in a small bowl. Whisk a little of the hot soup into beaten eggs. Pour egg mixture into soup stirring constantly. Taste for salt and adjust. If you reheat this soup, do so on a very low flame or in a double boiler.

PRESENTATION

Serve in warm, cream soup bowls topped with tiny florets of broccoli boiled in salt water until just tender. If cauliflower is used, sprinkle each serving with finely chopped parsley.

BOULA BOULA

A charming soup that fits into many occasions. It is quickly made, and I promise that your guests and family will rave over the results. An excellent soup used in demitasse cups.

2 packages frozen green peas
   (10 oz. package)
1½ cups water
4 cups canned, clear turtle bouillon
1 tablespoon grated onion

Grindings of black pepper
Salt
½ cup dry sherry
Thick cream (optional)

Combine peas and water in a saucepan. Bring to a boil rapidly. Cover, lower heat to moderate and cook 10 minutes, or until tender. Purée vegetable and water in a blender. Return to a clean saucepan.
    Strain any meat from turtle bouillon. Add bouillon to the soup. Blend in the grated onion and a few grindings of black pepper. Taste and adjust for salt. Bring combined ingredients to a boil. Add the sherry and remove from the burner.

PRESENTATION
    Thick cream may be floated on top of each serving. Try adding a light dusting of nutmeg on top of cream for a slightly different flavor. Or just pass the sherry carafe! Serves 6 to 8.

 # BUTTERNUT SQUASH SOUP

A delicate, creamy soup with a soft pumpkin color that is delightful for the opening of an important dinner party. Serves 6 to 8.

1 butternut squash, 1½ to 2 pounds
5 cups chicken broth, canned, cubes
   or your own make
⅓ cup finely minced onion

1 cup sour cream
Salt
Grindings of white pepper
Finely chopped parsley

Peel the squash, cut in half, and discard the seeds. Slice into 1″ pieces. Measure the chicken broth into a large saucepan and bring to a boil. Add the squash and onion. Lower heat to simmer. Cover the pan, and cook vegetables until tender, about 20 to 25 minutes. Remove from the burner and whirl soup in a blender. Return to a clean saucepan and add the sour cream. Taste for salt, adjust, and add a few grindings of pepper. Bring just to a boil. Serve in warm soup bowls garnished with finely chopped parsley.

COFFEE CAKES

SOUPS:

Cream of Leek
Cream of Celery
Black Mushroom
Clam Chowder

BASIC COFFEE CAKE DOUGH

The richness of eggs and butter produce a silky textured dough easy to manipulate in making a great variety of coffee cakes. The recipe is large; remember that the cakes freeze. It is always great to have extra goodies tucked away for emergencies and gifts. You can make two-thirds of the recipe or divide in half. In either case, use 2 packages of yeast.

3 packages dry or compressed yeast
¼ teaspoon ginger
2½ cups warm water
1 cup dry skim milk
1 cup melted butter or margarine

¾ cup sugar
1 teaspoon salt
4 eggs, lightly beaten
Grated rind of 1 lemon
11 to 12 cups flour

Combine yeast, ginger, and water in a large mixing bowl. Stir with a fork until dissolved. Set aside 10 minutes, or until bubbling. Blend in the dry milk, butter, sugar, salt, eggs, and grated rind. Beat in 4 cups of flour with a rubber spatula until batter is smooth. Gradually add sufficient flour to form a soft, workable dough (refer to Techniques, page 11). Turn out on a lightly floured board and knead until smooth and satiny, about 12 minutes. Sprinkle board and hands with more flour if needed, but do not let dough become dry. Place in a large warm, greased bowl, turning to coat the top. Cover loosely with plastic wrap and a towel. Place in a protected area and allow to rise until doubled, about 1½ hours. Punch down, knead in bowl lightly, recover and let double again, about 1 hour. Turn out on a floured surface, knead lightly, cover, and let rest 10 to 15 minutes. The dough is now ready to form into any of the following coffee cakes.

BLUEBERRY BRAID

2 cups fresh or frozen blueberries
  (unsweetened)
½ cup sugar
3 tablespoons cornstarch
Grated rind 1 lemon
2 tablespoons lemon juice

Streusel Topping:
⅓ cup flour

2 tablespoons sugar
1 teaspoon cinnamon
Grated rind 1 lemon
2 tablespoons soft butter
¼ Basic Coffee Cake Dough
1 egg beaten with 1 tablespoon
  milk

Combine blueberries, sugar, cornstarch, grated rind, and lemon juice in a saucepan. Bring to a boil, lower heat to simmer, and cook until thick, stirring occasionally. Set aside to cool. Prepare streusel topping:

combine flour, sugar, grated rind, cinnamon, and butter in a small bowl. Work with hands or a fork until mixture becomes crumbly.

Roll ¼ of Basic Coffee Cake Dough in a rectangle, 9x18″. Place dough on a large, greased baking sheet. Pat dough back into shape. With a rubber spatula, spread blueberry filling down the center third of the rectangle. With a small, sharp knife slit dough at 1″ intervals on both sides of the filling. Fold strips across the filling at a slight angle, alternating from side to side. Cover and let rise until doubled, about 1 hour. Brush with egg wash. Sprinkle streusel topping over the cake. Bake in a 350° oven 25 to 30 minutes. Serve immediately or cool on a wire rack.

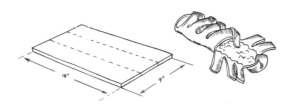

PRUNE SWIRL

2 cups dried pitted prunes	Grated rind 1 lemon
1½ cups boiling water	1 teaspoon lemon juice
1 cup sugar	¼ Basic Sweet Coffee Cake Dough
¼ teaspoon cloves	Confectioner's Icing, page 268

Combine prunes and boiling water in a saucepan. Bring to a simmer and allow to cook until water is absorbed. Do not allow to burn; stir frequently. Add sugar, cloves, lemon rind, and juice. Beat with a rubber spatula until well mixed. Set aside to cool. This is sufficient filling for 2 cakes.

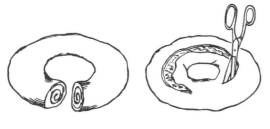

Roll ¼ Basic Dough into a 10x20″ rectangle. With a rubber spatula spread ½ of prune filling over the oblong to within ½″ of edges. Roll from long side jelly roll style. Pinch edge to seal. Place on a greased baking sheet seam side down. Make a circle and insert ends together. Pinch to seal. With kitchen shears cut ½″ into the center and make a slash completely around the circle. Press down lightly with your hands. Cover and let rise 1 hour. Bake in a preheated 350° oven 25 to 30 minutes. Remove from oven and cool on a wire rack. Dribble with Confectioner's Icing flavored with vanilla or lemon juice. If desired, a second cake may be made with remaining filling. The filling may also be frozen or used for Kolachy buns. It is excellent made into a braid; follow directions for the Blueberry Braid.

APRICOT TEA RING

2 cups dried apricots
1½ cups boiling water
1 cup sugar
2 tablespoons brandy
¼ teaspoon cinnamon

⅛ teaspoon nutmeg
½ teaspoon lemon juice
¼ Basic Coffee Cake Dough
Confectioner's Icing, page 268

Cook apricots and boiling water over medium heat until liquid is absorbed, stirring frequently. Do not allow to burn. Add the sugar, brandy, cinnamon, nutmeg and lemon juice. Beat until mixture is fairly smooth. Set aside to cool. Makes sufficient filling for 2 cakes.

Roll ¼ Basic Coffee Cake Dough into a 10x16″ rectangle. With a rubber spatula, spread ½ of apricot filling over the oblong to within ½″ of edges. Roll jelly roll style and pinch the edges together. Place on a greased baking sheet, seam side down. Make a circle; insert ends together and pinch to seal. Make 1″ slashes with scissors around the top of cake at 1″ intervals. Press cake slightly with hands. Cover and let rise until doubled, about 1 to 1½ hours. Bake in a preheated 350° oven 25 minutes or until golden. Cool on a wire rack. If serving immediately, frost while warm with Confectioner's Icing flavored with brandy or lemon juice. A second cake may be made or freeze remaining filling for a future use.

LEMON-COTTAGE CHEESE COFFEE CAKE

2 cups well drained cottage cheese
4 egg yolks
6 tablespoons sugar
2 tablespoons flour
Grated rind 1 lemon
2 tablespoons lemon juice
1 tablespoon soft butter

½ cup dark raisins
½ Basic Coffee Cake Dough

Glaze:
½ cup sugar
3 tablespoons milk
Grated rind 1 lemon

Combine drained cottage cheese, egg yolks, sugar, flour, grated rind, lemon juice, butter, and raisins. Stir until well mixed. This is sufficient filling for 2 coffee cakes.

Divide ½ of Basic Dough in two equal portions. Roll one piece in a 11x18″ rectangle. Place on a greased baking sheet. Reshape dough on pan. Spread ½ of cheese filling down center third of rectangle. Fold remaining thirds on top, envelope style. Pinch side and ends to seal thoroughly. Carefully turn cake so seam is on the bottom. Cover and let rise about 45 minutes. Repeat with remaining dough.

Combine sugar, milk, and lemon rind. Brush the glaze over coffee cakes. Bake in a preheated 350° oven 25 minutes or until golden brown. Cool on wire racks.

CHOCOLATE CHIP CAKE

For all you chocolate lovers, here is a coffee cake that is spectacular to see and luscious to eat.

½ Basic Coffee Cake Dough
1½ cups semi-sweet chocolate chips

Glaze:
¾ cup semi-sweet chocolate chips

¼ cup butter
2 tablespoons light corn syrup
½ teaspoon vanilla extract
Confectioner's Icing (optional)

Roll ½ of Basic Coffee Cake dough in a long rectangle, 12x22″. Sprinkle dough with 1½ cups of chocolate chips to within ½″ of edges. Roll tightly jelly roll style from the long side. Pinch side to seal. Place in a well greased bundt or tube pan, seam side down. Insert ends together. Cover and let rise until doubled, about 1 hour. Bake in a preheated 350° oven 30 minutes. Cool on a wire rack.
Glaze:
Combine the ¾ cup chocolate chips, butter, and corn syrup in a saucepan. Cook and stir over medium heat until chocolate is melted and mixture is smooth. Add the vanilla. Dribble glaze over the cooled cake.

VARIATIONS
The 1½ cups chocolate chips can be kneaded into the dough rather than sprinkled over a rectangle.

Frost coffee cake with Confectioner's Icing, page 268. Pour half the chocolate glaze over the white icing — most spectacular.

APPLE-RAISIN SWIRL

Allow this apple loaf to cool completely before cutting. It is excellent sliced and oven toasted for breakfast.

¼ *Basic Coffee Cake Dough*
1 *cup apples, peeled, cored*
   and coarsely grated
½ *cup dark raisins, rinsed in*
   hot water and dried

½ *cup sugar*
1 *teaspoon cinnamon*
1 *egg mixed with 1 tablespoon*
   water

Roll ¼ Basic Coffee Cake Dough in a rectangle, 10x15". Spread prepared apples over the dough to within ½" of edges. Scatter raisins on top. Combine sugar and cinnamon. Reserve 1 tablespoon. Sprinkle sugar mixture over apples. Roll tightly jelly roll fashion from the short side. Pinch the side and ends to seal. Place in a greased 9x5x3" loaf pan. Pierce 6 times with a toothpick. Cover and let rise until doubled or just curved over top of pan, about 1 hour. Brush with egg wash and sprinkle top with reserved tablespoon of sugar mixture. Bake in a preheated 350° oven 40 to 45 minutes. Remove from oven and cool in the pan on a wire rack 10 minutes. Loosen loaf with spatula as there may be a sticky sugar seepage. Turn loaf out and let cool before slicing.

COCONUT SWIRL

An exceptionally easy coffee cake to make that is marvelous to have when a friend drops by for coffee.

¼ *Basic Coffee Cake Dough*
¼ *cup sugar*
2 *tablespoons melted butter*

¼ *cup moist, flaky coconut*
1 *tablespoon milk*
1 *teaspoon grated lemon rind*

Divide ¼ basic Coffee Cake Dough in 2 equal portions at end of second rising. Roll one part in a rope 30" long. Roll the remaining portion in a 32" rope. Brush a 9" round cake pan with soft butter. Starting from the center of pan, wrap the 30" rope around itself. Where it ends, begin with the 32" strand and continue around until the pan is full. Combine the sugar, butter, coconut, milk, and lemon rind. With a soft pastry brush, spread topping over the swirl. Cover and let rise 45 minutes. Bake in a preheated 350° oven 25 to 30 minutes, or until golden in color. Remove to a wire rack and allow to cool in the pan 10 minutes. Turn out on a tray and serve while warm.

KUCHENS

Following are three delightful Kuchens. A Kuchen is an Old World coffee cake usually made with fruit or jam topped with streusel. Any of the Kuchens may be baked in a foil pan, cooled, wrapped, and frozen.

MARMALADE KUCHEN

¼ Basic Coffee Cake Dough
½ cup orange marmalade

Streusel Topping:
½ cup soft butter
¼ cup flour

½ cup sugar
¼ teaspoon cinnamon
1 teaspoon grated lemon rind
½ cup slivered almonds

Cut off ¼ Basic Coffee Cake Dough. Pat dough in 12″ round, or a 10x15″ greased cake pan. If dough resists, let it rest a few minutes. Pat evenly over the pan.

Spread marmalade over the dough. Combine butter, flour, sugar, cinnamon and grated rind. Work with hands or a fork until well mixed and crumbly. Add the almonds. Sprinkle streusel topping over the marmalade. Cover and let rise until doubled, about 45 minutes to 1 hour. Bake in a preheated 350° oven 30 to 35 minutes. Serve while warm or cool on a wire rack.

BLUEBERRY KUCHEN

¼ Basic Coffee Cake Dough
Melted butter or margarine
2 cups fresh or frozen blueberries
*   (unsweetened)*

Streusel Topping:
¾ cup sugar
¾ cup flour

½ cup soft butter
Grated rind 1 orange
Grated rind 1 lemon

Brush an 8x12″ baking dish with melted butter. Set aside. Roll ¼ Basic Coffee Cake Dough into a rectangle. Place dough in prepared baking dish and press into corners. If dough resists, cover and let rest while you prepare the streusel topping. Combine sugar, flour, butter, and grated rinds. Blend well with a fork or your hands until mixture is crumbly. Sprinkle the blueberries over the dough. Spread the streusel topping over the blueberries. Cover and let rise 30 minutes. Bake in a preheated 350° oven 40 minutes. Let cake cool in the pan on a wire rack 10 minutes. Serve while warm.

APPLE KUCHEN

¼ *Basic Coffee Cake Dough*
Streusel Topping:
¾ *cup sugar*
¾ *cup flour*
½ *cup soft butter*

1 teaspoon cinnamon
Grated rind 1 lemon
½ *cup chopped almonds*
2 large apples, peeled, cored, and thinly sliced

Roll ¼ Basic Coffee Cake Dough in a rectangle, 8x12". Place in a greased baking dish, 8x12". Press dough into corners. Cover and let rest while you prepare the streusel topping. Combine sugar, flour, butter, cinnamon, and grated rind. Blend with a fork or your hands until mixture is crumbly. Add the chopped almonds. Overlap the apple slices in rows on top of dough. Spread streusel topping over the apples. Cover and let rise 30 minutes. Bake in a preheated 350° oven 30 minutes. Cool on wire rack 10 minutes. Serve while warm.

ALMOND TOPPED COFFEE CAKE

A magnificent, high coffee cake with swirls of cinnamon inside, topped with almonds that is good served either hot or cooled.

Melted butter or margarine
½ *cup slivered almonds*
½ *Basic Coffee Cake Dough*

1 cup Cinnamon-Sugar, page 131
1 cup raisins, scalded and dried

Brush a Bundt or Swirl baking pan heavily with melted butter. Sprinkle almonds over bottom of pan. Set aside.

Roll ½ Basic Coffee Cake Dough in a rectangle, 10x22". If dough resists, cover and let rest a few minutes. Brush rectangle with melted butter to within ½" of edges. Sprinkle with Cinnamon-Sugar. Scatter raisins over sugar mixture. Roll tightly jelly roll style from the long side. Pinch the edge to seal. Place in prepared pan and insert ends together. Cover and let rise until doubled, about 45 minutes. Bake in a preheated 350° oven 40 minutes. Cool on a wire rack.

CINNAMON COFFEE CAN CAKE

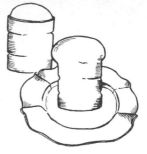

¼ Basic Coffee Cake Dough
Melted butter or margarine
½ to 1 cup Cinnamon-Sugar, page 131
½ cup raisins, rinsed in hot water
   and dried
½ cup chopped nuts (optional)

1 pound clean coffee can
Confectioner's Icing, page 268

Roll ¼ Basic Coffee Cake Dough in a 10x15" rectangle. If dough resists, cover and let rest a few minutes. Brush with melted butter to within ½" of edges. Sprinkle Cinnamon-Sugar over the oblong. Scatter raisins and nuts over sugar mixture. Roll tightly jelly roll style from the short side. Pinch edge and ends to seal. Drop the roll into a well buttered coffee can. Cover and let rise about 40 minutes or until dough reaches top of can. Bake in a preheated 350° oven 35 to 40 minutes. Remove coffee can to a wire rack for 10 minutes. Turn bread out to cool. Place cake in center of a pretty plate or tray. Dribble Confectioner's Icing over the top, allowing to drip down the sides. Serve warm or cooled.

ORANGE ALMOND SWEET BREAD

Here is one of my favorite coffee cakes to keep frozen for an emergency or as gifts. The dough is unusually good so I have included a variation: a Cinnamon-Caramel Tea Ring.

The Dough:
2 packages dry or compressed yeast
½ cup warm water
1 cup warm milk
½ cup sugar
½ cup melted butter or margarine

1 teaspoon salt
3 eggs, lightly beaten
6 to 7 cups flour

The Filling:
½ cup soft butter
Grated rind 1 orange
¾ cup honey
1 cup almonds, finely chopped
1 cup golden raisins, rinsed
   in hot water and dried

½ cup chopped, candied
   orange peel
1 egg beaten with 1
   tablespoon water
Slivered almonds

161

Sprinkle yeast over the warm water, stirring with a fork until dissolved. Set aside. Combine the milk, sugar, butter, and salt in a large mixing bowl. Add the beaten eggs and yeast mixture; stir until well blended. With a rubber spatula, beat in 3 cups of flour until mixture is smooth. Gradually add sufficient flour to form a soft, workable dough that pulls away from sides of the bowl. Turn out on a lightly floured surface. Knead until smooth and satiny, about 10 minutes. Be careful to keep dough from becoming dry (refer to Techniques, page 11). Place in a warm, greased bowl, turning to coat the top. Cover loosely with plastic wrap and a towel. Allow to double in bulk, about 1½ hours. Punch down, recover, and let double again, about 45 minutes. Turn out on a floured board, knead lightly, cover and let rest 15 minutes.

While dough is rising, prepare the filling. Combine butter, grated rind, and honey, mixing until smooth and light. Roll dough in a large square ¼" thick, about 16x16". With a rubber spatula, spread the orange mixture over the dough to within ½" of edges. Scatter the almonds, raisins, and orange peel over the filling. Roll jelly roll style so that an open end faces you. Pinch side to seal. Flatten roll with your hands. With a rolling pin, press again; roll back and forth until the roll is about 1" high. With a dough scraper or sharp knife, divide flattened roll lengthwise to make 3 strips. Cut each strip in half, making 6 portions. Twist 3 strips together and place in a well greased 9x5x3" loaf pan. Repeat with remaining 3 strips. Don't worry if the dough breaks in places, or if you and the dough are greasy. Regardless, you will have a beautiful bread when finished. Cover and let rise until curved over tops of pans, about 45 minutes. Brush loaves with egg wash. Decorate with slivered almonds. Bake in a preheated 350° oven 45 minutes. Remove from oven and let cool in pan 10 minutes. Loosen bread with a spatula and turn out on wire racks to cool. Do not attempt to slice bread until thoroughly cooled.

CINNAMON-CARAMEL TEA RING

An elegant coffee cake that is beautiful placed on a tall cake plate. With a little variation, the cake can be turned into a Christmas centerpiece with a candle in the center.

Topping:
2 tablespoons melted butter or
    margarine
¾ cup dark corn syrup
1 tablespoon lemon juice
½ Orange Almond Dough, at end
    of first rising

Melted butter or margarine

Filling:
½ cup brown sugar, packed
½ cup golden raisins, rinsed
    in hot water and dried

Combine the 2 tablespoons melted butter, corn syrup, and lemon juice in a small bowl. Set aside. Roll the rested dough in a 10x12" rectangle. Brush lightly with melted butter to within ½" of edges. Combine the brown sugar and raisins. Sprinkle over the rectangle. Roll tightly jelly roll style from the long side. Pinch side to seal. Cut in 1" slices. Brush a 10" tube pan with melted butter (be sure that center is not removable or syrup will leak through). Place one ring of rolls standing up on edge around the tube pan. Arrange a second row on the inside so that you have 2 circles of rolls. Pour half the syrup over rolls. Cover and let double in bulk, 45 minutes to 1 hour. Remove towel and pour remaining syrup over rolls. Bake in a preheated 350° oven 30 to 35 minutes. Let cool in pan on wire rack 10 minutes. Invert on rack or plate.

CHRISTMAS VARIATION

Slice ½ cup green or red candied cherries to include in the filling. Sprinkle whole cherries on bottom of prepared tube pan. Proceed as directed.

SALLY LUNN

An English batter bread that has been used in our country for several generations. It may be served hot out of the oven for dinner or sliced and toasted for breakfast.

¼ cup warm water	*½ cup sugar*
1 package dry or compressed yeast	*1 teaspoon salt*
1 cup warm milk	*3 eggs, beaten*
½ cup melted butter or margarine	*4 cups unbleached white flour, approximately*

Sprinkle yeast over the warm water, stirring until dissolved, (refer to Ingredients, page 7). Set aside. In a large mixing bowl, combine the milk, butter, sugar, salt, and eggs. Beat in 1 cup of the flour until smooth. Stir in the yeast mixture. Add 1 cup of flour at a time, beating well after each addition. Beat until batter is light and creamy. This may be done with an electric mixer or rubber spatula. Cover and let double in size, about 1 hour. Stir the batter down, pour in a well buttered 10" tube pan and spread evenly. Cover and let double in bulk, about 1 hour. Bake in a 350° oven 35 to 40 minutes. Check with a cake tester for doneness. Turn out on a wire rack to cool or serve immediately with lots of good butter!

LEMON-CHEESE COFFEE CAKE

One of the loveliest of coffee cakes that has been a "must" for each cooking class. If you want to please your family and friends, plus showing off a little, then this is your cake!

2 packages dry or compressed yeast
½ cup warm water
4 eggs
1 cup melted butter or margarine
1 cup sour cream
½ cup sugar
½ teaspoon salt
Grated rind 1 lemon
5 to 6 cups flour

Filling:
1 large package cream cheese
  (8 oz.)

½ cup sugar
2 eggs
2 teaspoons lemon juice

Topping:
1½ cups apricot jam or
  preserves
1 teaspoon lemon juice
Powdered sugar

Sprinkle yeast over the warm water, stirring with a fork until dissolved. Set aside. In a large mixing bowl, whisk the eggs thoroughly. Blend in the butter, sour cream, ½ cup sugar, salt, and grated rind. Stir in the yeast mixture. Beat in 2 cups of flour with a rubber spatula until batter is smooth. Gradually add sufficient flour to make a soft, workable dough. Turn out on a floured board and knead until dough is smooth, about 5 to 8 minutes. An extremely rich dough does not require a long kneading and can easily absorb too much flour. Be careful not to use more than ½ cup flour beyond specified amount. Place in a warm, greased bowl. Cover loosely with plastic wrap and towel. Let double in bulk, about 1½ to 2 hours.

Punch down the dough, knead lightly, cover, and let rest 10 minutes. Prepare the filling: stir the cheese until smooth in small bowl of electric mixer. Beat in the sugar until creamy. Add eggs one at a time, beating well after each addition. Blend in the lemon juice.

  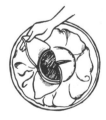

Brush a 3 quart ring mold with melted butter. Sprinkle board with flour in a circle. Turn out the dough. With a rolling pin, roll dough in a large circle 24 to 25″ in diameter. Fold in half and lay over ½ of the mold. Unfold the dough and carefully fit down into bottom of mold; be careful not to break dough. If there are breaks, repair by pinching dough together. You will have 1 to 2 inches of dough hanging like a skirt outside the ring. Pour in the cheese filling. Lift overlapping dough over the filling by folding in large pleats around the cake. Press folds against inside ring. Cut a cross in center hole with scissors. Fold each triangle back over the folds of dough. Cover and set aside to rise about 30 minutes, or until dough comes to ¼" of the top. Bake in a preheated 350° oven 40 minutes. The top will be quite brown due to richness of dough. Let cool in pan 10 minutes. Turn out on wire rack. When cooled, the cake may at this point be frozen and finished later.

PRESENTATION

Turn the cake over so that the bottom becomes the top. Place on a large round tray. Heat the apricot jam with lemon juice in a small skillet until bubbling lightly. Spoon over cake and allow to cool. Sieve a small amount of powdered sugar over the cake for a final touch.

SWEDISH COFFEE BREAD

Several years ago an American Field Service student from Sweden lived in our home during a school year. Svante brought recipes and many ideas of the wonderful Swedish Coffee Cakes and breads. Here is a lovely dough, redolent with cardamom, a favorite spice of Swedish bread makers, that may be made into a wonderful variety of both cakes and breads.

2½ cups warm milk	2 teaspoons ground cardamom
2 packages dry or compressed yeast	1 cup melted butter or
1 cup sugar	margarine
1 teaspoon salt	8 to 9 cups flour

Measure warm milk into a large mixing bowl. Sprinkle in the yeast, stirring with a fork until dissolved. Blend in the sugar, salt, cardamom, and butter. Beat in 4 cups of flour until the batter is smooth. Gradually add sufficient flour to make a workable dough. Turn out on a lightly floured board and knead until smooth and elastic. Place in a warm, greased bowl, turning to coat the top. Cover loosely with plastic wrap and a towel. Set aside to rise until doubled, about 2 to 2½ hours (refer to Techniques, page 12).

Punch down the dough, turn out on a floured surface and knead lightly. Cover and let rest 10 to 15 minutes. The dough is ready to form into any of the following breads and rolls.

CARDAMOM TWIST

Cardamom Filling:
(sufficient for 3 twists)
½ cup soft butter
2 cups powdered sugar
1 teaspoon cardamom
Grated rind 1 orange
2 tablespoons orange juice

Swedish Coffee Bread Dough
1½ cups golden raisins, rinsed
and dried (optional)
Pine nuts or slivered almonds
1 egg beaten with 1
tablespoon milk

Combine butter, sugar, cardamom, grated rind, and orange juice. Beat until light and creamy.

When Swedish Coffee Dough has rested, divide in 3 portions. Set aside 2 pieces and cover. Roll one part in a long rectangle, 8x28″. With a rubber spatula, spread ⅓ of filling over the oblong to within ½″ of edges. Sprinkle ⅓ of raisins over butter mixture, if desired. Roll tightly from the long side. Pinch edge to seal. Place on a greased baking sheet, seam side down and twist into a figure 8. Insert ends and pinch to seal. Flatten with hands slightly. Cover and allow to double, about 1½ hours. Repeat directions with remaining 2 portions of dough.

Brush twists with egg wash. Sprinkle with almonds or pine nuts. Press nuts lightly into the dough. Bake in a preheated 350° oven 40 minutes. Do not be disturbed if some filling oozes out; it will not harm the bread. Remove with 2 spatulas on a wire rack to cool or serve immediately. Makes 3 coffee cakes.

COFFEE BRAIDS

½ Swedish Coffee Bread Dough
1 egg beaten with 1 tablespoon milk

Cinnamon-Sugar, page 131
Chopped almonds

When Swedish Dough has rested, divide ½ of dough in 3 portions. Working from the center out to the ends, roll each piece into 21″ ropes. Cross ropes in the center and braid out to each end. Place braid on a greased baking sheet, cover, and let rise until almost doubled, about 1 to 1½ hours. Brush with egg wash. Sprinkle with Cinnamon-Sugar and chopped almonds. Bake in a preheated 350° oven 30 to 35 minutes. Cool on a wire rack.

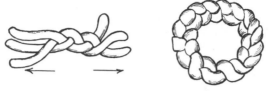

ROUND BRAID
Roll the 3 ropes of dough in 26″ lengths. Braid, place on a greased baking sheet and form in a circle. Pinch ends together. Let rise and bake as described above.

CINNAMON RINGS AND ROLLS

RING No. 1
You will need: ½ Swedish Coffee Bread dough at end of rising period, melted butter, Cinnamon-Sugar (page 131), and Confectioner's Icing. Roll dough in a rectangle, 15x24″. Brush with melted butter to within ½″ of edges. Sprinkle with Cinnamon-Sugar. Roll tightly, jelly roll style from the long side. Pinch side to seal. Place in a greased 10″ tube pan. Make long slashes with kitchen scissors 1″ apart around top of loaf. Cover and let rise until doubled, about 1½ hours. Bake in a preheated 350° oven 40 minutes. Turn out on a wire rack to cool. Frost with Confectioner's Icing while still warm.

RING No. 2
You will need ½ Swedish Coffee Bread Dough at end of resting period, melted butter, and Cinnamon-Sugar (page 131). Roll dough in a thin rectangle, 15x24″. Brush with melted butter to within ½″ of edges. Sprinkle with Cinnamon-Sugar. Roll tightly jelly roll style from the long side. Pinch side to seal. Place on a greased baking sheet. Form the dough in a circle, inserting ends together and pinching to seal. With kitchen 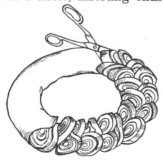 scissors, cut deep slashes at a slight angle 1½″ deep and ½″ apart. As you slash, pull alternating slices to the right and then left. Press the cake lightly with your hands so that slices lay against each other. This makes a most intriguing, handsome coffee cake. Delightful to serve as the slices may be pulled apart easily. Cover and let rise until not quite doubled, about 1 hour. Bake in a preheated 350° oven 25 minutes. Cool on wire rack.

RING No. 3

Swedish Coffee Bread dough is excellent as a Christmas ring. Follow directions on page 220 for Christmas Tea Ring. Use ½ the Swedish Dough to make a large, beautiful holiday cake. Bake in a preheated 350° oven 30 to 35 minutes. If serving immediately, frost while still warm with Confectioner's Icing, page 268.

BUTTERFLY ROLLS

You will need: ¼ Swedish Coffee Dough, melted butter, and Cinnamon-Sugar (page 131). Roll dough in a rectangle, 8x14″. Brush with melted butter. Sprinkle with Cinnamon-Sugar. Roll tightly from the long side. Pinch side to seal. Cut in 1½″ rolls. With a sharp knife, cut 2 slices in each roll, 1″ deep and ½″ apart. Place on a greased baking sheet and spread slices apart in a butterfly fashion. Cover and let rise 1 hour. Bake in 350° oven 15 to 20 minutes. Cool on wire rack. Leave plain or frost with Confectioner's Icing, page 268.

KUGELHOPF

A beautifully molded coffee cake from Austria that is particularly delicious with either a glass of wine or hot coffee. The cake becomes even better after two or three days.

1 cup golden raisins	1 cup butter or margarine
½ cup almonds, finely chopped	1 teaspoon salt
2 tablespoons cognac	6 eggs
1 package dry or compressed yeast	Grated rind 1 lemon
¼ cup warm water	Melted butter
1 cup warm milk	Whole or sliced almonds
1 cup sugar	for decoration
5 cups sifted all purpose flour	Powdered sugar (optional)

Combine raisins, chopped almonds, and cognac in a small bowl. Set aside.

The Sponge: In a mixing bowl, sprinkle yeast over the water, stirring with a fork until dissolved. Blend in the milk and ¼ cup of sugar. Beat in 2½ cups of flour until mixture is smooth. Cover bowl with a towel. Set aside until sponge has doubled, about 1 hour.

Grease a Kugelhopf pan thoroughly with melted butter. Place whole or sliced almonds in the bottom design of mold.

Measure the ¾ cup of remaining sugar, butter, and salt in a large mixing bowl. Beat until smooth and fluffy, preferably with an electric mixer. Add eggs one at a time, beating well after each addition. Stir down the sponge and add to butter mixture with 1½ cups of flour. Beat until smooth. Stir in the fruit-nut mixture, grated rind, and remaining flour. Mix well. Pour batter in prepared Kugelhopf mold. Cover with a towel. Let batter rise to ½″ of the top, about 1½ to 2 hours. If batter rises higher, there will be spillage while baking. Bake in a preheated 350° oven 50 to 60 minutes. If a glass mold is used, reduce heat to 325° (refer to Techniques, page 14). Remove from oven. Let remain in mold on a wire rack 10 minutes. Turn out and cool. Powdered sugar may be sifted over cake when ready to serve.

POTICA

A luscious, elegant coffee cake that stems from the Balkan countries. When this cake is served, your guests will wonder how you did so many swirls!

The Dough:
2 packages dry or compressed yeast
¼ cup warm water
3 egg yolks
½ cup warm milk
1 cup melted butter or margarine
¼ cup sugar
½ teaspoon salt
3 cups sifted flour

Sprinkle yeast over the warm water, stirring with a fork until dissolved. In a mixing bowl, beat egg yolks lightly. Blend in the yeast mixture, milk, butter, sugar, and salt. With a rubber spatula, beat in the sifted flour until mixture is smooth. Cover bowl with plastic wrap and a towel. Refrigerate overnight.

The Filling:
3 egg whites
½ cup white sugar
2 cups ground walnuts or almonds
½ cup golden raisins, rinsed in
    hot water and dried
½ cup brown sugar, packed
1 teaspoon cinnamon or
    grated lemon rind

The next morning: Beat egg whites until softly stiff. Slowly add the ½ cup white sugar, beating constantly until mixture is meringue-like. Combine ground nuts, raisins, brown sugar, and cinnamon or grated rind. Fold into the meringue.

PREPARATION OF CAKE

Brush a Bundt pan thoroughly with melted butter. Remove dough from refrigerator. Divide in 2 portions. Return one portion to refrigerator. On a floured surface, roll dough into a rectangle, 10x18″. Spread half the meringue filling over the rectangle to within ½″ of edges. Roll up jelly roll style from the long side. The dough is very tender; use your dough scraper to assist in the rolling process. Pinch edge to seal and place roll in prepared Bundt pan seam side down. Overlap the ends. Remove the second portion of dough and repeat above directions. Place the second roll on top the first. Cover and allow to rise 45 minutes. Bake in a preheated 350° oven 45 minutes. Check for doneness with a cake tester. Let cool in pan 10 minutes. Remove to wire rack. While still warm frost with Confectioner's Icing (page 268).

CARAMEL BUBBLE LOAF

Another delightful loaf that people seem to enjoy so much — such fun to pull off the "bubbles". Children especially like the little balls of cake. This recipe has a luscious syrup running through it and may easily be turned into a beautiful Christmas cake.

1 package dry or compressed
    yeast
¼ cup warm water
1 cup warm milk
½ cup sugar
½ teaspoon salt
1 egg
¼ cup melted butter or
    margarine

1 teaspoon vanilla extract
4 to 5 cups flour

Glaze:
½ cup melted butter or margarine
½ cup sugar
1 teaspoon cinnamon
½ cup chopped nuts
Dark or golden raisins, rinsed
    in hot water and dried

Sprinkle yeast over the water, stirring with a fork until dissolved. In a mixing bowl, combine milk, sugar, salt, egg, butter, and vanilla extract. Blend ingredients well. Add the yeast mixture and 2 cups of flour. Beat until mixture is smooth. Gradually add sufficient flour to make a soft dough. Turn out on a lightly floured board and knead until smooth and elastic, about 10 minutes. Place in a warm, greased bowl, turning to coat the top. Cover loosely with plastic wrap and towel. Set aside in a warm spot to double in bulk, about 1½ hours. Punch down, knead lightly in the bowl, recover, and allow to rise again, about 1 hour. Turn the dough out on a floured surface. Knead 1 minute, cover, and let rest 10 minutes.

Prepare glaze by combining melted butter, sugar, cinnamon, and nuts. Cut off pieces of dough the size of a walnut. Roll roughly in a ball. Dip tops into the glaze and place in a well buttered 10″ tube or 2 loaf pans, 8½x4½x2½″. Pile the balls in 2 layers glaze side up. Scatter raisins among the balls. Pour remaining glaze over the top. Cover with a towel and allow to double, 45 minutes to 1 hour. Bake in a preheated 350° oven 40 to 45 minutes. The smaller pans will take about 35 minutes. Invert immediately on a serving platter or rack with foil underneath to catch excess syrup. Serve warm or cool and freeze.

CHRISTMAS BUBBLE LOAF

Brush a 10″ tube pan thoroughly with melted butter. Make a topping with the following ingredients: combine 3 tablespoons corn syrup, 3 tablespoons butter, and ½ cup packed brown sugar. Heat until sugar dissolves. Pour in bottom of prepared pan. Distribute whole blanched almonds, green and red cherries over the topping. Prepare Caramel Bubble Loaf as directed, placing the balls of dough on the topping.

CREAM OF LEEK SOUP

A soup similar to Vichyssoise but quickly and easily made with an unusually fine flavor. Serves 8.

4 cups sliced leeks, white part only
2 cups diced potatoes
6 cups chicken broth, your own
*   make or canned*
1 cup thick cream

3 tablespoons dry Vermouth
*   or a dry white wine*
Salt
Finely chopped parsley

Combine leeks, potatoes, and chicken broth in a soup pot. Bring to a boil, lower heat to simmer, and cook until vegetables are tender, about 20 minutes. Whirl this mixture in a blender, returning to a clean soup pot. Place soup back on medium heat. Slowly add the cream and wine, stirring constantly. Taste for salt. Bring soup to a simmer and serve immediately. This soup freezes well or can be made the day before serving. When reheating, do so slowly stirring occasionally. Serve in warm soup bowls, garnished with finely chopped parsley.

CREAM OF CELERY SOUP

A lovely pale, green soup healthful and refreshing at any time of the year since we always have such an abundance of celery.

1 head of celery, about 4 cups
*   chopped*
¾ cup chopped onion
¼ cup butter
4 cups hot chicken broth

2 cups milk
3 tablespoons cornstarch
Salt
½ cup light cream
Finely chopped celery leaves

Wash celery thoroughly, trim, and chop into small pieces, including part of the leaves. In a large saucepan, melt the butter. Add the celery and onion. Sauté over medium heat for 10 minutes, stirring occasionally but do not allow to discolor. Add the chicken broth. Lower heat to simmer and continue cooking partially covered until vegetables are very tender, about 30 minutes. Purée soup in blender or put through a sieve. Return blended soup to a clean saucepan. Combine the cornstarch and milk; slowly add to the soup, stirring constantly. Bring just to a boil and taste for salt. Add the cream and heat but do not allow to boil. Serve in warm soup bowls with finely chopped celery leaves as a garnish.

BLACK MUSHROOM SOUP

½ pound fresh mushrooms
  (preferably dark brown variety)
½ cup dried mushrooms, soaked 30
  minutes in water to cover
5½ cups beef broth, your own make
  or canned
2 tablespoons cornstarch
¼ cup water

Grindings of black pepper
1 teaspoon lemon juice
¼ cup dry Vermouth
Whipped cream

Wash mushrooms and remove stems. Chop mushrooms finely and set aside. Drain the dried mushrooms thoroughly. Measure broth into a saucepan. Add the mushroom stems and dried mushrooms. Bring to a boil, lower heat to simmer and cook 30 minutes uncovered. Strain broth into a clean saucepan. Discard dried mushrooms and stems. Add the chopped mushrooms to the strained broth and bring to a boil. Combine the cornstarch with ¼ cup water. Stir mixture into boiling soup. Lower heat to simmer and add the black pepper, lemon juice, and Vermouth. Simmer lightly 10 minutes.

PRESENTATION

Pour soup in warm soup bowls. Float 1 tablespoon whipped cream on top of each bowl. Run under broiler about 2 minutes to brown. Serves four.

CLAM CHOWDER

One of the most popular soups in the United States is a hearty New England Clam Chowder. Here is my version with an added fillip of white wine.

2 cans of clams (8 ounce)
3 cups diced potatoes
½ cup finely diced onion
1 bay leaf
½ teaspoon thyme
1 cup water

Grindings of black pepper
¼ lb. lean salt pork, diced
¼ lb. butter or margarine
¼ cup flour
2 cups light cream
3 tablespoons dry white wine

Strain the clams over a soup pot. Reserve clams. To the clam juice add diced potatoes, onion, bay leaf, thyme, water, and a few grindings of black pepper. Bring to a boil, reduce heat to simmer, and cook until potatoes are almost done. Stir in reserved clams.

Sauté the diced salt pork over medium heat until crisp. Add the butter, allow to melt and whisk in the flour. Let the roux bubble a few minutes but do not allow to burn. Stir in 1 cup of hot soup. Beat vigorously until smooth. Add this mixture to the soup pot and allow to cook over medium heat until hot, stirring occasionally. Blend in the cream and wine. Taste for seasoning and adjust. Heat but do not allow to boil. Serves 6 to 8.

AN EXCITING ASSORTMENT OF BREADS

SOUPS:

Lobster Bisque
Cream of Spinach
Meat Ball
Mary's Soup Stew
Corn Chowder

LEMON TWIST

A big showy loaf with a light lemon flavor that is perfect for a dinner party of 10. Serve the bread hot on a large wooden board and slice at the table.

1 package dry or compressed yeast	½ cup melted butter or margarine
¼ cup warm water	2 eggs, slightly beaten
¾ cup warm milk	Grated rind and juice of 1 lemon
⅓ cup sugar	4½ cups flour, approximately
½ teaspoon salt	1 egg beaten, with 1 tablespoon water

Sprinkle yeast over the water, stirring with a fork until dissolved. Set aside. In a large mixing bowl, combine the warm milk, sugar, salt, and butter. Blend well with a rubber spatula. Stir in the beaten eggs, grated rind, and juice. Beat in 2 cups of flour until the mixture is smooth. Add the yeast mixture. Gradually add sufficient flour to make a soft dough. Turn out on a lightly floured board. Knead until smooth and satiny, about 10 minutes. Place in a warm, greased bowl, turning to coat the top. Cover loosely with plastic wrap and towel (refer to Techniques, page 12). Set in a protected spot to double in bulk, about 1 to 1½ hours.

Punch the dough down and turn out on a floured board. Knead lightly, cover, and let rest 10 minutes. Divide dough in half. Roll each portion into a strip 30″ long. Place one strip vertically and the other horizontally, crossing in the middle. Lift the top end of the vertical length down to the left side of its bottom end. Then, lift the left end of the horizontal length up and over the 2 lower strips. Repeat this with

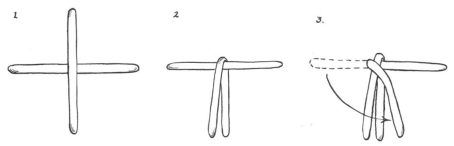

the right end of the same strip. Alternate with the top left and right strips until dough is used. Pinch ends together. Place twist on a greased baking sheet. Cover and allow to rise half doubled in size, about 45 minutes. Brush twist with the egg wash. Bake in a preheated 325° oven 10 minutes. Increase heat to 350° and bake 35 minutes longer. Remove to a wire rack.

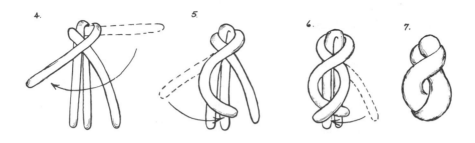

TRIPLE ORANGE LOAVES

Orange juice, rind, and candied peel are used to make this a triple flavored bread. It is amazingly delicious toasted and served with orange marmalade adding a fourth orange flavor! Made with grapefruit,* this bread has a piquant, haunting taste.

2 packages dry or compressed yeast	6 tablespoons melted butter or margarine
⅓ cup warm water	Grated rind 2 large oranges
2 cups warm orange juice	1 cup ground candied orange peel
½ cup sugar	1 teaspoon salt
6 to 7 cups flour	2 eggs, lightly beaten

The Sponge: In a mixing bowl, sprinkle yeast over the warm water, stirring with a fork until dissolved. Add the orange juice, sugar, and 2 cups of flour. Beat mixture with a rubber spatula until smooth. Cover with a towel and let double in bulk, about 45 minutes.

Meanwhile prepare the grated rind and candied orange peel. When the sponge is bubbling, stir in the butter, grated rind, ground orange peel, salt, and eggs. Gradually add enough of the remaining flour to make a soft dough. Turn out on a lightly floured board and knead until smooth and elastic, about 10 minutes. Place dough in a warm, greased bowl, turning to coat the top. Cover loosely with plastic wrap and a towel. Allow to double in bulk, about 1½ hours. Punch the dough down and turn out on a floured board. Knead lightly. Cover and let rest 10 minutes. Shape into 3 loaves (refer to Techniques, page 13). Place in greased 8½x4½x2½″ loaf pans. Cover and allow to rise until just curved over tops of pans. Bake in a preheated 350° oven about 50 minutes. Cool on wire racks.

*GRAPEFRUIT LOAVES

Substitute grapefruit juice for the orange juice. It is difficult to grate the skin of grapefruit; with a potato peeler cut off the skin of one grapefruit and chop very finely. Use the chopped grapefruit rind in place of the oranges. Candied grapefruit is difficult to find. Either make your own or use the candied orange peel as in the original recipe. Proceed as directed for the Orange Loaves.

HERB BREAD

Here is one of the most tantalizing, aromatic breads with several variations. Have this bread baking at the time friends walk in for a party — they will be devoted to you forever.

2 packages dry or compressed yeast	1½ teaspoons oregano
2½ cups warm water	1 teaspoon thyme
2 teaspoons powdered chicken stock	Optional herbs: marjoram,
½ cup hot water	savory, rosemary
3 tablespoons sugar	½ teaspoon salt
½ cup melted butter or margarine	8 to 9 cups flour
1½ teaspoons basil	

Combine yeast and the 2½ cups warm water in a large mixing bowl. Stir with a fork until dissolved (refer to Ingredients, page 7). In a small bowl, blend the powdered chicken stock and ½ cup hot water. Blend the sugar, dissolved chicken stock, and butter into the yeast mixture. Beat in 3 cups of flour until smooth. Stir in the basil, oregano, thyme, and salt. (You may use any combination of herbs desired.) Gradually add sufficient flour to make a soft, workable dough. Turn out on a floured surface and knead until smooth and satiny, about 10 minutes. Round in a ball and place in a warm, greased bowl. Cover loosely with plastic wrap and a towel. Set aside in a warm, protected spot to double in bulk, about 1 hour.

Punch the dough down. Turn out on a lightly floured surface and knead 2 or 3 minutes. Cover and let rest 10 minutes. Shape in 3 loaves and place in greased 8½x4½x2½" loaf pans. Cover and let rise to tops of pans, about 40 minutes. Bake in a preheated 350° oven 40 minutes. Remove and cool on wire racks.

VARIATIONS

The recipe will make 16 miniature loaves, 2x2x4''. Shape loaves, place in greased pans, cover, and allow to rise 30 minutes. Bake in preheated 350° oven 20 to 25 minutes, or until golden brown. For ease of handling, place loaf pans on a baking sheet. Serve as individual loaves on small bread boards. Another variation is to chill loaves thoroughly, preferably 24 hours. Cut in thin slices and toast in a preheated 300° oven about 45 minutes or until crisp. Serve with cocktails or a soup.

CHEESE HERB BREAD

Grate 2 cups of sharp cheddar cheese. Add to the bread dough when stirring in the herbs. Another delicious addition is 2 teaspoons of caraway seeds. Proceed as directed.

ANADAMA BREAD

There are several delightful stories involved with the origin of this bread; here is my favorite. A pioneer lady named Anna went to the local village for supplies, leaving her husband to mind the house and her rising dough. The husband was most unhappy and to spite her, he flung the cornmeal into the dough, yelling, "Anna, damn her, she went off and left me with this dough." Amazingly, the bread was most tasteful and so was called Anadama!

2 cups boiling water
1 cup cornmeal
¾ cup dry skim milk
2 teaspoons salt
⅓ cup butter or margarine

½ cup molasses
2 packages dry or compressed
  yeast
½ cup warm water
6 to 7 cups flour*

Measure the boiling water into a large mixing bowl. Slowly stir in the cornmeal, blending until well mixed and free of lumps. Add the dry milk, salt, butter, and molasses. Mix well and set aside to cool.

In a small bowl, sprinkle yeast over the warm water. Stir with a fork until dissolved. Add yeast mixture to the cooled cornmeal mixture. Beat in 3 cups of flour until smooth. Gradually stir in sufficient flour to make soft, workable dough. Turn out on a floured surface; knead until smooth and elastic, about 10 minutes. Place in a warm, greased bowl, turning to coat the top. Cover loosely with plastic wrap and towel. Set aside in a warm spot to double in bulk, about 2 hours. Punch down the dough, turn out on a floured surface and knead lightly. Cover and and let rest 10 minutes. Shape in 3 loaves (refer to Techniques, page 13). Place in greased 8½x4½x2½″ loaf pans. Cover and let curve over tops of pans, about 1 hour. Bake in a preheated 350° oven 35 minutes. Remove loaves and cool on wire racks.

*VARIATION

Substitute 2 cups stone ground whole wheat flour for 2 cups of white flour. Proceed as directed.

ELSIE'S CHEESE BREAD

An excellent multi-purpose bread, easily made, and a beautiful dough to handle. The bread is enjoyable for sandwiches and delicious toasted for poached eggs.

2 packages dry or compressed yeast
½ cup warm water
1¾ cups warm milk
3 tablespoons sugar
2 teaspoons salt

2 tablespoons melted butter
or margarine
2½ cups grated American or
Cheddar cheese
6 to 7 cups flour

Sprinkle yeast over the warm water, stirring with a fork until dissolved (refer to Ingredients, page 7). In a large mixing bowl, combine the milk, sugar, salt, and melted butter. Blend well. Add the yeast and grated cheese. Beat in 2 cups of flour until mixture is smooth. Gradually add sufficient flour to make a soft, workable dough that pulls away from sides of the bowl. Turn out on a lightly floured board. Knead until smooth and satiny, about 10 minutes. You will find this a lovely dough to manipulate — very responsive. Place dough in a warm, greased bowl, turning to coat the top. Cover loosely with plastic wrap and a towel. Allow to rise until doubled, about 2 hours.

Punch down and let rise again, about 1 hour. Turn out on a floured surface, knead lightly, cover, and let rest 10 to 15 minutes. Shape in 2 loaves and place in 9x5x3″ greased loaf pans or divide in 3 portions for 8½x4½x2½″ pans. Cover, and let rise until just curved over tops of pans, about 1 hour. Bake in a preheated 375° oven 40 minutes for larger loaves and 35 for smaller ones. Remove from pans and cool on wire racks.

MINIATURE LOAVES

The recipe will make 14 to 16 small loaves, 2x2x4″. Grease pans, fill each half full of dough, cover, and let rise to tops of pans, about 30 minutes. Bake in preheated 375° oven 25 minutes. Serve as individual loaves or slice and toast for cocktails and soups.

ADOBE BREAD — A TRIBUTE TO THE SUN

It is interesting that one of the most popular Indian breads is similar to French. As with Indian Fry Bread, the origin may have come from the Jesuit Priests. Adobe ovens are free standing and conical shape so that with this construction a marvelous crust is created. One form of the bread symbolizes the sun and its streaming rays.

2 packages dry or compressed yeast *2 teaspoons salt*
2 cups warm water *6 cups flour, approximately*
3 tablespoons melted shortening

Sprinkle yeast over the warm water in a mixing bowl. Stir with a fork until dissolved. Blend in the shortening and salt. Beat in 3 cups of flour until the batter is smooth. Gradually stir in enough more flour to make a soft dough that pulls away from sides of the bowl. Knead lightly in the bowl. Transfer dough to a warm, greased bowl, turning to coat the top. Cover loosely with plastic wrap and a towel. Allow to rise until doubled in bulk, about 1½ hours. Punch down. Turn out on a floured board and knead 4 or 5 minutes, adding more flour if necessary to cut stickiness. Cover and let rest 10 minutes.

METHODS OF MOLDING

1. Divide dough in half. Prepare 2 round loaves as described under French Bread, page 67. Place on a greased baking sheet. Cover and let rise 15 minutes. Bake in a hot 400° oven 45 minutes. Cool on a wire rack.

2. Sun Shape: Roll half the dough in a circle 9″ in diameter. Fold ½ of dough over like an envelope almost to the other edge. Make 6 slashes with kitchen shears two-thirds of the way into the dough from the circular side. Place on a greased baking sheet and spread the fingers apart. Repeat with remaining dough. Cover and let rise until doubled, about 1 hour. Bake in a preheated 350° oven 50 minutes. Cool on a wire rack.

DILLY CASSEROLE

Several years ago, "Dilly Bread" appeared on the American scene capturing the acceptance of many cooks. It is a quick, easy, and tasteful bread. For variety, try caraway seed in place of the dill.

1 package dry or compressed yeast
¼ cup warm water
1 cup creamy cottage cheese,
*   heated to lukewarm*
2 tablespoons sugar
1 tablespoon minced or grated onion

1 tablespoon melted butter
2 teaspoons dill seed
1 teaspoon salt
¼ teaspoon soda
1 egg
2½ cups sifted flour

Sprinkle yeast over the warm water, stirring with a fork until dissolved. In a large mixing bowl, combine the warm cottage cheese, sugar, onion, butter, dill seed, salt, soda, and egg. Mix thoroughly with an electric mixer or rubber spatula. If you have a heavy mixer with a flat beater, this is excellent for any batter bread. Add the yeast mixture to the cottage cheese mixture. Gradually stir in the flour until you have a stiff batter. Beat until smooth. Cover with plastic wrap and towel. Set aside in a warm spot to double in bulk, about 1 hour. Slap the dough down with a rubber spatula and beat thoroughly. Pour into a well greased 2 quart casserole or soufflé dish. Let rise 40 minutes or ¼" from the top. Bake in a preheated 350° oven 50 minutes, or until golden brown. Remove and brush top with melted butter. Loosen with a spatula. Serve while still warm on a round tray.

CORIANDER-HONEY LOAVES

Aromatic loaves redolent of ancient spices have been a favorite of each class. No wonder the European hunted for easier routes to the land of spices. Excellent served with honey-butter, page 251.

2 packages dry or compressed yeast
½ cup warm water
¼ teaspoon ginger
½ teaspoon sugar
2 eggs
¾ cup honey
1½ tablespoons coriander

1 teaspoon cinnamon
½ teaspoon cloves
1½ teaspoons salt
½ cup melted butter
1½ cups warm milk
7 cups flour, approximately

In a small bowl, combine the yeast, water, ginger, and ½ teaspoon sugar. Stir with a fork until dissolved and set aside. In a large mixing bowl, whisk until smooth the eggs, honey, coriander, cinnamon, cloves, and salt. Blend in the yeast mixture, butter, and milk. Beat in 3 cups of flour until smooth. Gradually add flour, small portions at a time, until a soft, workable dough is formed. Be careful in the addition of flour as the dough can easily become dry. Turn out on a lightly floured board and knead until smooth and elastic, about 10 minutes. If dough remains sticky, rub soft butter on hands and continue kneading. Place in a warm, greased bowl, turning to coat the top. Cover loosely with plastic wrap and towel. Allow to double in bulk, about 2 to 2½ hours.

Punch down and turn out on a floured surface. Knead lightly, cover, and let rest 10 minutes. The recipe will make 3 loaf pans, 8½x4½x2½" or round loaves in a 2 quart and 1 quart soufflé bowls. Shape loaves, place in greased pans or bowls, cover and let double, about 1½ hours, or until just curved over tops of pans. Bake in a preheated 300° oven, 45 minutes for small loaves and 55 for the larger bowl. Loosen sides with spatula and carefully turn out on wire racks to cool.

SOUTHERN PECAN BREAD

An unusually fine cinnamon-swirled bread, crunchy with pecans on the inside and encrusted with whole nuts on the outside. An ideal gift as the recipe can be made into nine beautiful small breads.

2 packages dry or compressed yeast
¼ cup warm water
1¼ cups warm milk
½ cup sugar
1½ teaspoons salt
6 cups flour, approximately

• • •

¾ cup melted butter or margarine
½ cup honey
3 eggs, slightly beaten

1 cup golden raisins, scalded
  and dried
¾ cup finely chopped pecans
Melted butter or margarine
1 cup sugar
1 tablespoon cinnamon
Whole pecans
1 egg beaten with 1 teaspoon
  water

The Sponge: Sprinkle yeast over the warm water; stir with a fork until dissolved. In a large mixing bowl, combine the warm milk, ½ cup of sugar, salt, yeast mixture, and 3 cups of flour. Beat until smooth. Cover and let double in bulk, about 45 minutes.

Stir down the sponge. Add the melted butter, honey, eggs, and blend well. Stir in the raisins and chopped pecans. Gradually add sufficient flour to make a soft, workable dough that leaves sides of the bowl. Turn out and knead on a lightly floured board until smooth and satiny, about 10 minutes. Place dough in a warm, greased bowl, turning to coat the top. Cover loosely with plastic wrap and a towel (refer to Techniques, page 12). Let double in bulk, about 1½ hours.

Turn dough out on a floured board, knead lightly, cover and let rest 10 minutes. Divide in 3 portions. Roll one piece into a rectangle, 8x14". Brush with melted butter leaving ½" free edge. Combine the 1 cup of sugar and cinnamon. Sprinkle 1/3 over the rectangle. Roll up jelly roll style from the short end. Pinch the side and ends to seal. Repeat with remaining dough. Grease 3 loaf pans, 8½x4½x2½". Arrange 8 Whole pecans in bottom of each pan. Place prepared swirls seam side down in the pans. Cover and let rise until doubled or just curved over tops of pans, about 45 minutes. Dip whole pecans in the beaten egg and water; make a pattern on top of each loaf. Use any number of pecans you wish but press them firmly into the dough. Bake in a preheated 350° oven 45 to 50 minutes. Turn loaves out on wire racks to cool.

SMALL LOAVES

The recipe will make 9 smaller loaves, 6x3x2". Divide dough into 9 portions. Roll each into a rectangle, 6x7". Brush with melted butter and sprinkle with the cinnamon-sugar. Roll jelly roll style from short ends. Pinch side and ends to seal. Decorate greased pans with pecans. Place swirls in prepared pans and proceed as directed. Reduce baking time 35 to 40 minutes.

MONKEY BREAD

I have not been able to determine where this bread obtained its name. But it is fun to make and eat as the process always brings smiles and conversation.

	⅓ cup sugar
2 packages dry or compressed yeast	*1 teaspoon salt*
¼ cup warm water	*3 eggs, lightly beaten*
1 cup warm milk	*6 to 7 cups flour*
½ cup melted butter or margarine	*Melted butter or margarine*

Sprinkle yeast over the warm water; stir with a fork until dissolved. In a large mixing bowl, blend in the warm milk, butter, sugar, salt, and eggs. Add the yeast mixture. Beat in 3 cups of flour until mixture is smooth. Gradually add sufficient flour to make a soft, workable dough. Turn out on a floured surface and knead until smooth and elastic, about 10 minutes. Round into a ball, place in a warm, greased bowl, turning to coat the top. Cover loosely with plastic wrap and towel. Allow to double in a protected spot, about 1½ hours (refer to Techniques, page 12).

Punch the dough down. Turn out on a lightly floured board and knead lightly. Cover and let rest 10 to 15 minutes. Divide dough in 2 portions. Roll each half in a rectangle 10x14″. With a sharp knife or dough scraper, cut dough in diagonals about 3″ in length and 1½″ wide. Dip each piece in melted butter. Place in a greased tube pan or 2 loaf pans, 8½x4½x2½″. The easy way is to cut all the pieces of dough, hold loaf or tube pan on edge, and arrange by alternating one piece with another. Cover and let rise until doubled, about 30 minutes. This is an active dough; watch the rising carefully. Bake in a preheated 375° oven 45 minutes. Remove from oven and cool in pan 10 minutes. Turn out on serving tray or wire racks.

POPPY SEED BRAIDS

A bread that is delicious hot or cooled and exceptionally fine for toasting. A favorite of my daughter-in-law, Margaret, who makes it in miniature pans to use sliced and toasted for soups.

2 packages dry or compressed yeast	½ cup poppy seeds
¼ cup warm water	½ cup chopped pitted prunes
1 cup warm milk	Grated rind 1 lemon
¼ cup melted butter or margarine	6 cups flour, approximately
¼ cup sugar	Confectioner's Icing, page 268
1 teaspoon salt	Chopped nuts (optional)
2 eggs, lightly beaten	

Combine yeast and water in a small bowl. Stir with a fork until dissolved. In a large mixing bowl, blend thoroughly the milk, butter, sugar, salt, and eggs. Beat in 1 cup of flour until smooth. Stir in the yeast mixture, poppy seeds, prunes, and lemon rind. Gradually add sufficient flour to make a soft, workable dough. Turn out on a lightly floured board and knead until smooth, about 5 minutes. Place in a warm, greased bowl, turning to coat the top. Cover loosely with plastic wrap and towel. Set aside in a warm spot to double in bulk, about 2 hours, (refer to Techniques, page 12). Punch down, turn out on a floured surface, and knead lightly. Cover and let rest 10 minutes.

Divide dough in 6 portions. Roll 3 pieces in 18″ ropes. Braid strands together, beginning in the center and working out to each end. Place on a greased baking sheet and tuck ends under. Repeat with remaining 3 portions. Cover and let rise until double, about 1 to 1½ hours. Bake in a preheated 350° oven 40 minutes. Remove to a wire rack. Frost while still warm with Confectioner's Icing and sprinkle with chopped nuts if desired.

MINIATURE LOAVES

The recipe will make 8 to 9 small loaves. Divide dough, place in greased pans, 2x2x4″, cover and let rise to tops of pans. Bake in a preheated 350° oven about 20 to 25 minutes. Cool for 24 hours, slice and toast in a slow oven (300°) until crisp.

ANISE LOAVES

An unusually flavorful bread that may be made into three golden loaves or two handsome braids.

2 packages dry or compressed yeast	Grated rind 1 lemon
¼ cup warm water	2 tablespoons lemon juice
2 cups warm milk	2 tablespoons anise seeds
½ cup melted butter or margarine	6 to 7 cups flour
6 tablespoons sugar	1 egg beaten with 1 tablespoon water
1 teaspoon salt	Untoasted sesame seeds

Sprinkle yeast over the warm water, stirring with a fork until dissolved. In a large mixing bowl, combine milk, butter, sugar, salt, grated rind, lemon juice, and anise. Stir until well blended. Add the yeast mixture. Beat in 3 cups of flour until smooth. Gradually add enough more flour until the dough leaves sides of the bowl. Turn out on a lightly floured board and knead until smooth and elastic, about 10 to 12 minutes. Place dough in a warm, greased bowl, turning to coat the top. Cover loosely with plastic wrap and a towel. Set in a warm spot until doubled in bulk, about 1½ hours.

Turn out on a floured surface and knead lightly. Cover and let rest 10 to 15 minutes. Divide into 3 portions, mold into loaves and place in greased 8½x4½x2½″ loaf pans. Cover, and allow to double in bulk, about 45 minutes. Bake in a preheated 350° oven 35 to 40 minutes. Cool on wire racks.

BRAIDED LOAVES

Divide dough in 2 portions. Cut each portion in 3 equal pieces. Roll each piece into 18″ lengths. Braid 3 ropes together beginning at the center and working out to the ends. Place braids on greased baking sheets. Cover and allow to almost double, about 45 minutes. Brush with the egg wash. Sprinkle braids with sesame seeds. Bake in a preheated 350° oven 40 minutes or until golden brown. Cool on wire racks.

HONEY ALMOND BRAID

A fascinating bread to make that is full of the flavor of honey. Do not be concerned if any of the filling leaks out — doesn't seem to bother the flavor or appearance.

2 packages dry or compressed yeast
¼ cup warm water
1 cup warm milk
1½ teaspoons salt
1 teaspoon cardamom
½ cup sugar
⅔ cup melted butter or margarine
2 eggs, lightly beaten
Grated rind 1 large orange
6 cups flour, approximately

Filling:
1¼ cups ground almonds
1 cup honey
½ cup soft butter or margarine

Glaze:
2 tablespoons sugar
¼ cup honey
1 tablespoon butter

Sprinkle yeast over the warm water, stirring with a fork until dissolved. Set aside. In a large mixing bowl, combine milk, salt, cardamom, sugar and butter. Blend until ingredients are dissolved. Add eggs and grated rind. Add the yeast mixture. Beat in 2 cups of flour until the batter is smooth. Gradually add sufficient flour to make a soft, workable dough (refer to Techniques, page 10). Turn out on a lightly floured surface and knead until smooth and satiny, about 5 to 8 minutes. Place in a warm, greased bowl, turning to coat the top. Set in a protected area until doubled in bulk, about 1½ hours. Punch down, turn out on a floured surface, knead lightly, cover and let rest 10 minutes.

Combine ingredients for the filling and mix well. Divide dough in half; set aside one portion and cover. Cut the other half in 3 pieces. Roll each part in a 5x16″ rectangle. With a rubber spatula, spread 1/6 of the filling on each rectangle to within ½″ of edges. Roll each rectangle jelly roll style from the long side. Pinch side and ends to seal. Braid the 3 rolls together, beginning in the center and working out to each end.

Place on a greased baking sheet and tuck ends under. Repeat with remaining dough. Cover braids and let rise 30 minutes. Bake in a preheated 350° oven 30 minutes. Remove to a wire rack.

GLAZE

Combine the sugar, honey, and butter in a small saucepan. Bring to a boil, stirring constantly. Brush on the warm braids.

PRUNE LOAVES

Reminiscent of the old fashioned "light" bread, this is a simple recipe with a delicious addition of moist prunes. Makes 3 loaves.

2 packages dry or compressed yeast	*¼ cup sugar*
½ cup warm water	*1½ teaspoons salt*
1½ cups warm milk	*1½ cups pitted diced prunes*
¼ cup melted butter or margarine	*6 to 7 cups flour*

Sprinkle yeast over the warm water; stir with a fork until dissolved. In a large mixing bowl, combine the milk, butter, sugar, and salt. Add the yeast mixture and 2 cups of flour. Beat thoroughly until smooth. Stir in the diced prunes and enough more flour to make a soft, workable dough. Turn out on a lightly floured board and knead until smooth and elastic, about 8 minutes. Place dough in a warm, greased bowl, turning to coat the top. Cover loosely with plastic wrap and a towel. Allow to double in a protected spot, about 2 hours. Punch down and turn out on a lightly floured surface. Knead lightly, cover, and let rest 10 minutes. Shape in 3 loaves and place in greased 8½x4½x2½" loaf pans. Cover and let rise until just curved over tops of pans, about 1 hour. Bake in a preheated 375° oven 40 to 45 minutes. Cool on wire racks.

LEMON-NUT PULL APART BREAD

Two pretty loaves similar to monkey bread that are festive and flavorful, interesting to form, and fun to eat.

2 packages dry or compressed yeast
1 cup warm water
¾ cup dry skim milk
½ cup sugar
¼ cup melted butter or margarine
1 teaspoon salt
Grated rind 1 lemon

2 eggs, lightly beaten
4 to 5 cups flour

Filling:
1 cup sugar
3 tablespoons lemon juice
½ cup chopped pecans

In a large mixing bowl, sprinkle yeast over the warm water stirring with a fork until dissolved. Blend in the dry milk, sugar, butter, salt, grated rind, and eggs; mix thoroughly. Beat in 2 cups of flour until smooth. Gradually add sufficient flour to make a soft, workable dough. Turn out on a lightly floured surface and knead until smooth and elastic, about 10 minutes. Place in a warm, greased bowl, turning to coat the top. Cover loosely with plastic wrap and towel. Set aside in a warm spot to double in bulk, about 1½ hours.

Punch the dough down, turn out on a floured board and knead lightly. Cover and let rest 10 to 15 minutes. (Refer to Techniques, page 13). In a small bowl, combine the filling: sugar, lemon juice, and nuts. Mix thoroughly. Brush 2 loaf pans (8½x4½x2½″) with melted butter.

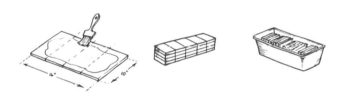

Divide dough in half. Roll one portion in a rectangle, 10x16″. Brush half the lemon mixture over the rectangle. Cut in 4x10″ rectangles. Stack on top of each other. Slice in 5 stacks 2″ wide and 4″ long. Place stacks in a row in prepared pan, cut side down. Follow these measurements, allow dough to completely relax, and the stacks will fit into the pan. Repeat directions with remaining dough. Sprinkle top of loaves with the following topping:

Combine in a small bowl 3 tablespoons flour, 3 tablespoons sugar, 2 tablespoons soft butter, and 1 teaspoon grated rind. Mix with a fork or your fingers until mixture is crumbly. Sprinkle over tops of loaves.

Cover and let dough rise 30 minutes. Bake in a 350° oven 35 to 40 minutes or until golden brown. Place pans on wire racks for 10 minutes. Remove loaves and allow to cool.

DOVE OF PEACE

A lovely, symbolic bird my cooking companion has given her own special creativeness. The dough is delightful to handle. Read the directions carefully and you can produce this handsome masterpiece.

1 package dry or compressed yeast	3 egg yolks
¼ cup warm water	½ cup warm milk
½ cup soft butter or margarine	5 to 6 cups flour
½ cup sugar	2 ounces almond paste
3 tablespoons grated orange peel	1½ egg whites
1½ teaspoons almond flavoring	Sliced and whole almonds
3 tablespoons brandy	1 egg white beaten with 1
½ teaspoon salt	tablespoon water
3 eggs	Granulated sugar

Combine yeast and water, stir with a fork until dissolved, and set aside. In the large bowl of an electric mixer, cream butter, sugar, orange peel, almond flavoring, brandy, and salt until mixture is fluffy. Beat in the eggs and egg yolks one at a time. (Cover egg whites and reserve.) With a rubber spatula, blend in the milk and yeast mixture. Beat in 2 cups of flour until batter is smooth. Add sufficient flour to make a soft, workable dough. Turn dough out on a floured board. Knead until smooth and elastic, about 10 minutes. If you have a heavy mixer, all the mixing and kneading may be done with the flat beater first and then change to the dough hook. Place dough in a warm, greased bowl, turning to coat the top. Cover loosely with plastic wrap and a towel. Let double in bulk, about 1½ hours.

Beat the almond paste in small bowl of an electric mixer with 1½ egg whites until of spreading consistency. Add more egg white, if needed. Set aside.

Turn dough out on a floured board, knead lightly, divide in half, and shape each portion in a smooth ball. Cover and let rest 10 minutes. Flatten one ball of dough with your hands and roll into an oval 11″ long and 6″ wide. If dough draws back, cover and allow to rest 5 more minutes. Place oval of dough on a greased baking sheet across the narrow dimension. Roll the remaining dough to make a triangle 14″ long and 6″ wide at one end. Lay the triangle across the oval. Twist the narrow end to make the head; pinch a tip to form her beak. Now twist the wide end over to form the tail. Pull the tail into a fan shape and cut gashes about two inches long to simulate feathers. To avoid portions of the bird browning too fast, place pieces of foil undeneath the tail and head.

With a rubber spatula, brush almond paste mixture on the tail and a 1″ border around edges of wings. Beat remaining egg white and water until frothy; brush over entire bird. Press whole almonds into almond paste border on the wings. Sprinkle the rest of wings heavily with sliced almonds. Dust wings with granulated sugar. Allow to rise 25 minutes, uncovered. Bake in a preheated 325° oven 45 minutes. Remove bird and cool on a wire rack.

NOTE

If desired, two small birds may be formed. Follow directions as described but reduce baking time to 35 minutes.

LOBSTER BISQUE

There is no greater way to begin a meal than by serving a creamy Lobster Bisque. Lobster tails are a bit more plentiful — so splurge and try this soup. Serves 6 to 8.

¼ cup butter or margarine
¼ cup celery, finely chopped
¼ cup carrots, finely chopped
½ cup onion, finely chopped
2 cloves garlic, minced
1 bay leaf
½ teaspoon thyme
2 pounds lobster tails in the shell

¼ cup brandy
5 cups fish stock, page 6
½ cup dry white wine
3 tablespoons butter or
    margarine
3 tablespoons flour
1 cup heavy cream
Salt

Melt the ¼ cup of butter in a deep skillet. Sauté the celery, carrots, onion, and garlic with the bay leaf and thyme. Cook 10 to 15 minutes, stirring occasionally, until vegetables are tender, but do not allow to discolor. Add the lobster tails. Sauté 10 more minutes, stirring constantly. Flame with the brandy. (Warm brandy in a small container, pour a tiny portion over lobster mixture, set fire to brandy in container and pour over ingredients, shaking skillet to keep flame going as long as possible.) Add the fish stock and wine. Bring to a simmer and cook 20 minutes. Remove the lobster. Take lobster out of the shell, dice, cover, and reserve. Discard the shells.

Whirl soup through a blender. In a clean sauce pan, melt the 3 tablespoons of butter. Whisk in the flour until smooth. Add blended soup all at once, stirring vigorously. Bring to a simmer and cook 10 minutes. Slowly add the heavy cream. Taste for salt and adjust. Add the diced lobster; heat thoroughly but do not allow to boil. Serve in warm soup bowls.

CREAM OF SPINACH SOUP

A smooth, tasteful soup, delicate in color that will please the most discriminating of guests. Serves 6 to 8.

¼ cup butter
¾ cup chopped onion
2 boxes frozen spinach
    (10 ounce size)
½ teaspoon salt
¼ teaspoon freshly ground black
    pepper

⅛ teaspoon freshly ground nutmeg
3 tablespoons flour
6 cups boiling chicken broth
2 egg yolks
½ cup heavy cream
Whipped cream
Nutmeg

192

Melt butter in a large saucepan. Sauté the onion until tender but do not allow to brown. Add the frozen spinach. Cover and cook until spinach is wilted. With a wooden spoon, stir in the salt, pepper, nutmeg, and flour until smooth and well blended. Add the chicken stock, stirring constantly. Simmer uncovered about 7 minutes, stirring occasionally until thickened. Whirl soup through a blender and return to a clean saucepan. At this point, the soup may be held several hours or overnight. It may also be frozen and finished later.

Blend egg yolks with the cream. Add a small amount of hot soup to the cream mixture. Slowly add cream mixture to the soup, stirring constantly. Allow soup to heat but not boil. Serve in cream soup bowls garnished with a dollop of whipped cream and a dusting of grated nutmeg.

MEAT BALL SOUP

Children love this soup as well as adults. An excellent choice to serve after a football game with lots of hot home made bread.

6 cups beef broth	1 teaspoon oregano
1¾ cups canned tomatoes	½ cup miniature pasta
¾ cup finely chopped carrot	Meat balls
1¼ cups chopped celery and leaves	Parmesan cheese

Combine the broth, tomatoes, carrot, celery, and oregano in a small soup kettle. Bring to a boil, lower heat, and simmer covered 15 minutes. Add the pasta and simmer until almost tender, about 10 to 15 minutes. In the meantime prepare the meat balls.

Meat balls:

2 slices stale homemade bread	1 tablespoon finely chopped
1 pound lean, ground beef	parsley
1 egg	1 tablespoon oil
1 clove garlic, minced	2 tablespoons butter
1 teaspoon salt	

Soak bread in water to cover. Squeeze water out and add bread to the ground beef. Stir in the egg, garlic, salt, and parsley. Mix thoroughly. Form in tiny balls, 1 teaspoon meat mixture for each ball. Melt oil and butter in a skillet. Sauté the meat balls until lightly brown. Drain on paper toweling. When the pasta is done, add the meat balls to the soup, and simmer about 5 minutes. Serve in large, warm soup bowls. Pass parmesan cheese and hot Italian bread as an accompaniment.

MARY'S SOUP STEW

When there is the first nip of winter in the air, I go immediately to purchase all the ingredients for this wholesome, steaming stew. A soup I have served my family for many years and have found a welcome gift when friends are ill.

4 pounds cubed stewing beef
4 or 5 marrow bones cut in 3″ pieces
3½ quarts water
1 teaspoon thyme
1 large bay leaf
3 sprigs fresh parsley
1 large onion, sliced

• • •

1 box mixed frozen vegetables
   (10 oz. size)

1 box frozen succotash
2 medium size onions, sliced
1 cup coarsely chopped celery
1 cup diced yellow squash or
   zucchini
1 cup chopped fresh or frozen
   cut asparagus
½ cup barley
Grindings of black pepper
Salt

Combine the cubed meat, marrow bones, and water in a large soup pot. Bring to a boil and skim. Add thyme, bay leaf, parsley, and sliced onion. Return to a boil, skim, lower heat, and simmer partially covered 3 hours. Allow soup to cool and skim off fat. (To cool quickly, set soup kettle in a sink filled with ice and water.) Remove bones and extract marrow. Discard bones and return marrow back to the soup. Add remaining vegetables down to the barley. Bring to a boil. Add barley with a few grindings of black pepper. Lower heat to simmer, taste, and adjust for salt. Allow soup to bubble lightly for 1 hour uncovered. Serve in large, warm soup bowls with hot bread. Serves 12.

VARIATION
On the second or third day, if there should be half the soup left, add 1 box of frozen cut okra and a Number 2 can of tomatoes. Recheck for seasoning.

FRESH CORN CHOWDER

My teaching companion, Sue, constructed this soup for a class session. It is everything you could want a creamy, fresh tasting, and hearty chowder to be. Serves 6.

3 cups fresh corn, about 4 ears
3 tablespoons butter
¼ cup sliced celery
¼ cup diced green pepper
½ cup chopped onion
1 medium potato, peeled and diced
1 bay leaf
1 pinch sage

Dash Cayenne pepper
Salt
Grindings of black pepper
2 cups hot water
1 cup heavy cream
1 cup milk
Minced parsley
Diced, crisp bacon

Cut the corn off the cobs with a sharp knife. Scrape cobs to remove remainder of corn. Purée 1 cup of the corn until smooth. Set aside. Melt butter in a 3 or 4 quart sauce pan. Saute celery, green pepper, and onion until soft but not brown. Add diced potatoes, bay leaf, sage, Cayenne, salt, pepper, and 2 cups of hot water. Cover and cook over moderate heat until potatoes are just tender. Add the pureed corn and remaining corn kernels, the cream, and milk. Stir and cook over medium heat about 10 minutes or until piping hot. Serve in warm soup bowls, sprinkled with either parsley or bacon.

INTERNATIONAL
BREADS

SOUPS:

Mexican Chicken — Caldo Tlalpeno
Belgian Endive
Bulgarian Curried
Greek Lemon
Italian Minestrone

ARMENIAN EGG BREAD

This is one of the most delightful and versatile breads in my book. A daughter-in-law obtained the recipe from her mother who lives in Beirut. The bread has a beautiful texture, golden in color, and can be molded in many shapes. I have tested and adapted this recipe for a variety of ideas. If you wish to divide the recipe, do not change the first three ingredients.

1 package dry or compressed yeast	1 tablespoon ground Mahleb*
½ cup warm water	1½ cups melted butter
⅔ cup flour	10 eggs, beaten
• • •	11 to 12 cups flour
1½ cups warm milk	1 egg beaten with 1 tablespoon
1½ cups sugar	water
1 teaspoon salt	Sliced almond or pine nuts

In a small mixing bowl, combine yeast and water, stirring until dissolved. Add the ⅔ cup of flour and beat until smooth. Cover with a towel and set aside until doubled and bubbling, about 45 minutes.

In a large mixing bowl, blend milk, sugar, salt, and mahleb. Stir in butter and eggs. Beat in yeast mixture and 4 cups of flour until smooth. Gradually add enough flour to make a soft, workable dough. Turn out on a floured board and knead until satiny and elastic, about 8 minutes. This is a large quantity of dough, but you will find it handles easily because of the lush richness. Place dough in a large, warm greased bowl. Cover loosely with plastic wrap and towel. Set in a warm, protected spot overnight.

The next morning at your leisure, punch down the dough. Turn out on a floured board and knead about 3 minutes. Cover, and let rest 10 to 15 minutes. It is now ready to shape into rolls, braids, or pan breads.

*If the Mid-Eastern spice, Mahleb is not available in your community, substitute the grated rind of 2 lemons. Refer to page 228.

ROLLS
Cut off pieces of dough about the size of a large egg. Roll and shape into round buns. Place on a greased baking sheet. Cover and let double, about 1 hour. Brush with egg wash. Decorate with sliced almonds, if desired. Be sure to press the nuts gently into the dough. Bake in a preheated 350° oven 15 to 20 minutes or until golden brown. Serve immediately or cool on wire racks.

SINGLE BRAID

Divide ½ the dough in 3 portions. Roll each part in 20″ ropes. Braid, beginning in the center and working toward each end. Pinch the ends together and tuck under. Place on a greased baking sheet. Cover and let rise 1 hour. Brush with egg wash. Decorate with almonds or pine nuts, if desired. Bake in a preheated 350° oven 35 to 40 minutes. Cool on a wire rack.

DOUBLE BRAID

Divide dough in half. Set one piece aside and cover. Cut off ⅔ of one portion of dough. Divide larger portion in 3 pieces. Roll in 16″ strips. Braid strips together, starting from the center and working toward each end. Place on a greased baking sheet. Divide the remaining ⅓ portion in 3 parts. Roll in 14″ strips. Braid as directed. Place the smaller braid on top of the larger. Press down and secure with several toothpicks. Cover, and allow to rise one hour. Brush with egg wash. Bake in a preheated 350° oven 35 to 40 minutes. Remove and cool on a wire rack.

NOTE

Read the recipe for Cholesterol Free Challah, page 236. Through further experimentation I have found the Armenian Bread to be excellent using Egg Beater. Substitute 2 cups of Egg Beater (2 boxes) for the 10 eggs and reduce butter (or margarine) to 1 cup. Proceed as directed. You will be pleased with the resulting bread.

CRUSTY ITALIAN LOAVES

Three loaves that are similar to French Bread but with the addition of oil a slightly different texture is created. The egg topping gives a shiny, golden crust.

3 packages dry or compressed yeast	3 tablespoons light oil
3 cups warm water	8 cups flour, approximately
1 tablespoon salt	1 egg yolk beaten with 1
3 tablespoons sugar	tablespoon milk

199

In a large mixing bowl, combine yeast and warm water, stirring with a fork until dissolved. Add salt, sugar, and oil, mixing until well blended. Beat in 3 cups of flour until mixture is smooth. Stir in sufficient flour to make a soft, workable dough. Turn out on a lightly floured board, knead until smooth and elastic, 10 to 15 minutes. Round in a ball and place in a warm, greased bowl, turning to coat the top. Cover loosely with plastic wrap and towel. Let double in bulk, about 1 hour. Punch down, knead lightly, recover, and let rise again until double, about 45 minutes to 1 hour.

Turn dough out on a lightly floured surface and knead 3 to 5 minutes. Cover and let rest 15 minutes (refer to Techniques, page 13). Divide in 3 portions. Shape in round or long loaves as described in French Bread. Place loaves on greased baking sheets. Cover and allow to rise 30 minutes. Make 3 long diagonal slashes in each loaf. Brush carefully with egg wash. Bake in a preheated 375° oven 15 minutes. Lower heat to 325° and bake 30 minutes longer. Remove loaves and cool on wire racks.

NOTE
If preferred, brush loaves with an egg white glaze for a harder, crisper crust; 1 egg white beaten with 1 tablespoon water.

CUBAN BREAD

In the charming old section of Tampa, Florida, called Yboe City, there are several delightful Spanish restaurants. Each has its own specialties but they all serve Spanish bean soup and Cuban bread. A simple bread very similar to French but started in a cold oven.

1 package dry or compressed yeast	1 tablespoon salt
2 cups warm water	6 to 7 cups flour
1 tablespoon sugar	Cornmeal

Combine yeast and warm water in a large mixing bowl. Stir with a fork until dissolved. Blend in the sugar and salt. Beat in 3 cups of flour until batter is smooth. Add enough more flour gradually to make a soft, workable dough. Turn out on a lightly floured surface and knead until smooth and elastic, about 10 minutes. Add small portions of flour if necessary to cut stickiness. Place in a warm, greased bowl, turning to coat the top (refer to Techniques, page 12). Set aside in a protected spot to double in bulk, about 1½ hours. Turn out on a floured surface, knead lightly, cover, and let rest 10 minutes.

Divide dough in half. Shape in 2 long loaves as suggested in French Bread, page 67. If desired, you can divide in 4 portions and form smaller loaves. Sprinkle a greased baking sheet lightly with cornmeal. Place loaves on prepared pan. Cover and let rise until almost doubled, about 45 minutes to 1 hour. Slash diagonally with a razor 3 times and brush with cold water. Place loaves in a *COLD* oven. Set temperature at 400° and bake 45 minutes. Bake smaller loaves 35 to 40 minutes. If a harder crust is desired, brush loaves with cold water twice during the baking process. Remove loaves and cool on wire racks.

GREEK MINT BREAD

A most unusually flavored bread made with intriguing ingredients. It is especially good used as an hors d'oeuvre or served as an accompaniment for soups. The recipe doubles easily.

1 cup warm water	*3 tablespoons crushed dried*
1 package dry or compressed yeast	*mint leaves*
⅓ cup oil	*½ cup black pitted olives,*
½ teaspoon salt	*chopped*
3 to 3½ cups flour	
4 tablespoons finely chopped onion	

In a mixing bowl, combine water and yeast, stirring with a fork until dissolved. Blend in the oil and salt. With a rubber spatula, gradually beat in sufficient flour to make a soft dough that pulls away from sides of bowl. Beat about 1 minute. Cover with a towel, set aside in a warm spot and let rise until doubled, about 1 hour.

Punch the dough down and turn out on a lightly floured surface. Pat the dough out and place the onion, mint, and olives on top. Knead until ingredients are well distributed. This is quite messy: add about ½ cup more flour if necessary. Cover and let rest 10 minutes. Grease an 8x12" baking pan. Spread the dough over bottom of pan evenly. Brush with a small amount of oil on top of dough. Cover and let rise until doubled, about 1 to 1½ hours. Bake in a preheated 400° oven 35 minutes. Cut in small squares and serve while warm.

VARIATION

The bread is excellent baked in miniature bread pans. Fill greased pans half full. Cover and let rise to tops of pans, about 1 hour. Bake in 400° oven 25 minutes. Let cool thoroughly. Slice and toast until crisp in a slow 300° oven about 45 minutes.

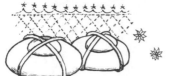

PORTUGUESE SWEET BREAD

A delightful sweet bread to use with coffee, a morning brunch, or on Easter Sunday decorated with an egg.

2 packages dry or compressed yeast	¼ cup melted butter
¼ cup warm water	4 eggs, lightly beaten
1½ cups warm milk	9 to 10 cups flour
1¼ cups sugar	1 egg beaten with 1 tablespoon
1½ teaspoons salt	water
	1 uncooked egg

Sprinkle yeast over warm water; stir with a fork until dissolved. Set aside. In a large mixing bowl, combine milk, sugar, salt, butter, and eggs. Blend thoroughly. Add the yeast mixture. Beat in 3 cups of flour until smooth. Gradually add sufficient flour to make a soft, workable dough that pulls away from sides of bowl. Knead thoroughly on a lightly floured board, adding only enough flour to cut stickiness, about 10 to 12 minutes. Place in a large, warm, bowl; cover with plastic wrap and a towel. Set aside in a protected spot to double in bulk, about 2½ hours. Doughs rich with eggs always take longer to rise (refer to Ingredients, page 9).

Turn the dough out on a floured board and knead lightly. Cover, and let rest 10 to 15 minutes. Shape in 2 round loaves and place in greased 10″ cake tins. Cover, and let rise until doubled, about 1 hour. Slash a cross in center with a razor. Brush with egg wash. Bake in a preheated 350° oven 40 to 45 minutes. Cool on wire racks.

EASTER BREAD

Cut off a small portion of dough. Divide remainder in 2 round loaves. Press an uncooked egg in center of each loaf. Cut small portion of dough in 4 pieces, roll in long strips and make a cross over each egg, tucking strips underneath the loaf. Proceed as directed.

IRISH BARMBRACK

A lovely, spicy bread full of raisins or currants that people in the British Isles love so much. It is a bread that keeps well and is usable for many occasions.

3 packages dry or compressed
   yeast
½ cup warm water
½ cup sugar
1½ teaspoons salt
1 teaspoon allspice
½ teaspoon cinnamon
Grated rind 1 lemon
1 cup warm milk

2 eggs, lightly beaten
¼ cup melted butter or margarine
1 cup raisins or currants
   rinsed in hot water and dried
½ cup chopped candied orange
   peel
5 to 6 cups flour
Confectioner's Icing, page 268

Sprinkle yeast over the warm water, stir with a fork until dissolved and set aside (refer to Ingredients, page 7). In a small bowl, combine sugar, salt, allspice, cinnamon, and grated rind. In a large mixing bowl, blend the milk, eggs, and butter. Add the sugar-spice mixture and stir until dissolved. Beat in the yeast mixture and 2 cups of flour until smooth. Add sufficient flour to make a soft, workable dough that pulls away from sides of the bowl. Turn out on a lightly floured board and knead until smooth, about 10 minutes. Place in a warm, greased bowl; cover with plastic wrap and towel. Allow to double in a protected area, about 1½ hours.

Combine raisins and orange peel. Sprinkle a tiny portion of flour over fruit and mix well. Turn dough out on a lightly floured board. Knead in the fruits until well distributed. Cover and let rest 10 minutes. Divide in 2 portions. Round into loaves and place on greased baking sheet. Cover and let double, about 1 hour. Bake in a preheated 350° oven 35 to 40 minutes. Cool on wire racks. Frost with Confectioner's Icing if desired.

ENGLISH CURRANT BREAD

A wedding in our family took us to Oxford, England. The English love of sweets and currants invaded the wedding cake, which turned out to be similar to a dark fruit cake full of currants, iced with marzipan topped with fluffy, white frosting. And the maitre d' would not allow it to be cut until the "proper time, madam".

2 packages dry or compressed yeast
½ cup warm water
1 cup warm milk
¼ cup melted butter or margarine
½ cup sugar
2 eggs, lightly beaten

1 teaspoon vanilla extract
5 cups flour, approximately
2 cups currants, rinsed in hot
   water and dried
Confectioner's Icing, page 268

Sprinkle yeast over the warm water, stirring with a fork until dissolved. In a mixing bowl, combine the milk, butter, sugar, eggs, and vanilla (refer to Ingredients, page 9). Beat in 2 cups of flour until smooth. Add the currants. Gradually stir in sufficient flour to make a soft, workable dough. Turn out on a floured surface and knead until smooth, about 5 to 8 minutes. Place in a warm, greased bowl, turning to coat the top. Cover loosely with plastic wrap and towel. Set aside in a protected spot until doubled in bulk, about 1½ hours. Turn out, knead lightly, cover, and let rest 10 minutes. Divide dough in half. Shape in loaves and place in 8½x4½x2½" loaf pans. Cover, and let curve over tops of pans, about 30 minutes. Bake in a preheated 350° oven 30 to 35 minutes. Cool on wire racks. Frost with Confectioner's Icing flavored with vanilla extract. If you wish to freeze the bread, do not frost until ready to use.

SWEDISH SAFFRON BRAIDS AND BUNS

Lovely, golden yellow braids and buns that would be handsome for a buffet table or served for a luncheon. The braids may also be sliced and toasted to serve with morning coffee.

¼ teaspoon saffron
1 tablespoon brandy
2 packages dry or compressed
  yeast
2½ cups warm milk
1 cup sugar
1 teaspoon salt
1 egg

1 cup melted butter or margarine
8 cups flour, approximately
¾ cup ground almonds
1 cup raisins, scalded and dried
1 egg beaten with 1 tablespoon
  water
Granulated sugar
Chopped almonds

Combine saffron and brandy in a small bowl; set aside to dissolve. Sprinkle yeast over warm milk in a large mixing bowl. Stir until dissolved. Blend in the sugar, salt, egg, butter, and saffron mixture. Beat in 3 cups of flour until smooth. Add the ground almonds and raisins. Stir in sufficient flour to make a soft dough. Turn out on a lightly floured board. Knead until smooth and satiny, about 8 minutes. Place in a warm, greased bowl, turning to coat the top. Cover loosely with plastic wrap and towel. Let double, about 1½ to 2 hours. Turn out on a floured surface, knead lightly, cover and let rest 10 minutes.

Divide in half. Cut ½ of dough in 3 portions. Roll in ropes 18 to 20" long. Braid ropes, starting from the center and working out to each end. Do not be afraid to pick braid up and turn for your convenience. Place on a greased baking sheet, tuck under the ends, cover, and let rise until doubled, about 1 hour. Brush with egg wash. Sprinkle with sugar and chopped almonds. Bake in a preheated 375° oven 35 to 40 minutes. Cool on wire racks.

With remaining dough, make a second braid or buns. Directions for buns are as follows: cut off pieces of dough the size of a large egg. Cup hand over a portion of dough and rotate quickly until smooth bun is formed. Place on a greased baking sheet. Repeat with remaining pieces of dough. Cover and let rise about 45 minutes to 1 hour. The buns may be left unadorned or brushed with egg wash as directed for braids. Bake in a preheated 375° oven 15 to 20 minutes or until golden brown. Serve while warm.

VIENNA LOAVES

A bread that originated in Vienna, but similar to both French and Italian loaves, has a crispy crust and is usually covered with flavorful sesame seed.

2 packages dry or compressed yeast
1½ cups warm water
1 tablespoon sugar
1 cup warm milk
1½ teaspoons salt
2 tablespoons melted butter
  or margarine

7 cups flour, approximately
1 egg white beaten with 1
  tablespoon water
Untoasted sesame seed

In a large mixing bowl, combine yeast, water, and sugar. Stir with a fork until dissolved. Blend in the milk, salt, and butter. Beat in 3 cups of flour with a rubber spatula until smooth. Gradually add enough more flour to make a soft workable dough. Turn out on a lightly floured board and knead until smooth and elastic, about 12 to 15 minutes (refer to Techniques, page 11). Place in a warm, greased bowl, cover loosely with plastic wrap and towel. Set in a protected spot to double in bulk, about 1 hour. Turn out on a floured surface and knead 4 to 5 minutes. Cover and let rest 10 minutes. Divide dough in 2 portions. Roll and shape each in a 12″ long loaf. Place on a greased baking sheet and taper the ends. Cover and allow to double in size, about 45 minutes. Make a slash down the center with a sharp razor 1″ deep, beginning and ending 1½″ from ends. Brush with egg white glaze and sprinkle liberally with sesame seed. Bake in a preheated 400° oven 40 minutes. Cool on wire racks.

SWISS EGG BRAIDS

Two delightful braids can be made with this easy Swiss Bread, one sweet and the other plain. Both make excellent toast.

2 packages dry or compressed
    yeast
½ cup warm water
1½ cups warm milk
¼ cup sugar
2 teaspoons salt
½ cup melted butter

3 eggs, lightly beaten
8 to 9 cups flour
1 egg beaten with 1 tablespoon
    water
Sesame seed
Poppy seed
Cinnamon-Sugar, page 131

Sprinkle yeast over the warm water, stirring with a fork until dissolved. In a large mixing bowl, combine milk, sugar, salt, and butter. Blend until ingredients are dissolved. Stir in the beaten eggs and yeast mixture. Beat in 3 cups of flour until batter is smooth. Gradually add sufficient flour to make a soft, workable dough (refer to Techniques, page 11). Turn out on a lightly floured board and knead thoroughly, about 10 to 12 minutes. Place dough in a warm, greased bowl; cover loosely with plastic wrap and towel. Set in a protected area until doubled, about 1½ hours. Punch the dough down, knead lightly, cover, and let rest 10 to 15 minutes.

BRAIDS

Divide dough in half. Cut one half in 3 equal portions. Roll in 3 smooth ropes, 18″ long. Braid the 3 strands, beginning from the center and working out to each end. Place on a greased baking sheet and tuck ends under. Repeat with remaining dough. Cover and let double, about 1 hour. Brush with egg wash and sprinkle liberally with sesame or poppy seed. Bake in a preheated 350° oven 35 minutes. Cool on wire racks.

CINNAMON BRAID

Divide dough in half. Cut one portion in 3 equal parts. Roll strands in 16″ lengths. Sprinkle ½ cup of Cinnamon-Sugar over a sheet of waxed paper. Roll each strand of dough in the sugar mixture. Braid the 3 ropes and place on a greased baking sheet. Tuck ends under. Repeat with remaining dough. Cover and let double, about 1 hour. Brush with egg wash. Bake in a preheated 350° oven 35 minutes. Cool on wire racks.

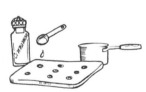

MORAVIAN SUGAR CAKE

A trip to one of the most charming areas in our country, the Pennsylvania Dutch region gave me this brown sugar coated coffee cake. These are hard working people and they love their breads and cakes to be big and hearty. This is one of my favorites and one that children especially love to eat and help make.

1 package dry or compressed yeast
⅔ cup warm water
1 cup warm milk
½ cup sugar
1½ teaspoons salt
½ cup melted butter or margarine
1 cup mashed potatoes (use instant)

2 eggs, lightly beaten
7 to 7½ cups flour
2 cups brown sugar
Melted butter
Cinnamon

Sprinkle yeast over the warm water, stirring until dissolved. Set aside. In a large mixing bowl, combine the milk, sugar, salt, and butter. Blend well. Stir in the potatoes (refer to Ingredients, page 8) and eggs with 2 cups of flour. Add the yeast mixture. Beat with a rubber spatula until smooth. Gradually add sufficient flour to make a soft, workable dough that pulls away from sides of the bowl. Turn out on a lightly floured board and knead until smooth and elastic, about 10 minutes. Round into a ball and place in a warm, greased bowl, turning to coat the top (refer to Techniques, page 12). Cover loosely with plastic wrap and a towel. Allow to double in bulk, about 1½ hours.

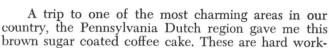

Turn the dough out, knead lightly, cover and let rest 10 minutes. Divide in 3 portions. Roll each into a rectangle 11x15″ and place on greased baking sheets. Smooth and pat out evenly with your hands. Brush with melted butter. Cover and let rise to ¾″ thickness, about 45 minutes. Sprinkle each cake with the brown sugar. Punch thumb deeply into the dough to make holes 1″ apart. Pour ½ teaspoon melted butter in each depression. With a pastry brush, sprinkle butter over the top. Now dust lightly with cinnamon. Bake in a preheated 350° oven 20 to 25 minutes. Serve immediately or cool on wire racks. You will find this cake to be better when served warm.

ARABIC BREAD

Simple ingredients compose one of the oldest yeast breads in the world taught me by a close friend of Lebanese heritage. Making Arabic bread is an easy but fast process. Read the recipe carefully. Gather all ingredients and utensils before beginning. The delightful part is that the bread freezes well so a large quantity may be made at one time.

1 package dry or compressed	1½ teaspoons salt
yeast	2 tablespoons sugar
¼ cup warm water	2 tablespoons melted shortening
1 tablespoon sugar	or oil
2 cups warm water	7 to 8 cups flour

Sprinkle yeast over the ¼ cup of warm water; add 1 tablespoon of sugar. Stir with a fork until dissolved. Measure the 2 cups of warm water into a large mixing bowl. Add the salt, remaining sugar, and shortening. Blend in the yeast mixture and 2 cups of flour. Beat with a rubber spatula until the batter is smooth. Add sufficient flour to make a soft, workable dough. Turn out on a floured surface and knead until smooth and elastic, about 10 minutes. Round into a ball and place in a warm, greased bowl, turning to coat the top. Cover loosely with plastic wrap and a towel. Set aside in a protected spot to rise until doubled, about 1½ to 2 hours.

Punch down the dough, knead lightly, cover, and let rest 10 minutes. Cut portions of dough off the size of a teacup. Round each in a ball, cover and let rise about 45 minutes. Roll each ball into a ¼″ thick circle, or 9″ in diameter. Spread these flat breads on a table, cover with a cloth, and let rest 30 minutes. Preheat oven to 500°. (If you have 2 ovens the process will be faster and easier. Turn second oven to broil.) Place a baking sheet on bottom shelf of preheated 500° oven. With a spatula slide a flat bread on the hot baking sheet. Let bake about 1 minute or just until puffed like a balloon but not browned. Remove pan and pop under the broiler (shelf at middle placement) until lightly browned — a matter of a few seconds so watch carefully! If you do not have the second oven, slide a shelf in quickly on middle placement and brown the bread under the broiler. Remove immediately. The bread will be quite puffed, golden brown, and then fall back to a flat bread. Place the hot bread under towels or a clean, doubled sheet to prevent drying. Repeat with remaining dough. When finished baking and the breads have cooled, they may be stacked, placed in plastic bags, and stored in the freezer.

LEBANESE SESAME SEED BISCUITS OR BREAD STICKS

A delicious little bread whose fragrance will add much to the cocktail hour. If served warm, the flavor of the Mid-Eastern spice will be much enhanced.

2 packages dry or compressed
yeast
½ cup warm water
1 cup margarine or butter
2 tablespoons oil
1 teaspoon mahleb, page 228

1 teaspoon salt
3 to 4 cups flour
1 egg beaten with 1 tablespoon
water
Untoasted sesame seed

Sprinkle yeast over the warm water, stirring with a fork until dissolved. Set aside. Combine margarine and oil. Beat until soft and creamy with a rubber spatula or electric mixer. Add the mahleb, salt, and 1 cup of flour. Stir until well mixed. Blend in the yeast mixture and sufficient flour to make a soft dough. Turn out on a floured board and knead until smooth, about 5 minutes. Place in a warm, greased bowl, turning to coat the top. Cover loosely with plastic wrap and a towel. Set in a warm spot to double in bulk, about 2 hours (refer to Techniques, page 11).

Turn dough out on floured surface and knead 2 minutes. Cover and let rest 10 minutes. Cut off portions about the size of a walnut, round into balls and place on a greased baking sheet. Cut off another portion and roll in a rope ½″ thick. Cut in 2″ pieces and form small circles, pinching ends together. Place on greased baking sheet. With a third portion, roll in a long rope ¼″ thick. Cut in 3 equal pieces and braid together. Cut braids in 2″ sections. Pinch ends together and place on baking sheet. **Bread Sticks:** Divide dough in half. Roll one portion into a rectangle ¼″ thick. With a dough scraper, cut in strips and roll into bread sticks. Place on greased baking sheet. (½ of dough will make about 30 thin bread sticks.) Cover biscuits or sticks and let rise until doubled, about 1 hour. Brush with egg wash and sprinkle liberally with sesame seed. Bake in a preheated 375° oven 15 to 20 minutes or until golden in color. These breads will keep indefinitely if packaged air tight.

PANETTONE

A high, light coffee cake favored by Italians at Christmas to serve with coffee or wine. The cake becomes better with a few days of age and will keep two weeks or more. This makes it ideal to have during the holiday season to serve unexpected guests.

½ cup golden raisins, rinsed in
    hot water and dried
¼ cup candied citron
2 packages dry or compressed yeast
½ cup warm water
½ cup melted butter
½ cup sugar

3 eggs
2 egg yolks
1 teaspoon salt
Grated rind 1 lemon
1 teaspoon vanilla extract
5 cups flour, approximately
Melted butter

Combine raisins and citron; set aside. Sprinkle yeast over warm water, stirring with a fork until dissolved. In a large mixing bowl, combine the butter, sugar, whole eggs, egg yolks, and salt. Beat with a rubber spatula until smooth. Add the yeast mixture, lemon rind and vanilla. Stir in 2 cups of flour until the batter is smooth. Gradually add sufficient flour to make a soft, workable dough that pulls way from sides of the bowl. Turn out on a floured board and knead until smooth and elastic, about 10 minutes. Cover and let rest 10 minutes. Pat dough out in a circle. Sprinkle a tiny portion of flour over mixed fruits. Transfer fruits to top of dough. Knead carefully until fruit is well distributed. Round dough in a ball, place in a warm greased bowl, turning to coat the top. Cover loosely with plastic wrap and towel. Set aside to double in a protected area, about 2 hours.

Turn the dough out on a lightly floured board and knead 3 to 4 minutes. Place in a well buttered 8 cup charlotte mold, or similar size baking dish. Brush top with melted butter, cover, and let rise until dough curves over top of pan, about 1½ hours. Slash a cross with a razor on top of dough. Brush again with melted butter. Bake in a preheated 400° oven 10 minutes. Reduce heat to 350° and bake 50 minutes. If top becomes too brown, cover with foil the last 20 minutes. Remove and cool on a wire rack.

FRENCH SAVARIN

There are few desserts that are any more spectacular than the lovely French Savarin and Baba au Rhum. Here is my version of these beautiful yeast cakes with several suggested variations.

2 packages dry or compressed yeast
¼ cup warm water
2 tablespoons sugar
½ teaspoon salt
2 cups flour

½ cup warm milk
4 eggs, lightly beaten
½ cup soft butter
Melted butter

Sprinkle yeast over the warm water, stirring with a fork until dissolved. Set aside. Combine and blend thoroughly the sugar, salt, and flour. Make a well in the dry ingredients. Pour in the yeast mixture, milk, and eggs. Beat vigorously with a rubber spatula or the flat beater of a heavy mixer 2 minutes or until you have a smooth, elastic batter. Cover with a towel, place in a warm spot to double in bulk, about 45 minutes.

Beat the dough down with a rubber spatula. Gradually begin to add the soft butter, a few pieces at a time. The important action now is to incorporate air into the dough. Try this method: beat the dough with your hand, slapping against the side of the bowl, lifting and letting it fall as you add the butter. This method of kneading is not too difficult as you are performing a downward motion which is easier than a circular one. If your bowl slips, place it on a wet tea cloth and slap away. The flat beater of a heavy mixer will do exceedingly well, but do try the hand method — great fun.

When all the butter is incorporated, brush a 4 cup Savarin mold with melted butter. Pour in the batter, spreading evenly. Cover and allow to rise just barely to the top, about 30 to 40 minutes. Watch carefully or you will have spillage in the oven. Bake in a preheated 400° oven 10 minutes. Lower heat to 350°. Bake 30 minutes longer.

While the cake is baking, prepare the following syrup: combine 2 cups water, 2 cups sugar, 3 slices orange and lemon peel cut off with a potato peeler to avoid any white portion. Bring to a rapid boil, lower heat, and let simmer 3 minutes. Remove from burner and add ½ cup brandy or Grand Marnier.

When the cake is done, remove from oven and turn out on a deep plate or platter. Pierce several places with a skewer or toothpick. Allow cake to cool 10 minutes. Slowly pour ½ of the syrup over the Savarin. Set aside for 1 hour. Drip remaining syrup on the cake.

PRESENTATION SUGGESTIONS

1. Pile fresh sugared strawberries or red raspberries in the center. The fruit may be marinated in a small amount of Kirsch if desired.

2. A macédoine of fresh fruits marinated in sherry and placed in center of cake.

3. Serve your favorite custard sauce or whipped cream with the fruits.

4. After cake is dripped and cooled, heat 1 cup apricot jam with 1 tablespoon lemon juice until bubbly. Spoon over Savarin and allow to cool. Heap a good vanilla ice cream in the center.

NOTE

If you wish to freeze the Savarin, cool thoroughly when removed from the oven. Wrap and store in the freezer. Finish the cake on the day you plan to serve.

BABAS AU RHUM

½ cup currants, soaked in
   3 tablespoons rum 1 hour
French Savarin Dough, page 210
Melted butter

Rum Sauce
Apricot Sauce, page 211
Fresh fruits
Whipped cream

Drain currants and pat dry on paper towels. When butter has been incorporated into the Savarin Dough, beat in the currants. Brush 12 Baba molds (2x2″), popover, or muffin tins of similar size with melted butter. Fill molds one-half full of dough. Set aside to rise uncovered about 1 hour or until dough is rounded over rim of mold. Place molds on a baking sheet for ease of handling. Bake in a preheated 375° oven 20 minutes or until golden brown. Remove and cool to warm on wire racks.

Rum Sauce
1 cup water
2 cups sugar
3 thin slices orange rind

3 thin slices lemon rind
¾ cup light rum

Combine the water, sugar, orange, and lemon rinds in a saucepan. Bring to a boil, lower to simmer, and cook 5 minutes. Stir in the rum and set aside until just warm. Place warm Babas in a pan or glass dish. Spoon syrup over the Babas. Let Babas stand in syrup, turning several times for 1 hour. Drain on a wire rack.

PRESENTATION
   Cover top of each Baba with apricot sauce if desired. Surround with fresh fruits such as raspberries, strawberries, or peaches that have been marinated in Kirsch or Sherry. Top with whipped cream.

ARGENTINE FRUIT BREAD

   A delicately textured bread that makes two round, golden loaves. Usually served as a holiday bread in Argentina, but delicious anytime with hot chocolate or coffee.

1 package dry or compressed yeast	⅓ cup sugar
	1 teaspoon salt
1 cup warm milk	4 eggs
2 cups flour	1 cup raisins, scalded and dried
• • •	⅓ cup chopped candied orange peel
¼ cup soft butter or margarine	3½ cups flour, approximately

The Sponge: Combine yeast and warm milk in a mixing bowl. Stir with a fork until dissolved. Set aside 10 minutes. Beat in the 2 cups of flour until smooth. Cover with plastic wrap and a towel. Set aside in a warm spot overnight.

The next morning: cream butter, sugar, and salt together in a small bowl of an electric mixer until light and fluffy. Add the eggs one at a time, beating well after each addition. Stir down the sponge with a rubber spatula and add the butter mixture. Blend in the raisins and orange peel. Gradually add sufficient more flour to make a soft, workable dough that leaves sides of the bowl. Turn out on a lightly floured board and knead until smooth and satiny, about 10 minutes. Cover and let rest 10 minutes. Divide dough in 2 portions. Round each piece of dough into a smooth ball. Place on a greased baking sheet. Cover and let double in bulk, about 1½ hours. Bake in preheated 350° oven 30 minutes. Cool breads on wire racks.

NORWEGIAN TEA BREAD

Norwegians love to use cardamom spice in breads and coffee cakes as do all northern European countries. When thoroughly cooled, cut this lovely bread into thin slices to serve for an afternoon tea.

¼ cup warm water	7 to 8 cups flour
2 packages dry or compressed yeast	2 teaspoons cardamom
2 cups warm milk	½ cup diced candied citron, pineapple, or orange peel
1 cup melted butter or margarine	
1 cup sugar	½ cup golden raisins
1 teaspoon salt	Melted butter

Combine water and yeast in a small bowl; stir with a fork until dissolved. Set aside. In a large mixing bowl, combine the milk, butter, sugar, and salt. Add the yeast mixture and beat in 3 cups of flour until smooth. Cover and set aside to double in bulk, about 45 minutes.

Mix the cardamom, candied fruit, and raisins together. Stir down the sponge and add the cardamom mixture. Gradually add sufficient flour to make a soft, workable dough (refer to Techniques, page 10). Turn out on a floured board and knead until smooth and elastic, about 8 minutes. Round into a ball and place in a warm, greased bowl, turning to coat the top. Cover loosely with plastic wrap and towel. Allow to double in bulk, about 2 hours. Punch down and divide dough in 3 equal portions. Shape into loaves and place in greased 8½x4½x2½" loaf pans. Cover and let rise to tops of pans, about 1 hour. Score the top of each loaf with a sharp knife or razor 3 times. Brush with melted butter. Bake in a preheated 375° oven 10 minutes. Reduce temperature to 300° and bake 40 minutes. Test with a cake tester for doneness. Remove loaves to wire racks.

MEXICAN CHICKEN SOUP
CALDO TLALPENO

This hearty recipe was given to me by a fine chef at the lovely Ramada Inn on the edge of Monterrey, Mexico.

2 quarts water
3 cloves garlic, peeled
1 two pound chicken, cut in small
  pieces or 4 chicken breasts
2 tomatoes, peeled and chopped
1 onion, finely chopped
¼ cup oil
1 cup yellow squash, diced
1 cup string beans, cut in
  pieces

1 cup canned chickpeas
  (Garbanzos)
½ cup rice, optional
3 teaspoons ground coriander
Salt to taste
Chile chipotle (available in
  cans)
Avocado for garnish

Bring the water to a boil in a soup pot. Add the garlic and chicken. Cover and allow to simmer about 30 minutes or until the chicken is done. Meanwhile, sauté the tomatoes and onion in the oil until soft. Remove chicken from the soup pot and strip off the meat. Dice and return to the kettle. Discard the bones. Add the tomato mixture, squash, string beans, chickpeas, rice, and coriander. Bring to a simmer and cook until vegetables are done. Adjust for salt. Add thinly sliced avocado to each serving. If the chile chipotle is not available to you, the soup is excellent without the hot chile.

BELGIAN ENDIVE SOUP

Would you like to impress your friends? Try making this charming but expensive soup — so delicate that it reminds you of silk velvet.

1 pound Endive, about
  3 large plants
3 tablespoons lemon juice
Boiling water to cover
2 large leeks, white part only
3 tablespoons butter

2 tablespoons flour
3 cups boiling chicken broth
1 cup warm cream
¼ teaspoon ground nutmeg
Grindings of white pepper
Salt

Trim base and outer leaves of the Endive. Wash thoroughly. Place in a saucepan with the lemon juice. Cover with boiling water. Allow to simmer 10 minutes. Drain well. Clean the leeks by slicing in half and place under running water. Chop both the drained endive and leeks finely. Melt butter in a clean saucepan. Sauté the leeks and endive until tender, about 10 minutes. Do not allow to brown. Stir in the flour with a whisk until smooth. Add the hot chicken broth all at once, stirring rapidly until creamy and free of lumps. Bring to a boil and reduce heat to simmer. Cover pan and cook lightly 20 minutes. Remove lid. Stir in the cream and nutmeg. Add a few grindings of white pepper. Taste for salt and adjust. Present in warmed, cream soup bowls. Six servings.

BULGARIAN CURRIED SOUP

A creamy, rich curried soup that would be perfect for a winter luncheon teamed with a fruit salad and Vienna, French, or Sour Dough bread. A good way to use left over chicken. Serves 8 to 10.

2 cups cooked, minced chicken	6 cups hot chicken broth
1 cup cream	2 tablespoons rice
¼ cup butter or margarine	Salt
¼ cup flour	Grindings of black pepper
1 tablespoon curry	Chopped toasted almonds

Combine chicken and ½ cup of cream. Set aside. Melt butter in a large saucepan. With a wooden spoon, blend in flour and curry. Cook 3 minutes, stirring constantly. Add 2 cups of chicken broth all at once. Stir vigorously until thickened and smooth. Allow to simmer 15 minutes, stirring occasionally. Add remaining broth, chicken mixture, and rice. Bring back to a simmer and cook until rice is tender. Add remaining cream. Taste for salt and adjust. Blend in a few grindings of black pepper. Reheat just to a boil and serve immediately in cream soup bowls topped with chopped toasted almonds.

GREEK LEMON SOUP

A tribute to the Greeks for giving us their traditional soup that is refreshingly delicate. The ingredients are simple and the soup easy to make.

2½ quarts rich chicken broth
½ cup rice
4 eggs
1 tablespoon water

½ cup strained lemon juice
Finely chopped parsley or
   fresh mint

Measure broth into a large saucepan. Bring to a boil and add the rice. Cover and cook until rice is tender. Beat the eggs and water until light and creamy. Slowly add the lemon juice, beating constantly. Gradually stir in 2 cups of hot broth. Blend into the remaining broth in the saucepan. Heat slowly, stirring constantly. Do not allow to boil or the eggs will curdle. Serve immediately in warm soup bowls garnished with finely chopped parsley or mint. The soup is excellent refrigerated and served thoroughly chilled.

ITALIAN MINESTRONE

There are as many versions of minestrone as there are cities in Italy. It is basically a peasant soup so that whatever is available can be thrown into the pot. My family and students have enjoyed this recipe.

1 pound mixed dried vegetables (beans, chick peas, lentils, fava
   beans) or two 7 ounce packages of Minestrone Soup Mix
1 quart beef broth
1½ quarts water
1 slice ham, ½″ thick
2 large onions, sliced

• • •

3 sprigs parsley
1 teaspoon dried marjoram
1 bay leaf
2 cloves garlic, minced
½ pound of 5 or 6 fresh vegetables (leeks, carrots, peas, green beans,
   zucchini, yellow squash, lima beans, asparagus, tomatoes)
2 cups celery, finely chopped
¼ pound spinach, washed and coarsely chopped
½ pound pasta (spaghetti, macaroni, linguine broken in small pieces
   or use the miniature pasta)
Salt and freshly ground black pepper
Grated Parmesan cheese

Soak dried vegetables overnight. The next morning, drain vegetables and transfer to a soup kettle. Add the beef broth, water, ham, and onions. Bring to a boil, skim, and lower heat to simmer. Cook partially covered about 1½ hours or until dried vegetables are tender.

Add the parsley, marjoram, bay leaf, garlic, fresh vegetables, celery, and spinach. Bring slowly to a boil. Add the pasta. Taste for salt and adjust. Stir in a few grindings of pepper. Simmer the soup until the pasta is just barely tender. Test vegetables for doneness, taste again for seasoning and cook longer if necessary. Remove ham, dice, and return to the kettle. Serve in large, warm soup bowls with Parmesan cheese as an accompaniment. Eight generous servings.

HOLIDAY
AND RELIGIOUS
BREADS

SOUPS:

> *Cream of Pumpkin*
> *Double Consomme*
> *Senegalese*
> *Matzo Ball*

HOLIDAY COFFEE CAKES

HOLIDAY TEA RING   CHRISTMAS TREE
DOUBLE CHRISTMAS WREATH   ST. LUCIA BUNS

CHRISTMAS DOUGH

2 packages dry or compressed
   yeast
½ cup warm water
1 cup warm milk
½ cup sugar

1 teaspoon ground cardamom
1½ teaspoons salt
½ cup melted butter or margarine
2 eggs, lightly beaten
6 to 7 cups flour

Combine yeast and warm water in a small bowl. Stir with a fork until dissolved. In a large mixing bowl, blend the milk, sugar, cardamom, and salt. Add the butter, eggs, and yeast mixture, blending well. Beat in 3 cups of flour until mixture is smooth. Gradually stir in just enough more flour to make a soft, workable dough that pulls away from sides of the bowl. Turn out on a lightly floured board and knead until smooth and satiny, about 10 minutes. Round in a ball and place in a warm, greased bowl, turning to coat the top. Cover loosely with plastic wrap and towel. Set in a warm spot to double in bulk, 1½ to 2 hours. Punch dough down, knead lightly in the bowl and allow to rise a second time, about 1 hour. Turn out on a lightly floured surface and knead 2 or 3 minutes. Cover and let rest 15 minutes (refer to Techniques, page 13). The dough is now ready to form into any of the following holiday cakes or rolls.

HOLIDAY TEA RING

If you wish to make a bread centerpiece for Christmas breakfast, place a large tea ring on a round tray, a big red candle in the center and surround with holly.

Christmas Dough at end of second
   rising
Melted butter
¾ to 1 cup Cinnamon-Sugar, page 267
1 cup raisins, rinsed in hot water
   and dried

1½ cups mixed candied fruit
½ cup chopped nuts
Whole candied red or green
   cherries
Confectioner's Icing, page 268

LARGE TEA RING
Roll the Christmas Dough in a large rectangle ¼" thick, about 13x23".

Brush with melted butter to within ½″ of edges. Sprinkle heavily with Cinnamon-Sugar. Spread the raisins, candied fruit, and nuts over the sugar mixture. Roll tightly jelly roll style from the long side. Pinch side to seal. Make a ring and insert ends together, pinching to seal. Place on a greased baking sheet. Flatten slightly with hands. With kitchen shears, cut slashes 1″ apart and 1½″ into the cake. Spread fingers apart and

  twist each slightly to lay flat against each other. Flatten again with hands. Cover and let double in bulk, about 50 minutes. Firmly press a candied cherry between each

finger. Bake in a preheated 350° oven about 30 minutes or until golden. Remove to a wire rack. If serving immediately, frost with Confectioner's Icing while still warm.

TWO SMALL RINGS
Divide Christmas dough in half. Roll each piece in a rectangle, 10x14″. Sprinkle half of filling ingredients over each rectangle and proceed as directed for the large ring. Bake 25 minutes.

DOUBLE CHRISTMAS WREATH

 When the Christmas Dough has rested, cut in ⅓ and ⅔ portions. Divide ⅔ of dough in half. Roll each piece in a 28″ smooth rope (roll from the center and work out to each end). Twist the 2 lengths together loosely and place on a greased baking sheet. Form a circle and pinch ends together. Divide the ⅓ portion in half. Roll each piece in 22″ lengths. Twist loosely together, place on baking sheet and form a circle. Pinch ends to seal. Cover and let double, about 1 hour. Bake in a preheated 350° oven 25 minutes or until a light golden color. Remove to wire racks and let cool thoroughly.

Prepare a double amount of Confectioner's Icing, page 268. Place the large wreath on a tray. Frost with the icing, allowing to dribble down sides. Immediately place the smaller wreath on top the larger one. Secure with a few toothpicks. Frost the top wreath (make more icing if necessary). Decorate with red and green candied cherries. Insert 4 long red or green candles through both cakes. Place in center of your Christmas table.

CHRISTMAS TREE

Let's build a Christmas tree for the children! Makes 2 trees.

Divide Christmas dough in half after resting period. Set one part aside and cover. Divide a portion in 18 pieces. Roll each piece in a 10″ strip. Hold one end of strip and roll dough around to make a coil. Pinch end to seal or tuck under the coil. Repeat with remaining portions of dough. Brush a baking sheet with melted butter. Place 1 coil at end of baking sheet. Place 2 coils just above the first to make a second row. On the third row, place 5 coils. Then place 4 in next row, 3 coils in the following row, then 2 and finally 1 coil at the top. Repeat with remaining dough on a second baking sheet. Cover and let double, about 45 minutes to 1 hour. Beat 1 egg with 1 tablespoon of water. Brush both cakes with egg glaze. Press a red or green candied cherry in the center of each coil. Bake in a preheated 350° oven about 20 minutes or until a golden color. Remove from oven and place on wire racks to cool.

ST. LUCIA BUNS

December the 13th, St. Lucia's Day begins Christmas for the Swedish household. The eldest daughter awakens her parents early in the morning with these charming little buns and hot coffee.

Christmas Dough   *1 egg beaten with 1 tablespoon*
Plump, dark raisins   *water*
                    Granulated sugar

Divide Christmas Dough in 24 pieces at end of resting period. Roll each portion in a smooth rope, 12″ long. Form each rope in an S shape and curve both ends in a coil. Cross 2 of these S shaped ropes to form an X. To make a larger bun, place a third rope across the X so there will be 6 fingers — makes a beautiful roll. Place buns on a greased baking sheet. Cover and let double, about 45 minutes. Brush buns with the egg glaze. Place a plump raisin in the center of each coil. Sprinkle lightly with granulated sugar. Bake in a preheated 350° oven 15 to 20 minutes or until golden brown. Cool on wire racks.

CHRISTMAS HOLIDAY BREAD

Here is a bread that smells like Christmas and tastes like Christmas. It may be made ahead and frozen to use later for your family or as gifts.

2 packages dry or compressed yeast	¼ teaspoon nutmeg
⅓ cup warm water	2 eggs, lightly beaten
2 cups warm milk	8 cups flour, approximately
½ cup melted butter or margarine	1 cup golden raisins
⅔ cup sugar	1 cup mixed candied fruits
1½ teaspoons salt	Confectioner's Icing, page 268
1½ teaspoons ground cardamom	Candied red and green cherries
1 teaspoon cinnamon	Tiny decorating candies

Sprinkle yeast over the warm water; stir until dissolved and set aside. In a large mixing bowl, combine the warm milk, butter, sugar, salt, and spices. Blend in the yeast mixture and beaten eggs. With a rubber spatula, beat in 3 cups of flour until batter is smooth. Add the raisins and candied fruits. Gradually add just enough flour to make a soft, workable dough. Turn out on a lightly floured board and knead until smooth and resilient, about 8 minutes. Round into a ball and place in a warm, greased bowl, turning to coat the top. Cover loosely with plastic wrap and a towel. Allow to double in bulk, about 1½ hours.

Turn out on a floured board and let rest 10 minutes (refer to Techniques, page 13). Form in 2 round loaves and place in greased 9" cake tins. An alternate method: divide dough in 3 portions. Roll in 3 smooth ropes, 16 to 18" long. Braid starting from the center and working out to each end. Place on a greased baking sheet and tuck ends under. Cover loaves and let rise until doubled, about 1 hour. Preheat oven to 350°. Bake round loaves 35 minutes. Bake the braid 40 to 45 minutes. Frost with Confectioner's Icing and decorate with cherries and decorating candies.

GERMAN CHRISTMAS STOLLEN

A traditional coffee cake that keeps well for several weeks. A delicious bread to have available during the holidays for guests as it is most delectable served with coffee, tea, or wine.

2 cups almonds, walnuts or pecans
   coarsely chopped
1 cup mixed candied fruit
1 cup golden raisins
¼ cup brandy
2 packages dry or compressed yeast
¼ cup warm water
1 cup warm milk
1 teaspoon salt

⅔ cup sugar
¼ teaspoon mace
1 cup melted butter or
   margarine
3 eggs, lightly beaten
Grated rind 1 lemon
7 cups flour, approximately
Brandy or Rum

Combine the nuts, candied fruit, and raisins with the brandy in a small bowl. Mix thoroughly and set aside.

Sprinkle yeast over the warm water; stir with a fork until dissolved. In a large mixing bowl, blend the milk, salt, sugar, mace, and melted butter. Add the eggs and grated rind. Stir in the yeast mixture and 2 cups of flour, beating until smooth. Add the nut-fruit mixture. Gradually stir in enough more flour to make a workable dough that leaves sides of the bowl. Turn out on a floured surface and knead until resilient. Add small portions of flour, if necessary, to cut stickiness. Round in a ball and place in a warm, greased bowl, turning to coat the top. Cover loosely with plastic wrap and towel. Let double in bulk, about 2½ hours.

Turn dough out on a lightly floured surface. Divide in half. Shape each half in an oval, 9x16″. Fold over like a Parker House roll, so that edges do not quite meet. Place on a greased baking sheet and brush with melted butter. Cover and let double, 1 to 1½ hours. Bake in pre-heated 350° oven 45 to 50 minutes. If cake becomes too brown, cover with foil the last 20 minutes.

VARIATION

The dough may be divided into 4 portions. Roll each piece in a 7x12″ oval and proceed as directed. Bake smaller cakes 40 minutes. Remove to wire racks.

OPTIONAL

Drip cakes with brandy or rum while still warm.

 **VANOCKA**

On the following pages are three traditional European Christmas breads. The Swedish Jule Kaga is a free standing, round loaf with no eggs and flavored with cardamom. The Czechoslovakian Hoska has a moderate amount of eggs and is molded into a three braided loaf. The Hungarian Vanocka is the richest — lots of butter and eggs. It is usually made into a four-tiered bread. All the breads may be baked in loaf pans or molded into simple braids.

3 packages dry or compressed
    yeast
⅓ cup warm water
2 cups warm milk
⅔ cup sugar
1 teaspoon salt
½ teaspoon mace
Grated rind 1 lemon

6 egg yolks, lightly beaten
1 cup melted butter or margarine
7 to 8 cups flour
1 cup golden raisins, rinsed in
    hot water and dried
1 cup chopped almonds
1 egg beaten with 1 tablespoon
    milk

Sprinkle yeast over the warm water, stirring with a fork until dissolved. Set aside (refer to Ingredients, page 7). In a large mixing bowl, combine milk, sugar, salt, mace, grated rind, egg yolks, and butter. Add yeast mixture. With a wooden spoon or rubber spatula, beat in 3 cups of flour until smooth. Stir in raisins and almonds. Gradually add enough flour to make a soft workable dough. Turn out on a lightly floured board and knead until smooth and elastic, about 10 minutes. Place in a warm, greased bowl, turning to coat the top. Cover loosely with plastic wrap and a towel. Allow to double in bulk, about 1 hour. Punch down, turn out on a floured surface, cover and let rest 10 to 15 minutes.

PREPARATION OF FOUR-TIERED BRAID

1. Cut dough in half, Divide ½ of dough in 4 pieces. Roll into smooth ropes, 20 to 22" long. Braid the four strands, starting from the middle and working out. Place braid on greased baking sheet. Press braid slightly. With a sharp knife, make a light slash down center of braid, leaving a 2" margin on both ends. Brush lightly with flour.

2. Cut off ⅓ of remaining dough. Divide in 3 portions. Roll in 18" lengths. Braid the 3 ropes, starting from the center and working out to each end. Do not be afraid to pick up a braid and adjust it for easy manipulating. Place braid on top the first one. Press down, make a slash down the center and dust lightly with flour.

3. Cut off ½ of remaining dough. Divide in 2 portions. Roll into 14" ropes. Twist the 2 lengths together. Place the twist on top the braids. Press down lightly and dust with a tiny portion of flour.

4. Roll the last piece of dough into a single strand — long enough to go across the braids and tuck underneath at each end. Secure braids with toothpicks. Cover and allow to rise half doubled, about 35 minutes. Brush braids with egg wash, allow to set 2 minutes and brush again. Place loaf in a preheated 325° oven 50 minutes. Cool on wire racks.

5. Loaf Pans: Divide dough in 3 portions, mold into loaves and place in 9x5x3" pans, or make 4 loaves, 8½x4½x2½". Cover and let rise until just curved over tops of pans. Bake in a preheated 350° oven 50 minutes for larger loaves and 40 for smaller breads. Insert cake tester; if it comes out clean, the loaves are done.

OPTIONAL

The pan loaves may be brushed with egg wash for a deep golden color if desired.

JULE KAGA

2 packages dry or compressed yeast
2½ cups warm milk
1 cup sugar
1½ teaspoons salt
2 teaspoons cardamom
1 cup golden raisins, rinsed in
    hot water and dried
½ cup candied red cherries, sliced

1 cup candied mixed fruit
1 cup melted butter
8 to 9 cups flour
Confectioner's Icing, page 268
Candied red or green cherries
Sliced almonds

In a large mixing bowl, combine yeast and milk, stirring with a fork until dissolved. Set aside. In a separate bowl, blend sugar, salt, and cardamom. Combine raisins, ½ cup candied cherries, and mixed fruit in a small bowl. Sprinkle with a tiny portion of flour to avoid sticking together.

Add melted butter and sugar mixture to yeast mixture, stirring thoroughly with a rubber spatula. Beat in 3 cups of flour until smooth. Stir in fruit mixture. Gradually add enough more flour to make a soft dough. Turn out on a lightly floured board and knead until smooth and elastic, about 10 minutes. Place dough in a large, warm, greased bowl, turning to coat the top. Cover loosely with plastic wrap and a towel. Set aside to double in bulk, about 2 to 2½ hours. Turn out on a floured surface. Cover and allow to rest 10 minutes. Shape in 2 round loaves or make one large loaf. Place on greased baking sheets. Cover and let double, about 1 hour. Preheat oven to 350°. Bake large loaf 55 minutes. Bake smaller loaves 40 to 45 minutes. Cool on wire racks. Frost with Confectioner's Icing. Decorate with candied cherries and almonds.

HOSKA

2 packages dry or compressed
    yeast
¼ cup warm water
1 cup warm milk
¾ cup sugar
½ teaspoon salt
½ cup melted butter or margarine
2 eggs, lightly beaten
6 to 6½ cups flour

¼ cup golden raisins, rinsed in
    hot water and dried
¼ cup candied pineapple, diced
¼ cup candied orange rind, diced
¼ cup chopped almonds
1 egg beaten with 1 tablespoon
    water
Sliced almonds

Sprinkle yeast over the warm water, stirring with a fork until dissolved. Set aside. In a large mixing bowl, combine warm milk, sugar, salt, butter, and eggs. Stir until well blended. Add yeast mixture. Beat in 3 cups of flour until smooth. Blend in raisins, pineapple, orange rind, and chopped almonds. Stir in enough more flour to make a soft, workable dough. Turn out on a lightly floured board and knead until smooth and resilient, about 10 minutes. Place in a warm, greased bowl, turning to coat the top (refer to Techniques, page 12). Cover loosely with plastic wrap and a towel. Allow dough to double in bulk, about 2½ hours. Turn out on a floured surface, flatten with hands and cover to rest 10 minutes.

Divide dough in 4 equal pieces. Set 2 portions aside and cover. Divide one part in 3 equal portions. Roll in strips 14 to 16″ long. Braid strips, starting in the center and working out to each end. Place braid on a greased baking sheet. Press down lightly. Make a ¼″ slash down the center leaving 2″ margin at both ends and dust lightly with flour.

Cut ⅔ off the second portion of dough; divide in 3 equal pieces. Roll into strips 12″ long. Braid and place on the first braid. Press braids down lightly with your hands. Make a ¼″ slash down center of second braid leaving 1″ margin at both ends and dust lightly with flour. Divide remaining ⅓ dough in 3 parts. Roll into 10″ strips and braid. Place on top of second braid. Press lightly and secure with toothpicks. Repeat directions with remaining 2 portions of dough. Cover each braid with a towel and allow to almost double, about 45 minutes to 1 hour. Brush with egg wash. Allow to set 2 minutes. Brush again. Decorate with sliced almonds, pressing them into dough lightly. Bake in a preheated 325° oven 45 to 50 minutes. Cool on wire racks.

GREEK NEW YEAR'S BREAD

A charming Greek girl lived in our city for a year as an American Field Service student. Our family visited her in Greece, and through Maria and her mother, learned much about Greek cookery and customs. This is an enchantingly flavored bread that may be turned into a New Year's loaf by kneading a penny into the dough. The person who receives the slice with the penny will have good luck through the next year.

2 packages dry or compressed yeast	1 teaspoon ground Mastic*
½ cup warm water	1½ teaspoons ground Mahleb*
1 cup warm milk	7 cups flour, approximately
¾ cup sugar	Soft butter
1 teaspoon salt	Untoasted sesame seed
½ cup melted butter	1 egg beaten with 1
3 eggs, beaten	tablespoon water
Grated rind 1 lemon	

Sprinkle yeast over the warm water, stirring with a fork until dissolved. In a large mixing bowl, blend the milk, sugar, salt, butter, eggs, grated rind, mastic, and mahleb. Add the yeast mixture and 3 cups of flour. Beat until smooth. Gradually add enough flour to make a soft dough. Turn out on a lightly floured board and knead until smooth and resilient, about 10 minutes. Place in a warm, greased bowl, turning to coat the top. Cover loosely with plastic wrap and towel. Allow to double in bulk, about 2 hours.

Punch down the dough and turn out on a floured surface. If you wish to make a New Year's bread, have 2 new pennies available. Divide dough in 2 portions. Knead 1 penny into each piece. Set aside to rest, 10 minutes. Brush 2 medium soufflé bowls or 10″ cake tins with soft butter. Sprinkle with untoasted sesame seed. Round each portion of dough in a ball. Place in prepared bowls; press down so that dough covers the bottom. Cover and let rise until double, about 2 hours. Brush with egg wash and sprinkle heavily with sesame seed. Bake in a pre-heated 350° oven 50 minutes. If loaves become too brown, cover with foil the last 15 minutes. Cool on wire racks.

BRAIDS

Divide dough in half. Cut one portion in 3 equal pieces. Roll each piece in a 16″ smooth rope. Braid the 3 lengths together beginning in the center and working toward each end. Place on a greased baking sheet and tuck ends under. Repeat with remaining dough. Cover and let rise about 1 hour. Brush with egg wash and sprinkle heavily with sesame seed. Bake in a 350° oven about 35 minutes or until a golden brown. Cool on wire racks.

*VARIATION

Mahleb and mastica may be obtained in import food shops. If you cannot obtain the Mid-Eastern spice, substitute ½ teaspoon each cinnamon and nutmeg plus ¼ teaspoon cloves. Proceed as directed.

EASTER BREADS

Following are three recipes for Easter breads made with the marvelous Armenian Egg Dough on page 198. It is one of the easiest of breads to manipulate besides being delicious to eat; you will find these breads enjoyable to handle and great fun for your children or grandchildren.

EASTER EGG TWIST

⅓ Armenian Egg Dough, page 198
6 uncooked tinted eggs*
1 egg beaten with 1 tablespoon water

Confectioner's Icing, page 268
Decorating candies

When the Armenian Egg Dough has rested, cut off ⅓ and divide in 2 equal portions. Roll each part in a 24 to 26" rope. Twist ropes together loosely and place on a greased baking sheet forming a circle. Pinch ends together to seal. Brush with egg wash, cover and allow to rise about 45 minutes. Bake in a preheated 350° oven 35 minutes. Cool on wire rack. Frost with Confectioner's Icing and sprinkle with tiny decorating candies. I do not recommend eating the eggs as they will have a slightly burned taste; mainly for decoration.

INDIVIDUAL EGGS

Cut off ⅓ of Armenian Egg dough and divide in 10 equal pieces. Roll each piece in a rope and fit around an uncooked tinted egg. Place on a greased baking sheet and pinch ends of dough to seal. Repeat with remaining dough. Cover and let double, about 45 minutes. Brush with egg wash made by beating 1 egg with 1 tablespoon of water. Bake in a preheated 350° oven about 20 minutes or until golden brown. Remove and cool on wire racks. Frost with Confectioner's Icing and sprinkle with decorating candies. Children will love having a baked Easter Egg sitting in artificial grass at their plates for Easter breakfast! Remember the egg will not be good to eat as the insides will be quite discolored from the baking.

VARIATION

If you wish to make the individual eggs a bit more elaborate, cut off extra dough and roll into long thin strips about ¼" thick. Cut 2 strips for each egg. Make a cross over the egg, tucking the ends underneath. Proceed as directed.

*Color uncooked eggs with any of the commercial dyes. Use very white eggs and you will have a brighter color. If you have no dye, use cake coloring. Add 1 tablespoon of vinegar to each cup of water. Sprinkle in cake coloring until you obtain the desired shade.

 ## EASTER EGG NEST

Divide Armenian Egg Dough in 2 equal portions. Set one piece aside and cover. Cut off ⅓ of one portion. Divide into 7 equal pieces. Roll each into a smooth ball. Place in a circle on a greased baking sheet with one ball in the center. They should be about ½" apart. Divide the larger portion of dough in 2 pieces. Roll into 30" ropes. Twist together and surround the "nest of eggs". Pinch ends to seal and secure with toothpicks. Cover and let rise 45 minutes. Bake in a preheated 350° oven about 30 minutes or until golden brown. Cool on a wire rack. Make a double amount of Confectioner's Icing, page 268. Take half the icing and divide into 4 small bowls. Color with four shades of cake coloring. Carefully ice the eggs with the different colors and sprinkle with an assortment of decorating candies. This is where you can have great fun creating on your own. Frost the twist with the remaining white icing. Color 2 cups of coconut with green cake coloring and sprinkle heavily over the frosted twist so that the eggs are surrounded by this lovely sweet grass. Beautiful for your Easter table and completely edible. You may repeat directions with remaining dough or make one of the other Easter Breads.

RUSSIAN KULICH

A traditional Russian bread complicated to make, but worth the effort for the dramatic result. Save different size coffee cans for this bread.

¼ cup rum
½ teaspoon saffron
½ cup mixed candied fruits, diced
½ cup raisins, rinsed in hot water
   and dried
½ cup toasted almonds, chopped
2 packages dry or compressed yeast
¼ cup warm water
2 tablespoons brown sugar
¾ cup soft butter

1 cup brown sugar
5 egg yolks
1 teaspoon vanilla flavoring
1 teaspoon almond flavoring
6 to 7 cups flour
1 cup warm cream
5 egg whites, stiffly beaten
Soft butter
Confectioner's Icing, page 268
Decorating candies

Combine rum and saffron in a small bowl. Set aside. In another bowl, combine candied fruits, raisins, and almonds. Sprinkle ½ cup flour over the mixture, stirring with your hands until ingredients are coated. Set aside. Sprinkle yeast over the water, add 2 tablespoons brown sugar and stir with a fork until dissolved. Cream the soft butter and 1 cup of brown sugar until fluffy. Beat in egg yolks and flavoring. If you have a heavy mixer, use the flat beater.

Measure 1 cup of flour in a large mixing bowl. Add the warm cream and beat with a rubber spatula until smooth. Stir in the yeast and butter mixtures. Fold in beaten egg whites. Cover bowl with a towel, place in a warm spot to double in bulk, about 1 hour (refer to Techniques, page 12).

When mixture has doubled, stir down. Blend in the rum and fruit mixtures. Gradually add enough flour to make a soft, workable dough. Turn out on a lightly floured board and knead 5 minutes. Place in a warm, greased bowl, turning to coat the top. Cover loosely with plastic wrap and towel. Set aside to double, about 1 hour.

Meanwhile, prepare choice of coffee cans. The recipe will make one large cake in a 3 pound can, a combination of a 2 and 1 pound cans, or 3 one pound cans. Brush chosen containers thoroughly with soft butter.

When dough has doubled, knead down lightly. Divide in desired number of portions. Drop dough into coffee can, press down and cover with a towel. Allow to rise ½" from the top, about 30 minutes. Do not let dough rise any higher or it will spill while baking. Place cans on a baking sheet. Bake in a preheated 350° oven 1 hour for large tins, 50 minutes for smaller cans. Check with cake tester for doneness. Remove loaves to a wire rack for 10 minutes. Loosen bread with a spatula and turn out to cool.

PRESENTATION

Place bread in the middle of a large tray or basket. Fluff imitation grass around the cake. Surround with piles of colored Easter eggs. Make Confectioner's Icing and dye it yellow with cake coloring. Dribble over top of bread so that it will run down the sides. Sprinkle with colored decorating candies. Thus it becomes a stunning center piece for your Easter table. When ready to serve, slice top off crosswise. As you cut off slices, the top can go back on the bread until finished.

HOT CROSS BUNS

Long a favorite in the British Isles, these delicious buns have become a tradition with many people in the United States. Make and freeze the rolls several weeks before Easter. Heat and frost before serving as they are best when warm.

1 package dry or compressed
    yeast
¼ cup warm water
1 cup warm milk
¼ cup melted butter or margarine
2 eggs, beaten
¼ teaspoon salt
⅓ cup sugar
½ teaspoon nutmeg

Grated rind 1 lemon
5 cups flour, approximately
½ cup dark raisins
¼ cup chopped citron or candied
    orange peel
1 egg beaten with 1 tablespoon
    water
White Icing*

Sprinkle yeast over the warm water; stir with a fork until dissolved. In a mixing bowl, combine and blend well the milk, butter, eggs, salt, sugar, nutmeg, and grated rind. Beat in the yeast mixture and 2 cups of flour with a rubber spatula until smooth. Add the raisins and citron or orange peel. Gradually add sufficient flour to make a soft, workable dough. Turn out on a lightly floured surface and knead until smooth and elastic, about 10 minutes. Place in a warm, greased bowl, turning to coat the top. Cover loosely with plastic wrap and a towel. Allow to double in bulk, about 1½ hours.

Turn dough out on a floured board, knead lightly, cover, and let rest 10 minutes. Cut into 16 equal pieces. Cup hand over a portion of dough and rotate quickly until a smooth bun is formed. Place on a greased baking sheet about 2″ apart. Repeat with remaining dough. Cover and let double, about 45 minutes to 1 hour. Brush with egg wash. Bake in a preheated 375° oven 20 minutes or until golden brown. Make a cross on each bun with the following icing.

*Beat 1 egg white until stiff. Add 1 teaspoon lemon juice and sufficient powdered sugar to make a thick, creamy icing.

GREEK TRINITY BREAD
AND
GREEK BREAD WITH A CROSS

The Greeks always seem to give special meaning for Easter with their beautifully shaped breads. Here are two lovely loaves that make thoughtful gifts or centerpieces as well as being delicious to eat.

2 packages dry or compressed
* yeast*
½ cup warm water
1 cup warm milk
⅔ cup sugar
1½ teaspoons salt
1 teaspoon ground Mahleb
* crushed Anise or Cardamom*

1 cup melted butter or margarine
3 eggs, lightly beaten
7 cups flour, approximately
1 cup raisins, scalded and dried
1 egg beaten with 1 tablespoon
* water*
1 uncooked tinted egg

Sprinkle yeast over the warm water, stirring with a fork until dissolved. In a large mixing bowl, blend the milk, sugar, salt, and spice. Stir in the butter, eggs, and yeast mixture. Beat in 3 cups of flour until batter is smooth. Add the raisins. Gradually stir in sufficient flour to make a soft, workable dough that leaves sides of the bowl. Turn out on a lightly floured board and knead until smooth and elastic, about 10 minutes. Place in a warm, greased bowl, turning to coat the top. Allow to double in bulk, about 2 hours. Punch down dough and turn out on a floured surface. Divide dough in half.

TRINITY BREAD

Cut half the dough in 3 equal pieces. Roll each in a smooth ball. Place on a greased baking sheet in a clover leaf shape about 1″ apart. Press each ball lightly with your hands. Cover and let rise until doubled, about 1 hour. Brush with egg glaze. Bake in a preheated 350° oven 25 to 30 minutes or until golden brown. Cool on wire racks. Loop a pretty ribbon around the seams of the three connected loaves. Tie a big bow in the center.

GREEK BREAD WITH A CROSS

Cut off ¼ of remaining dough and set aside. Roll the larger portion in a 21″ rope. Form a ring, pinch the ends to seal and place in a 9″ greased cake pan. Divide the smaller piece of dough in half. Roll each piece in a 10″ rope. Place the 2 ropes across the ring in the shape of a cross. Tuck ends of ropes under the ring. Press an uncooked red or purple egg in the center. Cover and let double, about 1 hour. Brush with egg glaze. Again press egg gently into the dough. Bake in a preheated 350° oven about 30 minutes or until a golden brown. Loosen gently from pan and let cool on a wire rack.

NOTE

Follow directions under Easter Egg Twist to dye the egg (page 229).

VALENTINE CAKE

This chapter would not be complete without a Valentine Coffee Cake. Decorated with frosting and red cherries, the cake makes a lovely gift for the children or a surprise for your husband.

2 packages dry or compressed yeast	2 eggs
¼ cup warm water	Grated rind 1 lemon
1 cup warm milk	Filling
½ cup sugar	Confectioner's Icing, page 268
1½ teaspoons salt	Candied cherries and
¼ cup melted butter or margarine	Decorating candies
4 to 5 cups flour	

Sprinkle yeast over the warm water, stirring with a fork to dissolve. Blend the milk, sugar, salt, and butter. Add 1 cup of flour and beat until a smooth batter with rubber spatula. Stir in the eggs, lemon rind, and yeast mixture. Add sufficient flour to make a soft, workable dough. Turn out on a lightly floured surface and knead until smooth and elastic, about 10 minutes. Round into a ball and place in a warm, greased bowl, turning to coat the top. Cover loosely with plastic wrap and a towel.

233

Allow to double in bulk, about 1 hour.

Punch down the dough, knead lightly, cover and let rest 10 minutes. Roll into a large rectangle, 15x24". Brush with melted butter to within ½" of edges. Prepare the following filling:

½ cup flour
½ cup brown sugar
¼ teaspoon salt

¼ cup soft butter
¼ cup chopped nuts (optional)

Combine the flour, sugar, and salt. Cut in the butter with a pastry blender or rub with your hands until crumbly. Add the nuts, if desired. Sprinkle filling over the rectangle of dough. Cut rectangle lengthwise in half. Roll each portion jelly roll style from the long side. Seal edges by pinching. Place each roll on a greased baking sheet, insert ends together and shape into a heart. (If you have a heart shaped pan, grease pan and fit one roll into the heart shape. Cover and let rise until doubled.) With kitchen shears, cut slashes 1" apart and 1" into the dough. Twist each finger to lay on its side. Cover and let rise until doubled, about 45 minutes. Bake either the free standing or pan bread in a preheated 350° oven 25 to 30 minutes. Cool on wire racks. Frost with Confectioner's Icing. Decorate with candied cherries and sprinkle with decorating candies.

CHALLAH

Jewish Challah is a magnificent egg bread used for dinner at the beginning of each Sabbath. The bread may be braided elaborately, simply, or made into loaves. With the help of a close Orthodox friend, the cholesterol problem has been solved as directed at end of the recipe

2 packages dry or compressed
  yeast
2½ cups warm water
¼ cup sugar
2 teaspoons salt
⅓ cup light oil

4 eggs, lightly beaten
8 to 9 cups flour
1 egg mixed with 1 tablespoon
  water
Poppy seeds

Sprinkle yeast over the warm water in a large mixing bowl. Stir with a fork until dissolved. Blend in the sugar, salt, oil, and eggs. Beat in 4 cups of flour with a rubber spatula until mixture is smooth. Add sufficient more flour to make a soft, workable dough. Turn out on a floured board and knead until smooth and elastic, 10 to 12 minutes. You will find this a responsive dough to handle. Place in a warm, greased bowl, turning to coat the top. Cover loosely with plastic wrap and a towel. Set aside to *triple* in bulk, about 1½ hours. Punch the dough down, turn out on a lightly floured surface and knead lightly. Cover and let rest 10 minutes (refer to Techniques, page 13).

THREE BRAIDS

Divide dough in 9 portions. Cover the pieces you are not working with. Roll 3 portions in smooth ropes, about 14" long. Braid together starting from the center and working out to each end. Tuck the ends under and place on a greased baking sheet. Repeat process with remaining dough. Cover braids and let rise until doubled, about 45 minutes. Brush with egg wash thoroughly and sprinkle liberally with poppy seeds. Bake in a preheated 375° oven 30 minutes. Cool on wire racks.

PAN LOAVES

Divide dough in 4 portions. Form into loaves and place in greased 8½x4½x2½" pans. Cover and allow to rise until just curved over tops of pans. Brush with egg wash and sprinkle with poppy seeds, if desired. Bake in a preheated 375° oven about 40 minutes or until golden brown. Cool on wire racks.

TWO BRAIDS (JACOB'S LADDER)

Divide dough in half. Cut one portion in 4 equal pieces. Roll into ropes 22" long. Arrange the 4 ropes in the shape of a cross with 4 ends meeting and overlapping in the center. Lift the ends of the 2 opposite

ropes and cross them over the other pieces to reverse their positions but still maintain the cross shape. Now lift and reverse the other pair of ropes in the same manner. Repeat the lifting and crossing process until the ropes weave completely into a braid. You will be pleased at the ease of this braiding as it literally forms itself as you go through the process. Tuck under the ends and place braid on a greased baking sheet. Repeat process with remaining dough. Proceed as directed for the other braids.

CHOLESTEROL FREE CHALLAH

Fleischmann's has now marketed a substitute for eggs called Egg Beater. This product works extremely well in breadmaking. I doubt that you can tell the difference from the real Challah. The salt content may be cut in half or eliminated.

2 packages dry or compressed
    yeast
2½ cups warm water
¼ cup sugar
2 teaspoons salt
½ cup melted margarine

1 cup Egg Beater
    (reserve 1 tablespoon for glaze)
10 cups flour, approximately
1 tablespoon Egg Beater mixed
    with 1 tablespoon water
Poppy seed

Follow directions for the Challah recipe. More flour is required because of increased liquid content. Margarine is for flavor; oil may be used if preferred. 1 tablespoon of Egg Beater mixed with water makes an excellent glaze.

CREAM OF PUMPKIN SOUP

An elegant soup in color and flavor. A perfect beginning for a Thanksgiving or Christmas dinner. Serves 8 to 10.

¼ cup butter or margarine
¾ cup coarsely chopped onion
3 tablespoons flour
2½ cups canned pumpkin purée
¾ teaspoon ginger
¼ teaspoon nutmeg

⅛ teaspoon white pepper
5 cups hot chicken broth
Salt
1 cup heavy cream
Whipped cream or Parsley

Melt butter in a large saucepan; sauté onion until tender, stirring occasionally. Whisk in the flour and cook over low heat until the roux is foamy. Remove pan from heat. Add the pumpkin, spices, pepper, and chicken broth. Bring to a boil and stir until smooth. Strain soup into a clean pan. Slowly add the cream and reheat but do not allow to boil. Taste for salt and adjust. Serve in warm soup bowls topped with either finely chopped parsley or a dollop of whipped cream.

DOUBLE CONSOMME

It takes a very short time to produce this beautiful, clear golden consomme. Restaurants color this lovely soup with caramel to make it dark, but I love the lighter, golden color. Wonderful served in demitasse cups or in a large tureen for a buffet.

3 egg whites, beaten until stiff
1 pound lean ground beef
½ cup parsley, chopped
½ cup celery and leaves, chopped
½ cup carrots, chopped
1 teaspoon peppercorns
1 bay leaf

½ teaspoon thyme
2 cups water
8 cups beef broth, canned
  or your own make
Salt
Dry Sherry

Combine the egg whites and meat. Stir thoroughly. Place the prepared vegetables, seasonings, meat mixture, and water in a soup kettle. Stir well with a wooden spoon. Add the beef broth and stir until you have a smooth mass. Bring to a boil over medium high heat, stirring frequently. Lower heat to simmer and let bubble lightly 1 hour. Remove from fire and allow to set 30 minutes. Strain soup through a wet cheese cloth placed in a colander over a clean pan. Taste for salt and adjust. Bring back to a boil and add a few tablespoons of sherry to your taste. Makes 4 to 5 cups of broth.

SENEGALESE SOUP

If you like unusual flavors with an exotic approach, this quick and easy curried soup will be a charming addition to your repertoire.

1 cup chopped onion	3½ cups chicken broth
2 stalks celery, chopped	1 chicken breast
1 medium apple pared, cored, and chopped	3 cloves
4 tablespoons butter	1 stick cinnamon
1 tablespoon curry powder	1 cup heavy cream
3 tablespoons flour	Toasted coconut*

Sauté onion, celery, and apple in the butter until soft. Blend in the curry and flour with a wooden spoon. Cook over low heat 5 minutes; do not allow to burn. Add the broth, chicken breast, cloves, and cinnamon. Cover and simmer 30 minutes. Strain soup through a fine strainer. Remove chicken breast and eat it for lunch — delicious. Return soup to the burner and slowly add the thick cream. Reheat but do not allow to boil. Serve hot garnished with toasted coconut.

*TOASTED COCONUT

Spread coconut in a shallow pan. Place in a 300° oven and toast until golden, about 20 minutes.

MATZO BALL SOUP

When a friend or member of your family is ill, nothing will be more heart warming than a pot of this great classic soup. This version has a distinctive fillip of nutmeg.

3 eggs, separated	¼ cup finely cut parsley
2 tablespoons cold chicken fat	¼ teaspoon nutmeg
Pinch salt	4 quarts chicken broth
¾ cup Matzo meal	

Combine and beat thoroughly the egg yolks, chicken fat and salt. In a separate bowl, beat the egg whites until softly stiff. Fold the egg yolk mixture into the beaten egg whites. Add the Matzo meal, parsley and nutmeg. Stir gently until well mixed. Chill 20 minutes. Remove from refrigerator. Wet your hands with water and form mixture into desired size balls. Drop into rapidly boiling chicken broth. Reduce heat to simmer, cover, and let bubble lightly 1 hour.

FAVORITE NON YEAST BREADS

SOUPS:

> *Cream of Tomato*
> *Chicken-Tomato-Wine Consommé*
> *Hot Tomato Bouillon*
> *Tomato Buttermilk*

BUTTERMILK BISCUITS

2 cups all purpose flour   ½ teaspoon soda
½ teaspoon salt   5 tablespoons shortening
4 teaspoons baking powder   1 cup buttermilk
Melted butter (optional)

Sift flour, salt, baking powder, and soda into a mixing bowl. Cut in the shortening with a pastry blender until mixture resembles coarse cornmeal. Make a well with a rubber spatula. Add buttermilk all at once and stir until a soft dough is formed and leaves sides of the bowl. Turn out on a floured board and knead about 1 minute. Pat or roll dough ½″ thick. Cut with floured biscuit cutter. Place biscuits on a greased baking sheet. Brush tops with melted butter if desired. Bake in a preheated 450° oven 12 to 15 minutes. Makes about sixteen 2″ biscuits.

BAKING POWDER BISCUITS

2 cups sifted all purpose flour
2½ teaspoons baking powder   ¾ cup milk
½ teaspoon salt   Melted butter
5 tablespoons shortening

Sift dry ingredients together into a mixing bowl. Cut in the shortening with a pastry blender until mixture resembles coarse cornmeal. Add milk gradually, stirring with a rubber spatula until a soft dough is formed. Turn out on a floured board and knead lightly 30 seconds. Pat or roll ½″ thick. Cut with a floured biscuit cutter. Place biscuits on greased baking sheet. Brush with melted butter if desired. Bake in a preheated 450° oven 12 to 15 minutes. Makes about twelve 2″ biscuits.

LEMON BISCUITS

2 cups sifted cake flour   ⅔ cup milk
2 teaspoons baking powder   • • •
½ teaspoon salt   4 tablespoons sugar
5 tablespoons butter or shortening   Grated rind 1 lemon
Grated rind 1 lemon   ¼ teaspoon lemon juice
Melted butter

Preheat oven to 450°.

Sift flour, baking powder, and salt into a mixing bowl. Cut in the butter with a pastry blender. Add grated lemon rind. Make a well in dry ingredients and add milk all at once. Stir quickly with a rubber spatula until mixture forms a soft dough. Turn out on a lightly floured board and knead 30 seconds. Roll or pat dough ¼" thick. Cut with 1½" floured biscuit cutter.

Combine sugar, grated rind of remaining lemon, and just enough lemon juice to make a crumbly mixture. Place half the biscuits in greased muffin tins. Brush tops with melted butter. Sprinkle the lemon-sugar mixture on biscuits. Top with remaining biscuits and press lightly together. Bake in preheated oven 10 to 12 minutes. Makes 24 biscuits.

PERFECT SWEET MUFFINS

The secret for excellent muffins is to have all ingredients ready, mix quickly and pop into a hot oven. Don't fret about lumps in the batter — they disappear in the baking. This recipe makes 12 large muffins.

2 cups sifted all purpose flour	2 eggs
½ teaspoon salt	1 cup milk
2 teaspoons baking powder	¼ cup melted butter or
¼ cup sugar	margarine

Preheat oven to 425°. Brush muffin cups thoroughly with melted butter.

Sift flour, salt, baking powder, and sugar into a mixing bowl. In a separate bowl, beat the eggs. Blend in the milk and butter. Make a well in the dry ingredients with a rubber spatula. Add liquid mixture all at once. Stir quickly just enough to moisten dry ingredients. Fill each muffin tin ⅔ full. Bake 20 to 25 minutes. Serve immediately. If smaller muffin pans are used, cut baking time 5 minutes.

MUFFIN VARIATIONS

Streusel Muffins: Combine ½ cup sugar, ¼ teaspoon cinnamon, ¼ teaspoon nutmeg, ½ cup flour, and ¼ cup soft butter. Work with your hands or a fork until mixture is crumbly. After filling greased muffin cups with batter, spoon 1 tablespoon of streusel topping over each muffin. Bake as directed.

Prune-Lemon Muffins: Add grated rind of 1 lemon to dry ingredients. Dice 1 cup pitted moist prunes and dust with a tiny amount of flour. Stir quickly into the batter. Bake as directed.

Raisin, Date, or Nut Muffins: Add 1 cup dark or golden raisins, chopped dates, or coarsely chopped nuts to muffin batter. Another option

241

is a combination of ½ cup of either fruit and ½ cup nuts. Bake as directed.

Orange Muffins: Add grated rind of 1 orange to dry ingredients. Substitute ½ cup orange juice for ½ cup milk. Proceed as directed.

Marmalade Muffins: Combine ¼ cup brown sugar with ¼ cup flour. Stir in 1 tablespoon orange juice and 2 tablespoons marmalade. Fill muffin tins half full of batter. Drop 1 teaspoon of marmalade filling on each muffin. Top with remaining batter. Bake as directed.

Coconut Muffins: Add 1 cup moist, flaky coconut to muffin batter. Proceed as directed.

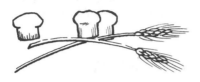

WHOLE WHEAT-RYE MUFFINS

1 cup whole wheat flour
1 cup rye flour
½ teaspoon salt
4 teaspoons baking powder

½ cup brown sugar
2 eggs, beaten
1 cup milk
⅓ cup melted butter or
  margarine
½ cup raisins or chopped nuts

Preheat oven to 425°.

Brush muffin cups with melted butter. Blend flours, salt, baking powder, and brown sugar in a mixing bowl. Combine the eggs, milk, and butter in a separate bowl. Make a well in dry ingredients with a rubber spatula. Quickly stir in the milk mixture until dry ingredients are just moistened. Add raisins or nuts if desired. Fill muffin tins ⅔ full. Makes 12 large muffins.

RAISIN-BRAN MUFFINS

1 cup sifted all purpose flour
2 teaspoons baking powder
½ teaspoon salt
¼ cup sugar
2 eggs, beaten

1 cup milk
2 tablespoons melted butter or
  margarine
1 cup bran flakes or buds
1 cup raisins, dark or golden

Preheat oven to 425°. Brush muffin tins with melted butter. Sift flour, baking powder, salt, and sugar into a mixing bowl. In a separate bowl, combine eggs, milk, butter, and bran flakes. Stir raisins in flour mixture and make a well. Beat in milk mixture, stirring just enough to moisten dry ingredients. Fill cups ⅔ full. Bake 20 to 25 minutes. Makes 12 muffins.

SPICY APPLE MUFFINS

2 cups sifted all purpose flour
2½ teaspoons baking powder
½ teaspoon salt
¼ cup sugar
¾ teaspoon cinnamon
¼ teaspoon nutmeg

1 egg
1 cup milk
⅓ cup melted butter or margarine
¾ cup pared, cored, and grated
    apples

Preheat oven to 425°. Brush muffin cups with melted butter. Sift flour, baking powder, salt, sugar, cinnamon, and nutmeg into a mixing bowl. In a separate bowl, blend the egg, milk, butter, and apples. Make a well in the dry ingredients with a rubber spatula. Pour in the milk mixture all at once. Stir just until ingredients are moistened. Fill cups ⅔ full. Bake 20 to 25 minutes. Makes 12 large muffins.

BLUEBERRY MUFFINS

A blueberry muffin is everyone's favorite. When blueberry season begins, buy several boxes, place in plastic bags and store in the freezer. Or if you prefer, make a quantity of muffins and freeze.

2 cups sifted all-purpose flour
¾ teaspoon salt
3 teaspoons baking powder
¼ cup sugar
2 eggs

¼ cup melted butter or margarine
1 cup milk
1 cup unsugared blueberries
    fresh or frozen

Preheat oven to 425°.

Resift flour with the salt, baking powder, and sugar into a mixing bowl. In a separate bowl, beat the eggs, butter, and milk until well blended. Lightly flour the blueberries so they will not sink in one spot. Make a well in the dry ingredients. With a rubber spatula, stir in the egg mixture rapidly, mixing just enough that dry ingredients are wet. Quickly fold in the blueberries. Fill well greased muffin tins ¾ full. Bake in preheated oven 20 to 25 minutes or until golden brown. Remove and serve immediately. Makes 12 large muffins.

NOTE
Try making miniature muffins for a luncheon. The recipe will make about 24. Bake in a 425° oven 15 minutes or until browned.

Split left over large muffins, butter and toast for breakfast — delicious with hot coffee or tea!

CORNBREAD

As with so many quick breads, the secret for a good texture in cornbread is fast mixing. The recipe is adaptable for either regular or stone ground cornmeal.

1 cup all purpose flour
1 cup yellow cornmeal
3 tablespoons sugar
2 teaspoons baking powder

¾ teaspoon salt
1⅛ cups milk
2 eggs
4 tablespoons melted butter

Preheat oven to 425°.

Sift dry ingredients into a mixing bowl. In a separate bowl, combine the milk, eggs, and butter, stirring until well blended. With a rubber spatula, make a well in the dry ingredients. Pour milk mixture in all at once. Stir quickly to just moisten the cornmeal mixture. Pour batter in a greased 7x11" or 8x8" pan. Bake 25 minutes. Serve immediately.

SOUTHERN SPOON BREAD

Serve heaping tablespoons of this light, golden bread on small plates with good butter and strawberry preserves. This recipe may be baked in a soufflé bowl or doubled and placed in a large, deep baking dish. Bake 15 to 20 minutes longer when doubled.

1 cup yellow cornmeal
3 cups milk
1 teaspoon salt
1 teaspoon baking powder

3 tablespoons melted butter or
   margarine
3 egg yolks, beaten
3 stiffly beaten egg whites

Combine cornmeal and 2 cups of the milk in a saucepan. Cook, stirring constantly until consistency of thick mush. Remove from heat and allow to cool 5 minutes. Add the salt, baking powder, butter, and remaining cup of milk. Blend thoroughly. Beat in egg yolks and fold in the egg whites. Pour in a well greased 2 quart soufflé bowl. Bake in a preheated 325° oven 1 hour. Serves 6 to 8.

POPOVERS

Most recipes for Popovers use the same ingredients. Where cooks disagree is the method of baking. After much testing, I have found the following directions most successful and easy.

2 eggs
1 cup milk
1 tablespoon melted butter

1 cup all purpose flour
(unsifted)
¼ teaspoon salt

Preheat oven to 450°.

Brush popover pans, muffin tins, or custard cups heavily with melted butter or margarine. If you want giant popovers, use deep ceramic or wide baking cups. Place individual cups on a baking sheet.

In a small bowl, whisk the eggs thoroughly. Add the milk, butter, flour, and salt. Beat quickly and vigorously with a whisk until batter is like thick cream. Pour cups one-half full. Bake in a 450° oven 15 minutes on the middle shelf. Reduce heat to 350° and bake 15 to 20 minutes. The muffins should be puffed, brown, crisp on the outside and moist inside. Serve immediately. The recipe doubles easily.

YORKSHIRE PUDDING

One of England's most famous puddings is simple to make and quite similar to Popovers. Formerly, the pudding was baked under a spitted roast so that it was full of good beef drippings — and a bit soggy too. Now, add beef drippings to a hot baking pan and cook just before serving the roast.

1 cup all purpose flour
Pinch of salt
2 eggs, beaten

1½ cups milk
1 tablespoon water

Sift flour and salt in a mixing bowl. Add the eggs and half the milk. Beat thoroughly with a whisk. Slowly add the remaining milk. Stir until batter is smooth. Set aside for 30 minutes. Preheat oven to 450°. Heat a 7x11″ pan with about ¼ cup beef drippings. Add water to the batter. Pour batter into hot pan. Bake in hot oven on middle shelf 25 to 30 minutes. Cut in squares and serve immediately.

Yorkshire pudding may be baked in popover or muffin tins. Heat tins until quite hot and add 1 tablespoon beef drippings to each cup. Fill cups half full of batter and proceed as directed. Bake until puffed and golden brown, about 25 minutes.

APRICOT BREAD

A favorite recipe given to me several years ago by a good friend and cook. A delightful bread to slice thin for afternoon tea.

Soak 1 cup of dried apricots in warm water 30 minutes. Drain and dice in ¼″ pieces.

1 cup sugar
2 tablespoons butter or margarine
1 egg
¼ cup water
½ cup orange juice

2 cups sifted all purpose flour
1½ teaspoons baking powder
½ teaspoon soda
1 teaspoon salt
½ cup chopped nuts

Beat together the sugar, butter, and egg thoroughly. Stir in the water, and orange juice. Sift dry ingredients together. Beat into the sugar mixture. Blend in the nuts and diced apricots. Pour the batter in a thoroughly greased 9x5x3″ loaf pan. Allow to stand 20 minutes. Bake in a preheated 350° oven 55 to 60 minutes. Remove from oven. Place pan on a wire rack to cool 5 minutes. Loosen sides with a spatula and turn bread out on a wire rack. Let cool before slicing.

BANANA BREAD

2 cups sifted all purpose flour
½ teaspoon salt
1 teaspoon baking soda
½ cup butter or margarine
1 cup sugar
3 eggs
3 large, ripe bananas

½ cup golden raisins, rinsed
in hot water and dried
½ cup chopped nuts
(optional)

Sift flour, salt, and baking soda together and set aside. In a mixing bowl, cream butter and sugar together until light and fluffy. Add eggs one at a time, beating well after each addition. If using an electric mixer, slice bananas and blend into egg mixture. If making bread by hand, mash bananas with a fork before adding to the batter. Beat in dry ingredients until well mixed. Add raisins and nuts. Bake in a well greased 9x5x3" loaf pan for 1 hour in a preheated 325° oven. Turn out on a wire rack. Do not slice until thoroughly cooled.

VARIATION

Substitute 1 cup unsifted stone ground whole wheat flour for 1 cup of white. Add 1 teaspoon grated orange rind and 2 tablespoons fresh orange juice to the butter mixture. Proceed as directed.

GOLDEN PUMPKIN BREAD

A moist, spicy cake-bread that smells like Thanksgiving and Christmas. An ideal holiday gift as the bread may be baked ahead in small loaf pans and frozen.

3½ cups sifted all purpose flour	4 eggs
1½ teaspoons salt	1 cup light oil
2½ teaspoons cinnamon	2 cups sugar
1½ teaspoons nutmeg	2 cups canned pumpkin
½ teaspoon cloves	1 cup chopped pecans
2 teaspoons baking soda	1 cup chopped mixed candied fruit

Sift flour, salt, spices, and baking soda together. Set aside. Sprinkle a small amount of flour mixture over the mixed candied fruits and set aside. In a mixing bowl, beat the eggs thoroughly. Blend in the oil, sugar, and pumpkin. Add dry ingredients and beat well until batter is smooth. Stir in the pecans and candied fruits. This amount of batter will make 1 large cake in a Bundt or 10" tube pan plus an 8½x4½x2½" loaf pan. Brush pans well with melted butter. Pour two-thirds of batter in Bundt pan and remaining third in the loaf pan. Bake in a preheated 350° oven 65 minutes. Check with a cake tester. Turn out on wire racks to cool. For 1 pound loaf pans, cut the baking time to 40 minutes. Makes 6 small loaves.

DATE BREAD

The unusual addition of cheese makes this a moist bread with a charming flavor. Excellent served alone or made into sandwiches with a filling of cream cheese mixed with chopped candied ginger.

2 cups diced dates
1 cup boiling water
⅓ cup butter or margarine
¾ cup brown sugar, packed
1 egg
1 cup grated American or
   cheddar cheese

1½ cups sifted all purpose flour
½ teaspoon salt
1 teaspoon baking soda
½ cup whole wheat flour
½ cup chopped walnuts

Pour boiling water over the dates and set aside while preparing the remaining ingredients. Brush a 9x5x3″ loaf pan with melted butter. Preheat oven to 350°. In a mixing bowl, combine butter, brown sugar, and egg, beating until smooth. Stir in the cheese and date mixture. Sift the flour with salt and baking soda. Beat flour mixture into the cake batter. Add the whole wheat flour and mix until smooth. Stir in the chopped walnuts. Pour into prepared pan. Bake 55 minutes. Turn out on wire rack. Do not attempt to slice the bread until thoroughly cooled.

HONEY ORANGE SOY LOAVES

An unusually delicious non-yeast bread, enriched with soy flour, aromatic with orange juice that is quickly and easily made. And men love it!

½ cup margarine or butter
1 cup honey
3 eggs
Grated rind of 2 large oranges
4 cups sifted all purpose flour
½ cup soy flour

4 teaspoons baking powder
1 teaspoon baking soda
1 teaspoon salt
1½ cups orange juice
1½ cups chopped nuts
   (pecans, walnuts, or almonds)

Cream the butter thoroughly. Gradually add the honey, beating until light and fluffy. Add eggs one at a time, beating well with each addition. Blend in the grated orange rind. Resift flour with soy flour, baking powder, soda, and salt. Add sifted dry ingredients alternately with the orange juice to the honey mixture. Beat for 1 or 2 minutes until batter is smooth and creamy. Stir in nut meats. Pour in 2 well greased 9x5x3″ loaf pans. Bake in a preheated 325° oven 1 hour. Test with a cake tester for doneness. Remove from oven and let stand in pans on a rack 5 minutes. Turn breads out to cool. Do not cut until thoroughly chilled.

ENGLISH FRUIT MALT LOAF

An English friend sent this delightfully simple recipe to me. It is moist and full of good dried fruit — I recommend it highly.

1 cup mixed dried fruit
1 cup All Bran or Bran Buds
1 cup sugar

1 cup buttermilk
1 cup self-rising flour

Remove any seeds from the dried fruit. You may chop the fruit but, personally I prefer to leave it whole as the bread is prettier when sliced.

In a large mixing bowl, combine the fruit, bran, sugar, and buttermilk. Stir until ingredients are well mixed. Cover bowl with a towel and allow to stand for 1 hour. Measure in the flour and blend well. Pour batter in a well greased loaf pan, 8½x4½x2½″. Bake in a preheated 350° oven 1 hour and 15 minutes. Allow to cool in pan on a wire rack 10 minutes. Loosen sides with a spatula and turn out on a rack. Let cool before slicing. The bread is delicious served buttered or spread with cream cheese for tea but we have also found it a great treat toasted for breakfast.

GRANDMOTHER'S COFFEE CAKE

One of the most delightful and tasteful coffee cakes that is quickly and easily made. An excellent choice for Christmas gifts as the cake freezes well so that several can be made ahead.

FILLING
½ cup brown sugar, packed
1/3 cup sifted flour
2 teaspoons cinnamon

¼ cup soft butter
Grated rind 1 large orange

Blend all ingredients with a pastry blender until crumbly. Set aside.

THE CAKE

¾ cup butter or margarine
1½ cups sugar
Grated rind 1 orange
3 eggs
3 cups sifted all purpose flour
2 teaspoons baking powder
1 teaspoon soda

½ teaspoon salt
1 cup sour cream
¾ cup golden raisins
1 cup powdered sugar
1 tablespoon Grand Marnier
3 tablespoons orange juice

Sift flour with baking powder, soda, and salt. Cream the butter, sugar, and orange rind until light and fluffy. Beat in eggs one at a time, stirring thoroughly after each addition. Add flour mixture to the creamed mixture alternately with the sour cream. Continue beating until mixture is smooth and creamy. Pour two-thirds of the batter into a greased bundt pan. Sprinkle the filling over the batter. Add the raisins and top with remaining batter. Bake in a preheated 350° oven 50 minutes or until cake tests done. Remove pan to wire rack and allow to cool 10 minutes. Turn cake out on a serving dish. Blend the powdered sugar, Grand Marnier, and orange juice until smooth. Spread over the warm cake.

CINNAMON SWIRL COFFEE CAKE

Almost as good as Grandmother's Coffee Cake! A creamy textured cake because of the sour cream, with a cinnamon filling that swirls through the center.

2 cups all purpose flour
1 teaspoon baking powder
¼ teaspoon salt
1 cup butter or margarine
2 cups sugar
2 eggs
1 cup sour cream

1 teaspoon vanilla flavoring
• • •
Filling:
½ cup brown sugar
1 cup chopped pecans
2 teaspoons cinnamon

Sift flour, baking powder, and salt together. Set aside. Mix the butter and sugar until light and creamy. Add eggs one at a time, beating well after each addition. Blend in the sour cream and vanilla. Stir in the dry ingredients until well mixed. Brush a Bundt pan thoroughly with melted butter. Combine the brown sugar, pecans, and cinnamon. Pour ½ of batter in prepared cake pan, spreading evenly. Sprinkle brown sugar filling over the batter. Spoon remaining batter over the brown sugar mixture. Bake in a preheated 350° oven 55 minutes. Check with a cake tester for doneness. Remove from oven and place on wire rack 10 minutes. Turn cake out to cool.

HOT SPICY GINGERBREAD

A family favorite that we sometimes neglect. Surprise everyone some cold Sunday morning with this delicious treat.

2¼ cups sifted all purpose flour
1 teaspoon baking soda
½ teaspoon salt
1½ teaspoons ginger
1 teaspoon cinnamon
½ teaspoon nutmeg

¼ teaspoon cloves
½ cup butter or shortening
2 tablespoons sugar
2 eggs
1 cup molasses
1 cup boiling water

Sift flour, soda, salt, ginger, cinnamon, nutmeg, and cloves together. Set aside. Combine butter, sugar, and eggs in a mixing bowl. Beat until light and creamy. Blend the molasses and boiling water together. Add the flour mixture to the butter mixture alternately with molasses and water. Begin with the flour and beat well after each addition. Pour batter into a well greased 7x12x2″ pan. Bake in a preheated 350° oven 40 to 45 minutes. Lower heat to 325° if a glass baking dish is used. Serve hot immediately with honey butter.

HONEY BUTTER
Mix equal amounts of soft butter and honey until creamy and light.

BLUEBERRY BUCKLE

A tasteful treat for Sunday brunch or coffee with the girls. When blueberry season arrives, make several in foil pans and freeze.

THE CAKE
½ cup butter or margarine
½ cup sugar
2 eggs
2 cups all purpose flour
¼ teaspoon salt

2 teaspoons baking powder
½ cup milk
2 cups frozen or fresh
   blueberries (unsugared)

Cream butter or margarine with sugar until fluffy Add eggs, one at a time, stirring well after each addition. Sift flour, salt, and baking powder together. Beat in the flour mixture alternately with milk until light and creamy. Pour into a well greased 9″ square cake pan or a deep pie plate. Sprinkle berries over the cake batter. Add the following topping:

½ cup sugar
½ cup flour
½ teaspoon cinnamon

½ teaspoon nutmeg
¼ cup soft butter or margarine

Combine all ingredients, mixing with a pastry blender or your hands until crumbly. Sprinkle over the blueberries. Bake the cake in a preheated 350° oven 60 minutes. If using a glass baking dish, reduce heat to 325°. Cool cake in the pan on a wire rack or serve immediately.

IRISH WHOLE WHEAT BREAD

If you enjoy the true flavor of whole wheat, this version of Irish Soda Bread creates a wonderfully earthy taste. This is a recipe sent to me from England that will make 1 large or 2 small loaves.

3½ cups whole wheat flour
1 cup white flour
1 teaspoon baking soda

1 teaspoon salt
1½ cups buttermilk

Blend dry ingredients in a mixing bowl. Make a well in the center with a rubber spatula. Add enough buttermilk to make a thick dough. Mixing should be done lightly and quickly. If mixture becomes too stiff, add a bit more milk. The dough should be slack but not wet. Turn out on a lightly floured board. With floured hands, shape and flatten dough into a circle about 1½″ thick. Place on a greased baking sheet and slash a large cross over the top with a sharp knife or razor. This is to ensure even distribution of heat. Bake in a preheated 400° oven 40 to 45 minutes. Test with a skewer before removing from oven. Serve hot, cold, or as crisp toast. Bake small loaves 40 minutes.

BROWN BREAD LOAF

A quick, nutritious whole wheat bread that can be made in one and one half hours. Great toasted and served with scrambled eggs.

1 cup sifted unbleached white flour
2 teaspoons baking soda
1 teaspoon salt
1 cup brown sugar
2 cups stone ground whole wheat
    flour

3 tablespoons melted butter
    or margarine
¼ cup molasses
1½ cups buttermilk
1 egg, well beaten

Sift white flour, baking soda, and salt together in a mixing bowl. Blend in the brown sugar and whole wheat flour. Add the melted butter, molasses, buttermilk, and egg. Beat vigorously until the batter is smooth. Pour into a greased 9x5x3″ loaf pan. Allow to stand 20 minutes. Bake in a preheated 350° oven 45 minutes. Check with a cake tester for doneness. Turn loaf out on a wire rack to cool.

BUTTERMILK PANCAKES

2¼ cups sifted all purpose flour
1 teaspoon baking soda
2 teaspoons baking powder
1 teaspoon salt
2 teaspoons sugar
2 eggs
2 cups buttermilk
¼ cup melted butter or margarine

Sift dry ingredients into a mixing bowl. In a separate bowl, beat eggs until light. Add the buttermilk and butter. Combine the buttermilk mixture with the dry ingredients, stirring until smooth. Cook pancakes on a hot, greased griddle, turning once.

ORANGE PANCAKES

An unusually light pancake that has been a favorite of my family. Excellent served with orange honey, marmalade, or raspberry jam.

1 cup sifted all purpose flour
½ teaspoon salt
1½ teaspoons baking powder
2 teaspoons sugar

1 teaspoon grated lemon rind
1 cup fresh orange juice
1 egg, separated
2 tablespoons melted butter

Sift flour, salt, baking powder, and sugar together in a mixing bowl. In a separate bowl, combine the lemon rind, orange juice, egg yolk, and butter. With a rubber spatula, blend the orange juice mixture into the dry ingredients until smooth. Beat the egg white until softly stiff. Fold into the batter. Bake pancakes on a hot, greased griddle, turning once.

AILEEN'S ORANGE BREAD

This charming bread is full of aromatic lushness. It is so moist and full of orange flavor, the baking is a joy just to have the aroma floating in your kitchen.

2 oranges
¼ cup water
1 cup sugar
2 cups sifted all purpose flour
1 cup sugar

1 teaspoon baking powder
¼ teaspoon salt
1 cup milk
1 tablespoon melted butter
1 egg

Squeeze juice from the three oranges; drink the orange juice. Remove pulp from the skin — simply dig out what you can with your hands, don't worry about what's left. Leave the white part attached to the orange skin. Julienne the skin until there are 1½ packed cups of strips. Place strips in water to cover, bring to a boil, and cook until tender, about 10 minutes. Drain. Combine the ¼ cup of water and 1 cup of sugar in a saucepan. Add the orange strips, bring to a boil, and cook until almost dry, about 30 to 40 minutes. Discard any liquid left.

Sift flour, 1 cup sugar, baking powder, and salt into a mixing bowl. Add the milk, butter, and egg. Stir in the orange skins until batter is smooth and well mixed. Pour into a greased 8½x4½x2½" loaf pan. Let stand 20 minutes. Bake in a preheated 325° oven for 1 hour. Test with a cake tester and if not done, bake another 15 minutes. Remove from pan and cool on a wire rack. Do not attempt to slice until thoroughly cooled.

LEMON COFFEE CAKE

2 cups sifted all purpose flour
½ teaspoon salt
2 teaspoons baking powder
½ cup butter
⅔ cup sugar
Grated rind 1 lemon

2 eggs
½ cup milk
¼ cup lemon juice

Glaze:
½ cup powdered sugar
2 tablespoons lemon juice

Sift flour, salt, and baking powder together. Set aside. Cream butter and sugar together until light and fluffy. Add the grated lemon rind. Beat in eggs one at a time. Add dry ingredients alternately with combined milk and lemon juice, beating well after each addition. Bake in a greased 8½x4½x2½" loaf pan in a preheated 350° oven 1 hour. Remove from oven. Combine the powdered sugar and 2 tablespoons of lemon juice, stirring with a fork until smooth. Brush on hot cake. Allow to stay in pan 20 minutes. Remove cake and cool on a wire rack.

ORANGE COFFEE CAKE:

Substitute grated rind of 1 orange for the lemon. Use ¼ cup milk and ½ cup orange juice. Proceed as directed.

GLAZE:

Substitute 2 tablespoons orange juice for the lemon.

CREAM OF TOMATO SOUP

A refreshing soup that is quickly put together. A great emergency soup as most of us always have the following ingredients in the pantry. Serves 6.

5 tablespoons butter or margarine
1 tablespoon oil
1 cup chopped onion
3 cups canned or 1½ pounds fresh
 tomatoes
¼ teaspoon thyme
½ teaspoon basil

Grindings of black pepper
3 tablespoons flour
2 cups chicken broth
¼ teaspoon baking soda
½ teaspoon sugar
½ cup heavy cream
Salt

Melt butter and oil in a large saucepan. Sauté onions until tender, about 10 minutes. If using fresh tomatoes, core and chop coarsely. Add the tomatoes, thyme, basil, and a few grindings of black pepper to onion mixture. Bring to a simmer and cook 10 minutes. In a small bowl, whisk the flour and ½ cup broth until smooth. Slowly add to the soup, stirring constantly. Pour in remaining broth. Cover and simmer 25 minutes. Put soup through a fine sieve into a clean saucepan. Add soda and stir thoroughly. Blend in the sugar and cream. Stir and heat, but do not allow to boil. Taste for salt and adjust. Serve immediately in warm soup bowls.

CHICKEN-TOMATO-WINE CONSOMME

A chilled soup that is adaptable for a large buffet party as the recipe may easily be made in any quantity. It is even better if made a day or two ahead; refrigerate in glass jars or plastic containers.

2 cups chicken broth
½ cup tomato juice
1 clove garlic, peeled
1 teaspoon sugar

Salt to taste
Grindings of black pepper
Pinch of basil
½ cup dry white wine

Combine all ingredients except the wine in a saucepan. Bring to a boil, lower heat, and let bubble lightly 10 minutes. Strain through a fine sieve. Add the white wine and chill thoroughly. Suggestion for serving a large party: cover a round card table with a pretty cloth, place a large tureen of soup with small cups on the table in a spot where guests can easily serve themselves.

HOT TOMATO BOUILLON WITH LEMON

6 cups tomato juice
  (46 ounce can)
1 can condensed consommé
1 teaspoon prepared horseradish

1 teaspoon Worcestershire sauce
Dash of black pepper
1 lemon, thinly sliced

In a large saucepan, combine the juice, consommé, horseradish, Worcestershire, and pepper. Blend well. Add lemon slices. Bring to a boil over moderate heat. Serve immediately in warm soup bowls or cups. 10 servings.

TOMATO-BUTTERMILK SOUP

Combine equal amounts of tomato juice and buttermilk. Add a small amount of sweet basil. Stir thoroughly and refrigerate until completely chilled. A most delightful, refreshing soup to serve in pottery mugs on a hot summer day.

MISCELLANEOUS MEDLEY

PARTY BREADS, SANDWICH BREADS, BUTTERS, ICINGS, LEFTOVERS, DESSERTS

SOUPS:

Iced Medley of Fruits

Raspberry Wine

Fresh Fruit

Grape Soup with Dumplings

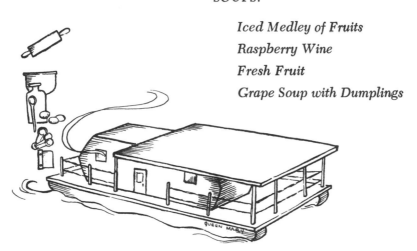

SWEET MUENSTER BREAD

An unusual and exciting bread that stems from middle Europe. This loaf has been so popular that it has been included in every class session. It can be frozen, served warm, room temperature, or chilled. Do not substitute any other cheese.

2 packages dry or compressed yeast
¼ cup warm water
1 cup warm milk
1½ tablespoons sugar

1½ teaspoons salt
½ cup melted butter
3 or 4 cups flour

Sprinkle yeast over the warm water, stirring with a fork until dissolved. Set aside. In a mixing bowl, combine the milk, sugar, salt, and melted butter. Blend well and add the yeast mixture. Beat in 2 cups of flour until mixture is smooth. Add sufficient flour to make a soft, workable dough. Turn out on a lightly floured board and knead until smooth and satiny, about 8 minutes. Round into a ball and place in a warm, greased bowl, turning to coat the top. Allow to double in bulk, about 1 hour. Punch the dough down and allow a second rising, about 30 minutes. Meanwhile prepare the following filling:

2 pounds Sweet Muenster cheese, grated or ground
1 egg

3 tablespoons melted butter

Brush a 10″ pie tin with melted butter. Punch the dough down, turn out on a floured board, cover, and let rest 10 to 15 minutes. Roll into a large circle 24 to 26″ in diameter. If dough resists, cover and let rest again. Fold circle of dough in half and lay across half the prepared pie tin. Unfold the dough. Carefully lift and press dough to fit into the pan leaving a skirt of dough draped over the rim. Mound the cheese on the dough forming it higher in the center. Pick up the skirt of dough and begin to pleat in loose folds around the mounded cheese, lifting and rotating the pan as you progress. Gather the ends on top together and twist into a knob. Take both hands and encircle the bottom of the knob and give a firm twist. If any dough is torn, pinch together firmly.

Set loaf aside 15 minutes. Give the knob one more twist. Bake in a preheated 375° oven 1 hour, or until golden brown. If top becomes too brown, cover with foil the last 15 minutes. Let bread cool in cake tin on a wire rack. Do not attempt to slice until the cheese has congealed. Reheat if you wish to serve warm.

LEBANESE PASTRY — SFEEHA

Many countries make delicious little meat pies for appetizers. The Lebanese are exceptionally good with all kinds of cocktail foods and this recipe is one of my favorites.

THE DOUGH
1 package dry or compressed yeast
1 cup warm water
3 tablespoons sugar

½ teaspoon mahleb (optional)
  (refer to page 228)
½ teaspoon salt
3 tablespoons oil
2 to 3 cups flour

Sprinkle yeast over the warm water in a mixing bowl. Blend in the sugar, mahleb, salt, and oil. Beat in sufficient flour to make a soft, workable dough that pulls away from sides of bowl. Turn out on a floured board and knead until smooth and elastic, about 10 minutes. Place in a warm, greased bowl, turning to coat the top. Cover loosely with plastic wrap and a towel. Set in a protected spot to double in bulk, about 1 hour. Turn out on a lightly floured surface, knead lightly, cover, and let rest 10 to 15 minutes (refer to Techniques, page 13). Cut dough in 24 equal pieces. Roll each in a ball, place on a greased baking sheet and press in a 3″ circle. Sprinkle meat topping over each. Press meat into the dough lightly. Bake in a preheated 400° oven, about 10 minutes, or until just browned on the edges. Serve immediately or cool on wire racks.

SPICY MEAT TOPPING
1 pound ground lamb or beef
1 cup finely chopped onions
⅓ cup pine nuts
3 tablespoons oil
2 tablespoons lemon juice

½ teaspoon salt
⅛ teaspoon each of cinnamon,
  cloves, and nutmeg
½ teaspoon dried mint

Sauté meat, onions, and pine nuts in the oil until onions are tender and the meat lightly browned. Add the remaining ingredients, stir thoroughly and cool.

NOTE

A delightful addition: When pomegranates are in season, sprinkle a few beautiful red seeds over each meat pie.

PAULINE'S PIZZA

A favorite food brought to our house boat was homemade pizza. With the help of my good friend, Pauline, we have designed the recipe in several parts with suggestions for variations.

HOMEMADE BISQUICK

8 cups sifted all purpose flour
¼ cup baking powder

4 teaspoons salt
1½ cups shortening

Sift flour with baking powder and salt into a mixing bowl. Cut in the shortening with a pastry blender until mixture looks like cornmeal. Place in a covered container (clean shortening can with plastic lid is excellent) and store in refrigerator. If well covered, the mixture keeps indefinitely.

PIZZA
Part 1.   The Dough

¾ cup warm water
1 package dry or compressed yeast
2½ cups homemade bisquick

Sprinkle yeast over the warm water in a mixing bowl. Stir with a fork until dissolved. Add the bisquick and beat vigorously with a rubber spatula. Turn dough out on a well floured surface. Knead until smooth and elastic, about 3 to 5 minutes. Divide in 4 pieces. Cover and let rest 10 to 15 minutes. Roll each portion in a thin circle 10″ in diameter. If necessary to make the rolling easier, place dough between 2 pieces of waxed paper. Place dough in greased pizza pans if you have them; if not on greased baking sheets or on foil pizza pans placed on a cookie sheet. Cover with the following sauce and garnishes.

Part 2.   Pizza Sauce
2 cans tomato paste (6 ounce size)
2 teaspoons oregano
1 teaspoon salt

1 can water
1 teaspoon water
Oil

Combine all ingredients except the oil in a saucepan. Stir and simmer 5 minutes to blend well. Spread the pizza sauce over the prepared dough. Sprinkle lightly with the oil.

Part 3.   Garnishes
This is where you can really let go and do your own "thing". Here are a number of suggestions which you may use in any combination. Add other ingredients that you particularly like.

A Must —
Grated Mozzarella and Parmesan cheeses

Brown and Serve sausage, cut in ¼"
  slices
Sautéed ground beef
Slices of pepperoni
Anchovies

Sliced canned mushrooms
Thinly sliced onions
Thinly sliced green pepper
Pitted sliced black olives
Chopped parsley

Sprinkle desired amount of grated Mozzarella over the Pizza Sauce. Top with any of the garnishes that your heart desires. Finally, sprinkle lightly with Parmesan cheese. Bake pizzas in a preheated 400° oven 20 minutes or until lightly browned on edges. Pizza may be frozen after the sauce and Mozarella cheese are on. When ready to cook, add the garnishes and Parmesan cheese.

SANDWICH BREADS

Following are two recipes for sandwich bread one white and the other a whole wheat. Both recipes are described first and then methods for molding and baking. To produce a finely textured bread, the dough must be thoroughly beaten and kneaded.

GRAHAM WHEAT SANDWICH BREAD

1 package dry or compressed yeast
2 cups warm milk
2 tablespoons sugar
1½ teaspoons salt
3 tablespoons butter or margarine

¼ cup light oil
2½ cups graham wheat flour
3 cups white flour, approximately

Sprinkle yeast over the warm milk in a large mixing bowl. Stir with a fork until dissolved. Blend in the sugar, salt, butter, and oil. With a rubber spatula or electric mixer, beat in the graham flour until mixture is very smooth. Gradually add sufficient white flour to make a soft, workable dough that pulls away from sides of the bowl. Turn out on a lightly floured surface and knead until smooth and resilient, about 10 to 12 minutes. Place in a warm, greased bowl, turning to coat the top. Cover loosely with plastic wrap and towel. Allow to double in bulk, about 1 hour. Turn out on a floured surface, knead 3 minutes, cover, and let rest 10 to 15 minutes.

WHITE SANDWICH BREAD

1 package dry or compressed yeast　*¼ cup melted butter or margarine*
¼ cup warm water　　　　　　　　*2 teaspoons salt*
2 cups warm milk　　　　　　　　*5 to 6 cups unbleached white*
⅓ cup honey　　　　　　　　　　*flour*

Sprinkle yeast over the warm water, stirring with a fork until dissolved. Set aside. In a large mixing bowl, combine the milk, honey, butter, and salt. Blend in the yeast mixture. Add 3 cups of flour and beat with a rubber spatula or an electric mixer until very smooth. Gradually add enough more flour to make a soft, workable dough. Turn out on a lightly floured board. Knead 10 to 12 minutes or until smooth and satiny. Round in a ball and place in a warm, greased bowl, turning to coat the top. Cover loosely with plastic wrap and towel. Allow to double in bulk, about 1½ hours. Punch the dough down, turn out on a floured board and knead 2 or 3 minutes. Cover, and let rest 10 to 15 minutes.

MOLDING AND BAKING OF SANDWICH BREADS

Preparation for sandwich loaf pan, 4x16": brush pan and bottom of lid thoroughly with melted butter. When either the Graham Wheat or White Sandwich dough has rested, pat and press evenly into the pan. If dough still resists, allow to rest a few minutes, and press out again. Push lid on the pan and let dough rise to within ½" of top, about 30 to 45 minutes. Bake in a preheated 375° oven 30 minutes. Remove lid and bake 10 more minutes. Turn out and cool on a wire rack.

Preparation for loaf pans, 9x5x3": You will need 2 loaf pans, 2 oblong cake pans and 2 bricks or heavy tiles. Brush the loaf pans and bottom of cake pans with melted butter. Divide dough in half after resting period. Roll each half in a rectangle, 9x12". Press out any bubbles. Fold in thirds like an envelope (refer to Techniques, page 13). Place in prepared loaf pans. Cover with cake pan, buttered side down, and place bricks on top. Let dough rise to ½" of top, about 30 to 45 minutes. Bake in a preheated 375° oven 30 minutes. Remove brick and cake pan. Bake 10 more minutes. Remove bread and cool on wire racks.

BREAD CASES

When the sandwich breads have cooled, wrap carefully and refrigerate for one or two days or until completely firm. With a sharp knife, cut a ¼″ slice from the top. Carefully slice around the inside, leaving a ½″ thick wall. Turn bread on side. Insert knife across the bottom but do not slice completely through. Gently push out the inner portion of bread. Place bread shell on a long tray. Slice the inside block of bread into desired shapes for thin sandwiches. Pile back into the bread case. Place on a long pretty tray and surround with greenery such as parsley or leaf lettuce.

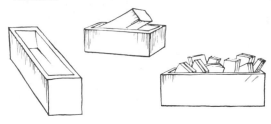

Round Bread Case: At end of the resting period, round either dough into a ball. Place in a well buttered 2½ quart soufflé or casserole dish with straight sides. Cover with a towel and let rise to within ¼″ of top. Bake in a preheated 375° oven 40 minutes or until golden brown. Cool on wire rack. Slice the top off; with a sharp knife cut out the center bread leaving a ½″ thick wall. (Be sure to refrigerate bread for at least one day.) Make 2 slits in bread top. Double a pipe cleaner and insert the two ends through the slits. Attach a big ribbon bow to the pipe cleaner. Sandwiches may be made for the bread basket and then topped with the gay lid— makes a fun centerpiece for a cocktail party.

BRIOCHE BREAD CASES

You will need: one recipe for brioche, page 69 and 2 coffee cans (2 pound size). Brush cans thoroughly with soft butter. Divide brioche dough in half. Place ½ of dough in each prepared coffee can. Press and pat dough down evenly. Set aside uncovered and let rise to within 1½″ of the top, about 2½ hours. Place cans on a baking sheet. Bake in a preheated 400° oven 10 minutes; reduce heat to 375° and bake 40 more minutes. Cool on wire racks 10 minutes. Gently loosen bread with a spatula and remove loaves. Allow breads to cool thoroughly, preferably overnight. With a sharp knife, slice off top of the bread. Insert knife down into the loaf and carefully slice around leaving a ¼ to ½″ thick wall. Turn loaf on its side and partially slice the bottom enough so that you can push out the inner portion. Thin, delicious sandwiches may be made with the brioche bread. Place bread case on a round tray and fill with the sandwiches. Make 2 slits in the bread top. Push the 2 ends of a pipe cleaner through the slits. Tie a bow with colorful ribbons and attach to the pipe cleaner so that you have a bread top with a beautiful bow to perch on the bread case.

SANDWICH LOAF

This may be made with either the whole wheat or white sandwich bread. Remove crust from all sides with a sharp knife. Carefully slice the bread length-wise in desired number of layers. Spread with a variety of fillings and stack on top of each other to form back into a loaf. Beat 2 large (8 ounce size) packages of cream cheese with enough sour or sweet cream to make a smooth, spreading consistency. Frost the sandwich loaf with the cheese mixture. Decorate with chopped parsley or pimiento and black olives in pretty designs. The sandwich loaf may be made a day ahead; wrap loaf carefully in plastic wrap and a slightly wet tea cloth. Refrigerate until ready to use. Remove from refrigerator and frost with cream cheese icing.

SUGGESTED SANDWICH FILLINGS
Water Cress: Combine 12 ounces of soft cream cheese with ¾ cup finely chopped water cress, 1 teaspoon grated onion, dash of salt and ¼ teaspoon pepper. Stir until smooth.
Pimiento-Cheese: Combine 2 cups grated American or cheddar cheese, ½ cup chopped pimiento, 2 tablespoons grated onion and 2 hard cooked chopped eggs with enough mayonnaise to make spreadable.
Deviled Ham: Mix 2 cans deviled ham (4 ounce size) with 1 cup cottage cheese and sufficient mayonnaise to make a spreading consistency.
Blue Cheese: Combine 6 ounces cream cheese, 1 ounce blue cheese, ½ cup ground nuts, ½ teaspoon grated onion, a dash of Worcestershire, 2 hard-boiled chopped eggs with enough mayonnaise to make a spreading mixture.
Chicken: Stir until smooth; 1 cup cooked ground chicken, ½ cup finely minced celery, ¼ cup ground almonds with ¼ to ½ cup of mayonnaise.
Crab: Combine 1½ cups cooked crabmeat, ½ cup finely minced celery, 1 tablespoon each of pimiento and green pepper with sufficient mayonnaise to make a spreading consistency.

Use any of the following thinly sliced tomatoes or cucumbers. Sliced smoked salmon or a good canned pâté thinned with mayonnaise. Use your own favorite sandwich fillings — do your own "thing" with these good home made sandwich breads.

BUTTER SPREADS AND MIXTURES

HERB BUTTER 1
1 cup soft butter
2 tablespoons lemon juice
4 tablespoons finely chopped shallots
4 tablespoons finely chopped chives
1 large clove garlic, minced
Grindings of white pepper
Pinch of following herbs: thyme, rosemary, tarragon

Combine and blend well all the ingredients. Place in a small crock or ramekin, cover and place in refrigerator. The butter will keep several weeks. For a variation, add 1 teaspoon of caraway seed.

HERB BUTTER 2
1 cup soft butter   *3 tablespoons finely minced*
1 teaspoon tarragon   *parsley*
½ teaspoon thyme

Mix all ingredients together. Keep refrigerated in a small covered jar. Variations: Add 1 teaspoon Dijon mustard for a piquant flavor. Eliminate the tarragon and use 1 teaspoon oregano.

HERB BUTTER 3
Combine 1 cup soft butter, 3 tablespoons finely chopped parsley, and 3 cloves finely minced garlic.

ORANGE CRUNCHY BUTTER
Cream 1 cup butter with 1 cup of sugar until fluffy. Stir in 6 small crumbled macaroons, grated peel of 2 oranges, 3 tablespoons finely chopped almonds, and 3 tablespoons brandy. A delicious mixture to spread on toasted bread.

CINNAMON-SUGAR
Combine 1 cup granulated sugar and 2 tablespoons cinnamon. Mix well. To keep a supply: measure 3 cups of sugar in a quart jar and add 6 tablespoons cinnamon. Cap, shake the jar well and label. Keep on your pantry shelf and use when any recipe specifies Cinnamon-Sugar.

CONFECTIONER'S ICING

To 1 cup of powdered sugar, add 1 teaspoon lemon juice plus just enough water or milk to make a thick frosting. Beat with a small whisk or fork until smooth and creamy.

VARIATIONS

A variety of flavorings may be used such as brandy, Grand Marnier, orange juice, vanilla extract, rum or any other essence that appeals to your taste.

LEFT-OVER BREAD

Never throw any bread away — there are so many things that can be done with stale or left-over bread, especially when it's your very own homemade. Here are suggestions:

1. One of the best uses is bread crumbs. I love having my own homemade bread crumbs so well, that I will occasionally take one whole loaf out of a batch and make it up into crumbs. Slice or break the bread and place on a large baking sheet. Place in a preheated 300 degree oven until golden in color, dry, and crisp. Allow to cool. Whirl through a blender or crush with a rolling pin. Store in a covered, labeled container. Keeps indefinitely.

2. Keep pieces of bread and store in the freezer for dressing. Home made dressing for your Thanksgiving turkey is a superb treat. Be sure to add whole wheat or rye as well as white; the combination of all three gives dressing a marvelous flavor.

3. Try bread crumbs in a meat loaf or with croquettes.

4. Croutons: Dice bread in small cubes. Sauté in a mixture of butter and oil. This may be done in the oven or in a skillet. Stir frequently until light brown and crisp.

5. There are all kinds of excellent desserts to be made with left-over bread. At the end of this chapter are several bread puddings that your family will love and are pleasing enough to serve guests.

HOW ABOUT A BREAD AND SOUP PARTY?

A marvellously, relaxing, and different way to entertain either a large or small group is to prepare breads and soups. If you have a spacious kitchen, do make it into a kitchen-clubroom party. If your kitchen is small, prepare a buffet in the dining room. So much of the food can be prepared ahead, that this will give you time to relax and enjoy your own party. If a hostess has a good time, her guests will be happy.

If the party is in the kitchen, have four soups bubbling on the stove with demitasse or small plastic cups for tasting each soup. The soups may be made ahead and frozen; thaw them the day of the party and pour into your prettiest pots. Prepare a variety of breads several weeks ahead and store them in the freezer. Heat all these good breads as the guests arrive. Or better yet, have one bread freshly baking so that with the aroma of the soups simmering, your guests will be sniffling happily as they walk in. You will love their comments and they will love you. If the dining room is used, place the soup on warming trays to keep them piping hot. Try to find some good home made butter or make several of the butter mixtures listed in this chapter. Fill a crock with crisp breadsticks to nibble on while cocktails are served. Prepare a large tray of fresh vegetables, a green salad or a fresh fruit salad. Serve a tray of cheese or make the Muenster Cheese Bread in this chapter. If you wish to be more elaborate prepare a sandwich loaf with a variety of delicious fillings. This, too, can be made the day before, wrapped in damp tea cloths and placed in the refrigerator. Frost the afternoon of the dinner. Another exceptionally fine dish that can be partially prepared ahead is a Brioche A Tête filled with your favorite paté or creamed seafood. Both the brioche and creamed dish can be made ahead, frozen, then reheated and put together just before serving.

If you prefer to maintain a simple menu, follow this easy and fun procedure. Select a wide variety of soups such as black bean, hot tomato bouillon, a creamed soup, and perhaps a hearty Minestrone. While serving cocktails (if you do), let the guests have the fun of stirring your soups, and peeking in the oven. Then serve just the hot soups and breads with plenty of good butter. Your guests will be happy and contented.

Dessert can be one of the elaborate coffee cakes such as the Potica, Lemon-Cheese cake, or a bread pudding. With hot coffee and tea, you will have a great finale for a distinctive and relaxing party.

ELECTION CAKE

My research has given me no clue as to the origin of this delicious cake. Regardless, it is redolent with spices and brandy — great for holiday time as well as an election night.

2 packages dry or compressed yeast
1 cup warm water
1 teaspoon sugar
4½ cups sifted all purpose flour
¾ cup butter
1 cup sugar
1 teaspoon salt
1 teaspoon cinnamon

½ teaspoon mace
½ teaspoon nutmeg
¼ teaspoon cloves
2 eggs
1 cup nuts
1½ cups golden raisins
½ cup brandy
Confectioner's Icing, page 268

Combine yeast, water, and 1 teaspoon sugar in a mixing bowl. Stir with a fork until dissolved. Add 1 cup of the flour and beat thoroughly with a rubber spatula or an electric mixer for 2 minutes. Cover and set aside to double, about 30 minutes.

Combine the remaining flour and spices. Cream butter and sugar until light and fluffy. Add eggs one at a time beating well after each addition. Stir in the yeast mixture and brandy. Add flour mixture gradually. Beat until smooth. Blend in the raisins and nuts. Pour into a well buttered 10″ tube or Bundt pan. Cover and let double, about 1½ hours. Bake in a preheated 350° oven 1 hour. Remove from oven and cool in pan 10 minutes. Turn out on a tray and frost cake while warm with Confectioner's Icing flavored with lemon juice or brandy.

BREAD PUDDING

This is one of the finest, plain bread puddings I have tasted. A recipe shared by a friend from Kansas, the Sunflower state — an excellent family dessert.

2 cans sweetened condensed milk
  (14 ounce size)
6 cups hot water
4 cups bread cubes
3 eggs, lightly beaten

3 tablespoons melted butter
½ teaspoon salt
1½ teaspoons vanilla flavoring
Grated rind 1 lemon
1 cup raisins (optional)

Combine the milk and hot water in a large mixing bowl. Add the bread cubes and allow to stand until lukewarm. Stir in the remaining ingredients. Pour into a 3 quart casserole or a 2 quart souffle bowl and individual custard cups. Place casserole in a shallow pan filled with 1½″ of hot water. Bake in a preheated 350° oven about 1 hour. Test with a silver knife; if it comes out clean the pudding is done. If not, bake 10 to 15 minutes longer. Serve warm or chilled. This pudding is so delicious that it needs no other adornment but cream may be offered as an accompaniment.

CHOCOLATE BREAD PUDDING

Chocolate even invades bread puddings! For those who are devotees of chocolate, here is a light and creamy dessert that will serve eight generously.

4 cups bread cubes	1 cup sugar
5 cups milk	1 tablespoon vanilla flavoring
4 squares bitter chocolate	2 egg whites
½ teaspoon salt	¼ cup sugar
5 eggs	

Place bread cubes in a 2 quart casserole or soufflé dish. Combine the milk and chocolate in a saucepan. Place over moderate heat until chocolate is melted, stirring occasionally. Beat eggs lightly; add sugar and salt. Continue beating until light and fluffy. Gradually add the milk mixture and vanilla flavoring. Pour over the bread cubes. Allow to stand 15 minutes so the bread can absorb the milk. Set bowl in a shallow pan with ½″ of hot water. Bake in a preheated 350° oven 50 minutes. Beat egg whites until softly stiff. Add the ¼ cup of sugar and continue beating until creamy and meringue stands in soft peaks. Spread meringue on top of pudding. Return to oven and bake 10 more minutes or until meringue is lightly golden.

NEW ORLEANS BRANDIED BREAD PUDDING

A rich and delicious pudding from fascinating New Orleans. It is typically southern Creole and will melt in your mouth.

4 cups bread cubes
½ cup raisins
5 eggs
1 cup sugar
1 teaspoon cinnamon
½ teaspoon nutmeg
3 tablespoons melted butter
5 cups hot milk

1 tablespoon brandy

Sauce:
2 eggs
1 cup sugar
3 tablespoons cornstarch
2 cups hot milk
½ cup brandy

Place bread cubes in a 3 quart casserole. Sprinkle raisins over bread. Beat the eggs until frothy and add the sugar stirring until light and creamy. Add the cinnamon, nutmeg, and butter. Gradually blend in the hot milk and brandy. Pour milk mixture over the bread. Allow to stand 15 minutes. Place bowl in a shallow pan filled with 1″ of hot water. Bake in a preheated 350° oven 1 hour. Remove and serve either warm or cooled with the following sauce:

SAUCE

Whisk the 2 eggs in top of a double boiler. Add the sugar and cornstarch. Slowly stir in the hot milk. Place pan over hot water, stirring until thick and smooth. Remove from heat and add the ½ cup of brandy.

MARMALADE BREAD PUDDING

A family favorite that disappears at one meal. The coating of marmalade over the custard gives a piquant flavor that is unusual and a feeling
of wanting just one more bite!

2½ cups soft bread cubes
1 quart hot milk
4 eggs
⅓ cup sugar
Pinch salt
1 teaspoon vanilla extract

2 tablespoons melted butter

Topping:
3 egg whites
4 tablespoons sugar
6 tablespoons marmalade

Combine bread and hot milk. Set aside 5 minutes. In the large bowl of
an electric mixer, beat eggs and sugar until light and fluffy. Blend in
the salt, vanilla, melted butter, and milk mixture. Pour in a 2 quart
casserole or soufflé bowl. Place bowl in a pan of hot water and bake in
a preheated 350° oven 45 minutes.

While the custard is baking, prepare the topping. Beat egg whites
until softly stiff. Gradually add the 4 tablespoons of sugar, beating constantly until mixture is creamy and stands in soft points. Remove custard from the oven. Spread marmalade over top of pudding with a rubber
spatula. Spread meringue on top. Reduce oven heat to 300°. Bake pudding 15 minutes or until meringue is lightly browned. Serve warm or
cooled.

ICED MEDLEY OF FRUITS

In the winter when a great variety of fresh fruits are scarce, give your family a delightful change with this lovely cold soup.

2 packages mixed frozen fruits   2 cups water
  (10 ounce size)   1 cup dry white wine
3 tablespoons lemon juice   Sour cream or whipped cream
3 cloves

Combine all ingredients except the cream in a saucepan. Bring slowly to a boil. Lower heat to a simmer, cover pan, and cook 20 minutes or until fruits are very tender. Discard cloves. Purée ingredients in a blender. Put blended soup through a fine sieve to remove any seeds. Refrigerate until thoroughly chilled. Serve in cold soup bowls garnished with a dollop of whipped or sour cream. For a different dessert, serve the soup in small cups with an almond cookie on the side.

 RASPBERRY WINE SOUP

A delicately colored refreshing soup that will add a charming difference to a meal.

2 packages frozen sweetened raspberries   Pinch of white pepper
  (10 ounce size)   Salt
1 cup dry white wine   ½ cup orange juice
1 teaspoon cornstarch   ½ cup dry white wine
1 tablespoon water

Combine raspberries and 1 cup white wine in a saucepan. Bring to a simmer and cook uncovered 15 minutes. Strain the mixture through a fine sieve. Return to a clean saucepan. Mix cornstarch with the water until dissolved. Blend into raspberry mixture. Bring to a boil and simmer 10 minutes, stirring occasionally. Remove from heat and skim. Season with a pinch of white pepper and salt to taste. Add orange juice and ½ cup of white wine. Chill thoroughly. Serve in demitasse cups to accompany a meal or as a summer dessert with cookies.

FRESH FRUIT SOUP

During the teen-age phase of our sons' lives, we floated each week-end on an enormous houseboat. The food that was invariably requested by their friends was this soup. We found that all ages enjoyed it!

3 tablespoons quick cooking
    tapioca
2 tablespoons sugar
2½ cups water
1 six ounce can frozen orange
    juice

3 cups fresh fruit—peaches, grapes,
    banana, strawberries, plums,
    melons, oranges, and apricots
1 tablespoon lemon juice

Combine the tapioca, sugar, and 1 cup of the water in a saucepan. Bring to a full, rolling boil, stirring constantly. Remove from burner. Blend in the orange juice until melted. Add remaining 1½ cups water. Cool 20 minutes. Stir, cover, and chill thoroughly. Prepare desired fruit and cut into bite size pieces. When soup is chilled, add the fruits and lemon juice. Serves about 8 hungry teen-agers. The recipe is easily doubled or tripled.

GRAPE SOUP WITH DUMPLINGS

A lovely, dark red soup that has a distinctive and unusual flavor. It may be used as a soup to accompany a meal or turned into a dessert with the addition of dumplings.

The Soup
1 can frozen grape concentrate
1 can water

2 cups grapefruit juice
Juice of 1 lemon or orange

Combine the grape concentrate, water, grapefruit, and lemon juice. Bring to a boil and simmer 5 minutes. Garnish with any of the following: to each serving add a tablespoon of sour cream or yogurt or cubes of avacado are a delightful addition.

The Dumplings
1 cup sifted all purpose flour
1½ teaspoons baking powder
½ teaspoon salt
3 tablespoons sugar

2 tablespoons soft butter
⅓ cup milk
1 egg, lightly beaten
1 teaspoon vanilla flavoring

275

Sift flour, baking powder, salt, and sugar into a mixing bowl. Cut in the butter with a pastry blender until crumbly. Combine milk, beaten egg, and flavoring. Add all at once to flour mixture and stir quickly just enough to dampen ingredients — don't worry about the lumps. Heat the soup in a skillet. Drop dumplings in by teaspoonsful. Cover and simmer 12 to 15 minutes. Serve in warm bowls with a dollop of whipped cream.

GLOSSARY

GLOSSARY

BAKE	To cook in a dry heat as in an oven
BAKING POWDER	A mixture of baking soda, cream of tartar and a starch used as a leavening agent in quick breads and cakes
BAKING SODA	A white crystaline salt (sodium bicarbonate) used in baking
BATCH	A quantity of combined ingredients for one operation as dough for baking
BATTER	A semi-liquid combination of flour and other ingredients
BEAT	Mixing thoroughly by repeatedly using a rapid rotary motion
BLEND	To lightly combine ingredients until well mixed
BOIL	To cook in a liquid over a brisk heat allowing to bubble constantly
BOUILLON	French term for stock or broth
BOUQUET GARNI	A bunch of herbs, usually thyme, bay leaf, and parsley tied together to be removed after flavor has been imparted to food
BUBBLE	A slow simmering of liquids where light bubbles rise to the surface. Also, allowing a sponge to become light and full of bubbles.
BROTH	Bouillon or stock
CLOVE OF GARLIC	One of the small bulbs within the large bulb of garlic
CARAMEL	A syrup made from scorched sugar used for coloring food products such as rye or pumpernickcl breads
COMBINE	To mix several ingredients together until well blended
CONSISTENCY	A degree of firmness
CONSOMME	A soup of enriched, concentrated, and clarified stock or bouillon
CREAM	To beat until ingredients are of a light and smooth consistency
CUT	Mixing together such ingredients as shortening, flour or sugar with a knife, fork, or blender. Also, to sever bread dough into several parts
DEGLAZING	Boiling of water or wine in a pan to release all

scrapings

DISSOLVE	To merge ingredients such as yeast and water until melted or liquified
DOUGH	A soft mass of moistened flour or meal thick enough to knead or roll with hands
DREDGE	To sprinkle or coat with flour or sugar
DUST	To sprinkle lightly with sugar, flour, or other ingredients
EGG GLAZE	The same as egg wash
EGG WASH	A combination of a whole egg, egg yolk, or white of an egg beaten with a liquid to brush on tops of breads
FISH STOCK	Addition of fish to a court bouillon or other liquid with herbs and vegetables giving a fish flavor to the broth
FOLD	A slow over and over stirring of ingredients to incorporate air
FROSTING	A coating or topping for bread or yeast cakes made from sugar combined with various liquids
GLAZE (breads)	Various combination of ingredients with a liquid to brush a thin coating over tops of breads
GLUTEN	An elastic protein substance characteristic of wheat flour giving adhesiveness to dough and the ability to retain gas
HERBS	Aromatic plants used in general cooking for sweet scent and flavor.
ICING	The same as frosting
JULIENNE	Vegetables cut in matchlike strips
LEAVENING	A substance such as yeast producing fermentation and lightness
MARROW BONE	A bone containing a soft tissue that is nutritive and edible
MIREPOIX	A finely chopped mixture usually of onions, carrots, herbs, and fat sautéed and used to enhance the flavor of soups
PROOFING DOUGH	To let dough rise in a warm bowl in a protected spot
PROOFING YEAST	Combine yeast with a small amount of warm water and sugar; allow to set 10 minutes until bubbles appear
PUNCH DOWN	A quick blow with a fist to deflate raised dough

PUREE	Food rubbed through a sieve or put through a blender
RESERVE	To retain or set aside ingredients for a future use
RESILIENT	Elastic capability of a dough to recover shape and size
REST	Allowing dough a period of relaxing before forming into loaves
ROUX	A cooked mixture of fat and starch used to thicken soups or sauces
SAUTE	Fried lightly and quickly in small amount of fat
SCALD	To bring to a temperature just below boiling
SCORE	To mark with lines or cut on surface of dough
SIMMER	To cook gently, keeping just below the boiling point
SKIM	To clear or take off scum or floating substance from a liquid such as soup
SLASH	To cut by sweeping strokes as with a razor on French bread
SOURDOUGH STARTER	A sponge composed of liquid and flour, potatoes or like ingredients allowed to ferment until actively bubbling and then used in making sourdough breads
SPONGE	A mixture of ingredients such as flour, water and sugar to which yeast has been added and allowed to ferment becoming light and bubbly
STEW	A dish of meat, fish, or poultry combined with vegetables and liquid slowly simmered for several hours
STOCK	The clear, flavorful, strained liquid produced by simmering meat or poultry, vegetables, and herbs for several hours
TURN OUT	To empty a container such as removing dough from a mixing bowl to a kneading board
WHIP	To beat with a fork or mixer into a froth

TABLE OF MEASUREMENTS
AND EQUIVALENTS

1 teaspoon		5 milliliters	
3 teaspoons	1 tablespoon	14½ milliliters	
4 tablespoons	¼ cup	58 milliliters	
2 tablespoons	1 fluid ounce	29 milliliters	
1¾ ounces	1 jigger	42 milliliters	
16 tablespoons	1 cup	235 milliliters	0.235 liters
1 cup	½ pint	235 milliliters	0.235 liters
2 cups	1 pint	470 milliliters	0.470 liters
4 cups	1 quart	940 milliliters	0.940 liters
16 ounces	1 pound	454 grams	0.454 kilograms
1 pound flour	3 cups	454 grams	705 milliliters
See below for Cup		0.454 kilograms	0.705 liters
Equivalent	4 cups, sifted	454 grams	940 milliliters
		0.454 kilograms	0.940 liters
*1 pound cornmeal	3 cups	454 grams	705 milliliters
		0.454 kilograms	0.705 liters
*1 pound butter	2 cups	454 grams	470 milliliters
		0.454 kilograms	0.470 liters
1 stick butter	½ cup or 8 tablespoons	113½ grams	116 milliliters
		0.113½ kilograms	0.116 liters
*1 pound grated cheese	4½ cups	454 grams	1056 milliliters
		0.454 kilograms	1.056 liters
*1 pound brown sugar	2½ to 3 cups	454 grams	586 milliliters or 0.586 liters to
		0.454 kilograms	705 milliliters or 0.705 liters
*1 pound granulated sugar	2 cups	454 grams	470 milliliters
		0.454 kilograms	0.470 liters
*1 pound confectioner's sugar	3⅓ cups	454 grams	783 milliliters
		0.454 kilograms	0.783 liters
*1 pound lump sugar	2 cups	454 grams	470 milliliters
		0.454 kilograms	0.470 liters
1 pint heavy cream	2 cups	470 milliliters	0.470 liters
	4 cups whipped	940 milliliters	0.940 liters
*1 pound raisins	2½ cups	454 grams	586 milliliters
		0.454 kilograms	0.586 liters
1 square chocolate	1 ounce or 2 tablespoons, grated	28 grams 29 milliliters	
*1 pound pitted dates	2 cups	454 grams	470 milliliters
		0.454 kilograms	0.470 liters
*1 pound nutmeats, chopped	4 cups	454 grams	940 milliliters
		0.454 kilograms	0.940 liters
1 lemon	3 tablespoons juice	43½ milliliters	
	3 teaspoons grated rind	14½ milliliters	
1 orange	about ½ cup juice	116 milliliters	0.116 liters
5 eggs	1 cup	235 milliliters	0.235 liters
9 eggs	1 pound	454 grams	0.454 kilograms
16 egg yolks	1 cup	235 milliliters	0.235 liters
8 to 10 egg whites	1 cup	235 milliliters	0.235 liters

*1 pound dried apricots	3 cups	454 grams	705 milliliters
		0.454 kilograms	0.705 liters
	4½ cups cooked	454 grams	1056 milliliters
		0.454 kilograms	1.056 liters
4 tablespoons dry whole milk Plus		58 milliliters	
1 cup water	1 cup milk	235 milliliters	0.235 liters
⅓ cup powdered skimmed milk Plus		78 milliliters	
¾ cup water		176 milliliters	0.176 liters
	1 cup	235 milliliters	0.235 liters
½ teaspoon dried herbs	1 tablespoon fresh	2½ milliliters	
		14½ milliliters	
1 cake of fresh yeast	2 tablespoons	29 milliliters	
1 package of dry yeast	¾ tablespoon	26 milliliters	
1 pound whole wheat flour, stone ground	3 1/5 cups	0.454 kilograms	752 milliliters
		454 grams	0.752 liters
1 cup whole wheat stone ground flour	5 ounces	145 grams	235 milliliters
		0.145 kilograms	0.235 liters
1 cup defatted wheat germ	4½ ounces	120 grams	235 milliliters
1 cup regular flour	3⅓ ounces	94½ grams	235 milliliters
		0.0945 kilograms	0.235 liters
½ cup regular flour	1 2/3 ounces	47 grams	117 milliliters
		0.047 kilograms	0.117 liters

SOURCES OF SUPPLY

ELAM MILLS

Broadview, Illinois 60153

EL MOLINO MILLS

3060 West Valley Blvd.
Alhambra, California 91803

WALNUT ACRES

Penn's Creek
Pennsylvania 18951

ARROWHEAD MILLS, INC.

P. O. Box 866
Hereford, Texas 79045

BYRD MILL CO.

RFD 5
Louisa, Virginia

AKIN'S SPECIAL FOODS

2052 Utica Square
Tulsa, Oklahoma 74104

HODGSON MILL ENTERPRISES

Hodgson Water Mill
Hwy. 181 Ozark County
Sycamore, Missouri 65758

INDEX

INDEX

MARY GUBSER's romance with bread-making began some years ago when there was a citywide bakers' strike in Tulsa, Oklahoma, where she lives. That was when she made her first loaf of yeast bread, and her family has turned up its collective nose at "store boughten" bread ever since. She has traveled extensively with her attorney husband, Eugene Gubser, always on the lookout for good food and interesting recipes. Her three sons added zest to her hobby on their own travels abroad as teenagers— by tramp steamer, hitchhiking, canoeing, cycling—by bringing home their reports of good breads, cheeses, and the pots of bubbling soup served in youth hostels.

When the Gubsers built a new home around a kitchen Mary Gubser designed herself, she ventured into teaching classes in bread-making with a cooking companion, Sue Schempf. Twenty students enrolled. Soup recipes were added to the curriculum. The classes mushroomed, the school was named Mary's Bread Basket, and it now has waiting lists. She then wrote and published privately MARY's BREAD BASKET AND SOUP KETTLE, which was so successful that it became necessary to reprint it with a New York publisher. Through these experiences, Mary Gubser learned that both amateur and accomplished cooks today want to take part in the exciting resurgence of "back to basics" and want to make their own good breads and soups at home.

A native Oklahoman, the author grew up in a Methodist parsonage, was graduated from the University of Oklahoma, and is now a grandmother. Her niece, Pat Loring Biggs, who illustrated this book, is a graduate of Oberlin College and a free-lance artist as well as a cooking hobbyist and the mother of six.

NOTES

NOTES

NOTES

NOTES

NOTES

Also available from Quill

Perfect Pies
A Complete Savory and Sweet Fare
of Unique Wholesome Pies
Diane Fine

More than 200 mouth-watering, wholesome, original pies for every season and every occasion. Includes comprehensive instructions on pie making and advice on inventing even more variations.
0-688-02799-7

The Cookie Bookie
Diane Fine and Ria Teale

Recipes for 45 scrumptious, nutritious, original, old-favorite, holiday, chocolatey, nutty, buttery, spicy cookies. Suitable for cookie bakers of *all* ages.
0-688-04179-5

**Jean Anderson's Green Thumb
Preserving Guide**
The Best and Safest Ways to Can and Freeze,
Dry and Store, Pickle, Preserve and Relish
Home-Grown Vegetables and Fruits
Jean Anderson

Recommended by Craig Claiborne on his personal list of best books for the cookbook library.
0-688-04190-6

Mother Earth's Vegetarian Feasts
Joel Rapp

How to eat better, enjoy each meal more, and spend less, with delicious vegetarian meals.
0-688-02213-8

The Complete Book of Chicken Wings
Joie Warner

Inexpensive, quick-to-cook, prepare-ahead recipes for parties, picnics, or meals in minutes.
0-688-05713-6

AVAILABLE AT YOUR LOCAL BOOKSTORE